Planning for Play, Observation, and Learning
in Preschool and Kindergarten

PLANNING for PLAY, OBSERVATION, AND LEARNING in PRESCHOOL and KINDERGARTEN

GAYE GRONLUND

 Redleaf Press®
www.redleafpress.org
800-423-8309

Published by Redleaf Press
10 Yorkton Court
St. Paul, MN 55117
www.redleafpress.org

Portions of this book were first published in *Focused Early Learning* by Gaye Gronlund, © 2003.

First edition 2013
Cover design by Jim Handrigan
Cover photograph © Segrey Galushko/Veer
Interior design by Ryan Scheife, Mayfly Design
Typeset in Whitman
Photograph on page 168 by Kathy Stewart
Photograph on page 188 by MediaDesigns, Inc.
Photograph on page 214 by Gail Holtz

Printed in the United States of America
19 18 17 16 15 14 13 12   1 2 3 4 5 6 7 8

Library of Congress Cataloging-in-Publication Data
Gronlund, Gaye, 1952-
    Planning for play, observation, and learning in preschool and kindergarten / Gaye Gronlund.
        p. cm.
    Includes bibliographical references and index.
    ISBN 978-1-60554-113-6 (pbk.)
    1. Play. 2. Education, Preschool—Curricula. 3. Kindergarten—Curricula. 4. Curriculum planning.   I. Title.
    LB1140.35.P55G76 2012
    372.21—dc23
                            2012032226

Printed on acid-free paper

To my children, Colin and Gwen, two wonderful adults now, but as children, two imaginative and wonderfully creative players, Mr. Earl and Melody Legs!

Contents

Acknowledgments

Heartfelt thanks to

- the New Mexico PreK Leadership and Consultants, who have continually refined my writings and put them into action, working toward high-quality preschool experiences for the four-year-olds of New Mexico
- my friend and colleague, Marlyn James, who supports and challenges my thinking and practice
- the early childhood practitioners who contributed their thoughts to this manuscript
- my editor, Jeanne Engelmann, whose help is invaluable

INTRODUCTION

The Wonders and Challenges of Teaching Young Children

. . . .

I have been in the field of early childhood education for thirty-six years. I have taught in a variety of early childhood settings: a cooperative nursery school, a university laboratory school, a Head Start program, special education preschool classrooms, and a public school kindergarten. As a consultant and an author, I have had the privilege of working with thousands of teachers around the country, helping them identify the best ways to implement recommended curricular and assessment strategies and meet the needs of the children in their unique settings.

Over the years, I have seen the expectations for preschool and kindergarten change dramatically. No longer is it enough to provide a fun, engaging social experience for young children. Teachers are held accountable for helping children achieve preschool and kindergarten standards that define expected performance—not only in the social domain but in other domains as well. And those domains are more traditionally academic in nature—literacy, mathematics, science, and social studies. It is not enough for early childhood educators to love and enjoy young children. They must also know their state's standards, plan curriculum incorporating those expectations, and conduct assessments that help them meet each child's needs. Academic learning is the focus now, and assessment of each child's learning is necessary.

I think this shift in early childhood education is *wonderful*! I also think it is *challenging*.

As I work with preschool and kindergarten teachers across the country, I hear their confusion and frustration about the challenging aspects of this shift. They feel they must push back against pressures for inappropriate early educational experiences for young children. They ask questions such as:

- How do I do implement developmentally appropriate practices when others demand more accountability?
- How do I plan for play experiences, give children choices, and not have absolute chaos?
- How do I focus on learning and standards and still nurture the joy of learning?
- Is it okay to plan teacher-directed activities? How much of my day should be devoted to group times and how much to play?
- How do I implement assessments that really show what the children are learning and how they are applying their skills?

And the question I hear most frequently is

- How do I write a lesson plan that shows everything I do that is intentional and preplanned and is also child focused and responsive, integrating all of what I know are best practices?

This book is my attempt to answer these questions.

The Wonders of Teaching Young Children

As I said earlier, I think there are wonderful parts to this shift in early education. Let's consider those wonderful parts. The development of early learning standards for preschool and kindergarten has occurred in all fifty states in America, and many states have developed or are developing standards or guidelines for infant/toddler development. The beauty of early learning standards is that they define reasonable expectations for young children at different age levels. Professionals in the field of early education have written most of these standards, and most are helpful in outlining what young children *can* do. No longer do teachers have to rely on sources such as developmental checklists and other information to piece together their knowledge base of child development. Early learning standards now serve as the reference point for planning curriculum and assessing young children's progress. Teachers have a common language grounded in research and endorsed by their state. This gives them a strong foundation from which to teach. That's good!

Clearly defined expectations and greater accountability professionalize the field of early childhood education. Unfortunately, inadequate wages still prevail for many early educators, but this may shift as the role of a preschool or kindergarten teacher is seen as more important in our society. In addition, more public and political attention is now focused on early childhood education. The importance of the early years is addressed routinely in the media with articles and reports about the long-term benefits of high-quality early childhood programs and the latest research in brain development. And governors across the country have implemented pre-K (public prekindergarten) programs and full-day kindergartens as ways of closing the achievement gap and providing children with equal opportunities to flourish. As early educators communicate with parents, helping them see connections between their child's development and early learning standards, they further the perceptions of professionalism in the field. Again, that's good!

And the Challenges—Teaching *Is* Rocket Science!

The shift toward more accountability and professionalism, while beneficial, is challenging as well. First, there are cautions to consider when implementing early learning standards. Everyone must understand the purpose of standards: they are reasonable expectations to serve as curricular goals. *Every child will NOT achieve every standard.* Unfortunately, politicians, policy makers, and parents have embraced the fallacy that each child will achieve each standard—that we can expect all preschoolers to recognize all of their letters, and all kindergartners to read by the end of the kindergarten year. Best practices for any age group, but especially for young children, recognize that each child develops and learns at his or her own pace, with strengths in some areas and weaknesses in others (NAEYC 2009). To make use of early learning standards most effectively, teachers use them as expectations by which they can measure each child's strengths as well as weaker areas of performance. Armed with this information, teachers can then plan curriculum that is individualized for each child, meeting each child where he is and helping him grow and learn from that point.

There are many ways to incorporate early learning standards without giving up the best approaches for teaching young children. Preschool and kindergarten classrooms can still be joyful, fun places where children thrive and love learning new things. Early learning standards can be integrated into play experiences both indoors and out. They can be part of daily routines such as snack, arrival and departure, bathroom time, and transitions. And standards can be part of small and large teacher-led group times. Preschool and kindergarten teachers do not have to do away with their play areas and extended playtimes in order to address early learning standards. Instead, they can embed standards throughout their curriculum in fun and engaging ways and communicate clearly to administrators and parents about that process.

Teaching in this way is hard work! It takes thoughtfulness, knowledge, and attentiveness to each child. In a presentation at a national conference, Barbara Bowman, former president of NAEYC and, until recently, head of the early childhood programs in Chicago Public Schools, showed a slide that said, "It *is* rocket science!" She explained that she presents this slide whenever she is talking with administrators, policy makers, politicians, and parents so that they see the depth of best practices in teaching young children. In the latest edition of *Developmentally Appropriate Practice* (Copple and Bredekamp 2009), or *DAP* as it is commonly called, teacher intentionality is emphasized much more than in the first two editions. To quote Barbara Bowman again, "What we do is not haphazard." Early childhood educators are intentional in setting up the environment, facilitating high-level play, planning for engaging group times, and knowing each child well. And all of this occurs while educators incorporate goals related to standards, assess children's performance, and build strong relationships with families. Teaching young children *is* rocket science!

The Value of Play

As I work with teachers, I hear them raise concerns about the multiple expectations to which they are held accountable. When trying to incorporate early learning standards in their classrooms, they wonder if they need to act more as instructors teaching children specific skills in small-group work, incorporating more pencil and paper tasks. They ask if playtime should be reduced so that more academic learning can be the focus. They wonder if they need to assess each child's performance through on-demand tasks or mini-tests. They question whether preschool and kindergarten classrooms now need to look more like classrooms for elementary grade students. Yet they also know young children, and they debate the rightness of "pushing down" curricular practices. They know it isn't right to use curricular practices from the next grade level—first-grade practices for kindergartners, and kindergarten practices for preschoolers, for example—to force academic learning at an earlier age. They know the value of play and its connection to learning for preschoolers and kindergartners.

The field of early childhood education has strong, research-based guidelines for best practices in curriculum and assessment, as outlined in the third edition of *Developmentally Appropriate Practice* (Copple and Bredekamp 2009). These recommendations emphasize that teachers recognize the learning styles and needs of children at different ages, as well as focus on each child's unique capabilities and cultural background. They do not endorse pushing down curricular practices. Instead, they define practices that are just right for preschoolers and kindergartners.

Play is still seen as a primary vehicle for learning even into kindergarten and the primary grades. Playtime is supported by an ever-growing body of research documenting the benefit of high-level play for children. Teacher intentionality is defined as facilitating learning through play experiences as well as teacher-led group times. The value of planning engaging activities that can address a range of individual children's abilities and the value of giving children choices are the focus throughout the *Developmentally Appropriate Practice* position statement and guidebook. Moreover, the connection between joy and learning is emphasized.

> Excellent teachers know . . . it's *both* joy *and* learning. . . . They go hand in hand. . . . Teachers are always more effective when they tap into this natural love of learning rather than dividing work and enjoyment. As some early childhood educators like to put it, children love nothing better than "hard fun." (Copple and Bredekamp 2009, 50)

Embracing developmentally appropriate practices does not mean teachers of preschoolers and kindergartners need to give up the fun in teaching this age group. Instead, teachers are clear about why they encourage play, plan specific activities, and work with children to help them get along with each other and love learning.

Frameworks for Play, Observation, and Learning

This book presents several frameworks for planning and reflection that attempt to capture what should really happen in preschool and kindergarten classrooms. These frameworks will help teachers "pull it all together" while integrating the very best curricular approaches they use every day in the classroom. Preschool and kindergarten children have unique needs and learning traits. The frameworks in this book are designed to help teachers organize the classroom and plan activities that will work with, rather than against, the needs and traits of this age group—not pushing down curricular practices that work with older children but representing those that are just right for young children.

Teachers of preschool and kindergarten children often combine a variety of curricular approaches and strategies that fall under the general heading of "developmentally appropriate practices." They incorporate aspects of environment-based learning centers with curriculum that emerges from children's interests. They integrate academic learning into hands-on exploration and play while paying very close attention to children's social and emotional development.

I think curriculum is truly represented by a teacher's plans. No matter what approach or curricular model she uses, her plans for the daily schedule, for the materials available, for facilitating play experiences, and for leading group times are the actual implementation of curriculum. Some curricular sets may provide a model planning framework, but teachers often tell me it's difficult to record the *actual* happenings in the classroom as they respond to children's interests, observe children's successes and challenges, and make adjustments to meet each child's needs. Their recorded plans include only their preplanned activities and materials, not the changes they make each day based on their observations of the children in action.

The frameworks presented in this book come originally from my book *Focused Early Learning: A Planning Framework for Teaching Young Children* (Gronlund 2003). Since the publication of *Focused Early Learning*, I have worked with hundreds of preschool and kindergarten teachers on the planning process. Through the experiences of these colleagues, I have realized some key components that should always be part of a planning framework. I have also learned that there are different ways to structure the written planning record to reflect those key components. So several models for planning and reflection will be presented here. You can review them and decide which ones might work best for your setting and your teaching and planning style. Planning and reflection are critically important aspects of intentional teaching. It's the process that is the focus. I hope the frameworks presented in this book will provide meaningful options and possibilities for professionals in the field of early childhood education.

Applying the Frameworks to Other Settings

Throughout this book, I refer to teachers and classrooms. The frameworks and curricular processes shared here can be used in preschool, pre-K (prekindergarten), and kindergarten classrooms in both private and public programs. In addition, they can be used in family child care settings as well as child care centers and nursery schools. Furthermore, special educators may apply the recommendations in this book to their work with young children with special needs. I invite those in different settings to consider the ideas shared and to make adaptations for their settings. In using the word *teacher*, I mean to include any adult who works with young children.

Field-Testing the Frameworks

Several early childhood professionals graciously agreed to share their experiences with planning for play, observation, and learning in their preschool and kindergarten classrooms. Their input is very important to me. I never want to make suggestions that are not based in real, everyday classroom life. Therefore, I am deeply grateful to my colleagues who have agreed to contribute to this book.

You will see comments from these early childhood professionals throughout the chapters and learn more about their successes and challenges with the planning process. They represent a variety of programs around the country. All of them have extensive experience working with young children, and all of them gave me honest, constructive feedback. Let me tell you about each one of them.

- **Mary Bliss:** Mary is currently Executive Director of the Christina Kent Early Childhood Center in Albuquerque, New Mexico. The program is a nonprofit preschool, enrolling children two to five years old, and has been serving working low-income families since 1919. Mary and her staff apply the principles and philosophy of Reggio Emilia in their staff development and practice. She has been teaching in New Mexico for twenty years in private and public preschools and kindergartens. She has a master's degree in early childhood education.

- **Laura Docterman:** Laura is a consultant with New Mexico PreK, providing support to teachers with curriculum, lesson planning, room environment, and teacher development. She has taught infants, toddlers, preschoolers, and kindergartners for sixteen years. She has a BS in early child multicultural education and is currently working on her master's in early childhood curriculum and instruction.

- **Suzanne Hegarty:** Suzanne has taught four-year-olds at St. Saviour's Church Nursery School in Greenwich, Connecticut, for eight years. She and her colleagues implement the Connecticut Preschool Assessment Framework through lesson planning and portfolio assessment. She has a BS in education and has also worked in the media center in an elementary school.

- **Sue Jeffers:** Sue has been teaching kindergarten at University School (a private, independent school) in Milwaukee, Wisconsin, for nineteen years. For ten of those years, she has served as cochair of the preprimary department. She has a BA in elementary education and early childhood certification.

- **Brenda Kofahl:** Brenda is PreK Program Specialist and Data Coordinator/K–3 Plus Program Manager in the Literacy Bureau, New Mexico Public Education Department. She has been an early childhood teacher, child care director, Head Start director, birth to age eight education coordinator, and an elementary principal. She taught full-day kindergarten in a visual and performing arts magnet school for nine years as well as teaching first and second grades. She also taught university-level early childhood courses and served for one year on the National Indian Head Start Directors' Board of Directors. She has a BS in elementary education and an MS in education.

- **Mary McQuiston:** Mary is Education and Development Manager for New Mexico PreK. She also teaches courses in early childhood multicultural education at the university level. She has been in the field of early childhood education since 1990 and has worked with infants, toddlers, and preschoolers in the roles of classroom teacher, supervisor, and trainer. She has a PhD in human services with a focus on early childhood care and education, an MA in educational thought and sociocultural studies, a BA in philosophy, and an AA in early childhood education.

- **Lauren Michael:** Lauren is a Training and Development Consultant for New Mexico PreK, providing training and on-site support to New Mexico PreK teachers. She has been in the field of early childhood education for eleven years and has taught in both infant/toddler and pre-K classrooms. She has a BA in early childhood and multicultural education and is currently in the process of completing an MA in early childhood curriculum and instruction.

- **Rosemary Neely:** Rosemary has been a Family Literacy Teacher in the Title I Even Start Family Literacy Program in the Albuquerque Public Schools, working with three-, four-, and five-year-olds for the past eight years. The primary focus of the program is to encourage family literacy. She has worked with young children for twenty years and has a BS in early childhood education and a master's in multicultural early childhood.

- **Robin Sampaga:** Robin is a kindergarten teacher, a Lead Mentor Trainer, and an Early Childhood Leader (ELL teacher, inclusion teacher) in Albuquerque Public Schools. She has taught preschool, kindergarten, and first, second, and third grades for twenty-eight years both in the United States and internationally. She has a BS in early childhood education and an MA in education.

- **Sarah Simms:** Sarah is Interim Consultant Program Manager for New Mexico PreK. She has worked in the field of early childhood education for twelve years with very diverse populations, including infants, toddlers, preschoolers, school-age children, and college students as a classroom teacher, a center mentor, and a program administrator. She has a degree in human development and family studies with an emphasis in early childhood education.

- **Kathy Stewart:** Kathy is Director of St. Saviour's Church Nursery School in Old Greenwich, Connecticut, and has worked with young children as a teacher and center director for more than twenty years. Over the past six years, she has worked diligently in partnership with the Greenwich Board of Education to provide high-quality professional development opportunities to the Greenwich early childhood education community with a focus on the intentional process of weaving together curriculum and early learning standards. She contributed a chapter to *The Storybook Journey: Pathways to Learning through Story and Play,* and coauthored an article about intentionality in action for *Young Children* in November 2011. She has a BA in English literature, has certification to teach kindergarten through sixth grade, and has a master's in public administration.

How to Use This Book

The process for planning described in this book encompasses the incredible number of accommodations and details in the life of a successful preschool or kindergarten classroom. This process will help teachers develop an ongoing record of the ways they integrate their own knowledge of child development with the specific needs and interests of the children they teach. This record can then become a tool for planning and reflection as well as for supervision and communication with families.

In addition to sharing planning and reflection frameworks, this book focuses on many aspects of teaching preschool and kindergarten children. Recognizing that some fine curricular approaches have been developed for preschool classrooms (such as the Creative Curriculum, the High/Scope curriculum, the Project Approach, the emergent curriculum, and the Reggio approach), this book does not attempt to reinvent the wheel. Instead, it offers ways to integrate the best of any developmentally appropriate approach into a cohesive whole, using the planning and reflection frameworks as the structure.

Chapter 1 will extend the definition of curriculum beyond a box, a book, or a set of materials and will explore curriculum in depth, defining it as a process that incorporates ongoing planning, observation, and individualization. Chapter 2 will introduce several planning and reflection frameworks to reflect the planning/observation/individualization cycle. The focus of chapter 3 will be on how to embed learning goals and academics in play, daily routines, and teacher-led group activities. Chapter 4 will address teachers' roles in planning and sustaining high-level play experiences for children. Those roles include setting up the environment for play, allowing ample time for high-level play to develop, and acting as play facilitators. In chapter 5, individualization and differentiation for each child will be discussed. Balancing adult-guided and child-guided activities will be explored in chapter 6, and building relationships with children and families is the focus of chapter 7. Chapter 8 focuses on integrating authentic assessment and curriculum. And last, chapter 9 revisits the planning/observation/individualization cycle and considers what happens when various elements are missing.

CHAPTER 1

Implementing Curriculum through the Planning/Observation/Individualization Cycle

The best curricular practices for preschool and kindergarten children revolve around knowledge of the traits of young learners. Because they are different from older children, they require teachers to use different approaches than those seen in elementary-grade classrooms. Let's consider some of the characteristics of young children.

Preschool and kindergarten children are active learners. They are not passive receptors or good listeners. Watching demonstrations or listening to lectures is not their primary mode for taking in new information. They are movers and shakers, wigglers and doers. They have energy to burn and the desire to try out things actively for themselves. They are risk takers, exploring their own capabilities and not always recognizing safety issues. They are builders and constructors. They are climbers and runners. They are scientists experimenting with new and exciting ways to use materials. They are artists and dancers, exploring their own creativity and freedom in space, figuring out how to express their unique selves.

Preschool and kindergarten children are just beginning to figure out written language and the power of stories. They understand quantities through real problems that arise and must be solved: How many crackers can we have for snack, or how many children can fit around a table? Young children express their feelings more through their behaviors than their words, and they often use their bodies to communicate; their verbal communication skills and vocabulary cannot yet keep pace with the intense emotions they experience over short periods of time.

Preschool and kindergarten children need a number of outlets to express their physical energy, to manipulate objects for learning, and to try things out for themselves. The classroom environment needs to provide opportunities for movement, exploration, and hands-on manipulation of objects. Teachers must carefully evaluate the daily schedule to make sure sitting and listening times are briefer than times for hands-on activities. And they must provide daily outdoor time to meet children's need to run, jump, and climb. Preschool and kindergarten teachers must do all of this in the name of curriculum.

Defining Curriculum

Defining curriculum in preschool and kindergarten classrooms is difficult. It entails so many more things than a literacy lesson or a science activity. Publishers have produced curriculum kits, curriculum books, curriculum materials, as well as curricular frameworks and approaches. I propose that *none* of these completely captures what happens between a skilled early childhood practitioner and her children—whether in a two and one-half hour program or in a full-day one. Curriculum is *everything* that goes on in a program, from the moment a child arrives until she leaves. Her experience throughout the time she is there impacts her learning and success.

Kathy: "Curriculum is so much more than a book or a kit—very straightforwardly, it's everything."

Laura: "I think it's very helpful to say curriculum is in everything. I have seen teachers say they understand this natural process, but it is not always being put into practice. Perhaps they don't trust it enough."

Curriculum cannot be limited to a box, a book, or a set of materials. It's a dynamic process of implementing plans and observing what happens. A teacher plans engaging activities and experiences for children—that's where the box, book, or materials may contribute. As she implements those plans, she observes to determine the success and involvement of each individual child as well as the success and involvement of the whole group. Based on what she observes, she makes adjustments—sometimes immediately, right in the moment, and sometimes after time has passed and she's reflected on what occurred. Skilled teachers are reflective more than reactive. They are thoughtful and intentional. They are observant and flexible. And the curriculum they implement is an evolving process of integrated teacher actions that take place in an ongoing cycle. The following graphic identifies five important steps in the curriculum process.

The Planning/Observation/Individualization Cycle

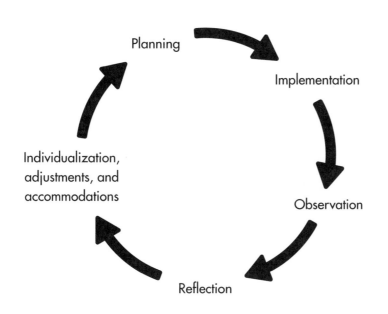

Let's look more closely at each of the steps in the curriculum process.

Planning

Skilled teachers plan activities and play experiences that are age appropriate for preschool and kindergarten children. The daily schedule includes a mix of child-chosen and teacher-led activities, with more time spent in child-chosen ones. These activities take place within the context of a classroom environment that is well organized and rich in possibilities.

Teachers plan for playtimes by choosing materials that engage children's interest and challenge their curiosity, thinking, and creativity. And teachers make plans to facilitate the children's play with those materials. They plan open-ended questions and suggestions that will sustain the children's engagement in what they are doing.

Teacher-led group times are planned with clear routines that help children settle in and participate. Large-group activities include dancing and movement games, singing and chanting, listening to stories, and planning for the day. For small groups, content goals are addressed through interesting, hands-on activities, such as a science experiment or a math or literacy game. Teachers write their plans so that they are clear about their goals for

Suzanne: "I've found that the process becomes circular. No one piece of the process can be successful on its own."

the week and can communicate with families about what will be happening at school.

Implementation

Next, teachers implement the planned-for activities and play experiences. They set out and prepare materials for both. Teachers know it's important to introduce the possibilities of play areas and materials from which children can select to develop high-level play. They may explain what children can do with the materials or present a challenge for a new way to use them. In this way, they guide curriculum—encouraging children to try new things or to think in different ways. Each child chooses an activity and goes to that area. Then the adults in the classroom move about the room, interacting with the children at different areas. They are ever watchful, seeing where they are needed and what actions will most effectively facilitate and enhance children's play.

Mary B.: "I feel better prepared because I plan—and I can still be flexible."

Teachers implement large-group times that are engaging and last only as long as children are interested. By starting with physical activity and moving to songs and fingerplays that settle children down, teachers find that children's attention gets more focused; then they are ready to listen to a story or watch a demonstration. For small-group work, teachers implement activities that are hands-on and have many possibilities. With a clear goal in mind, teachers choose materials that offer children different ways to practice that goal. For example, if sorting and categorizing objects is the goal, then small bins of buttons, beads, stones, shells, keys, screws, and bottle caps will engage the children more fully than only one bin of similar objects. Again, teachers are ever watchful, reading the signals of children's interest and ending the small-group time when it's best for the children.

Observation

Rosemary: "I like the emphasis on the dynamic process of planning and observation. There is an interplay between the two because it may not always be obvious to teachers that this is what they do, almost unconsciously."

Teachers watch the children in their care throughout the day. They observe the children in action as they play and as they participate in group times. They listen carefully to the children's words. They read the children's body language. They note the children's emotional tone. They see the lightbulb going on when a child understands a new concept or masters a new skill. They recognize the frustration when a child has difficulty with something or someone. As teachers watch, they may write down a few of their observations, keeping a record of what they see children doing for assessment purposes. They may take photographs of a child at work and at play. They may ask a child if they can keep a drawing, writing sample, or creation as part of an assessment portfolio.

Teachers observe the children individually and as a whole group. They pay attention when the noise level gets too loud in the block area or too quiet near the bathroom sink. They notice the areas of the classroom that are well used and those that are not. They watch to see the ways children use materials. These observations may require some immediate intervention but also provide information for future planning purposes.

Reflection

Good teachers need quiet time to think carefully about what's happening with each child. Time to reflect is a necessity. Replaying the day's mental videotape, reviewing observation notes, reflecting on those exciting teachable moments that worked as well as those activities that didn't are essential to providing quality early childhood education. Reflecting on what has been observed can help teachers achieve two things:

1. They can assess each child's performance and individualize curricular strategies to better meet the needs of each child.
2. They can consider what parts of their curriculum are working well for the whole group and what will need adjustment and change.

Individualization, Adjustments, and Accommodations

After reflection, teachers consider individual children's needs and adjust lesson plans. They make accommodations too. They also evaluate the way they handled a difficult behavior and rethink classroom arrangement. Based on their reflections, teachers adjust activities and change play experiences to accommodate both the needs of individual children and the needs of the group. To help children be successful, teachers make changes both spontaneously and after thoughtful planning.

Teachers make hundreds of accommodations spontaneously each day—they cut the story short because they see the group wiggling, or they decide to read another story because the children are so attentive. They pull out a set of materials or a piece of equipment on the spur of the moment to accommodate a child's deep interest or his need for physical motion on a day too rainy to go outside. Here's an example of a spontaneous accommodation for an individual child:

Sue: "Observation includes so many things—individual, group, and the use of the environment that has been set up. It isn't the time to reach conclusions, either. The curriculum circle has to go around a few times before that should happen."

Suzanne: "As always, time is the biggest challenge. Being able to thoroughly reflect on and discuss the observations we have taken through the week as well as apply those reflections in our plans for the following week can sometimes become tricky to find the time to do as a team."

Lauren: "One challenge that I remember being most difficult is the aspect of slowing down to really watch and listen to children and to reflect on your own practice. A day of teaching can be very hectic. However, I think that I would forget that slowing down and taking the time to reflect would eventually make the classroom less hectic, and I would be able to have more quality one-on-one and small-group interactions."

Ms. Anne sees Brandon trying to cut with scissors. As he turns them upside down, she notes his growing frustration and decides to move toward him and offer assistance. She carefully places her hand over his, turns his hand upside down, and helps him to make a snip. He smiles broadly. "You did it!" she says.

Preschool and kindergarten teachers also make hundreds of planned accommodations to help children learn or to build relationships. They seat certain children next to each other because they recognize that the pairing will be successful. Or they seat children on their own laps for just the same reason. They plan a change to the manipulative area because they notice that the puzzles are not being cared for, and they hypothesize that the available puzzles are too easy for many of the children. They plan ways to support children who are struggling with a particular skill and ways to challenge children in their areas of strength.

To make adjustments and accommodations in the curriculum to support the learning of individual children and of the group, teachers continually evaluate the following areas:

- available materials
- activity length
- level of physical involvement (active or passive)
- amount of teacher direction versus the amount of child choice
- activity themes (teacher-determined or based on children's interests)
- activity goals or goals for individual children

Whether spontaneous or carefully planned, all of these adjustments and accommodations are based on teachers' deep knowledge of the children, careful observation, and thoughtful reflection about the daily happenings in the classroom. Then the curriculum process begins again. Once teachers have reflected on individual and group needs, they plan, implement, and observe again. That's the curriculum process in action!

The Importance of Goals

On what is this curriculum process—this planning/observation/individualization cycle—based? How will a teacher know that her plans and adjustments are making a difference in children's learning? The answer to that question is LEARNING GOALS. *Everything a teacher does with the children is based on clearly defined, age-appropriate learning goals.*

Learning goals based on reasonable expectations for preschool or kindergarten children are the focus of the curriculum process. At all times, teachers must keep in mind learning goals in all domains (cognitive, physical, and social/emotional) that will support the healthy development of each child: learning goals that are just right for three- to six-year-olds. These learning goals may come from early learning standards or from assessment tools. Of course, it's ideal for assessment and curricular goals to be the same so teachers don't have to jump back and forth between different sources with differing expectations. Learning goals are at the core of preschool and kindergarten curriculum, as the graphic below illustrates.

The Planning/Observation/Individualization Cycle

Planning

Implementation

Age-appropriate goals integrated in all activities

Individualization, adjustments, and accommodations

Observation

Reflection

Notice that the learning goals at the center of this curriculum process are age appropriate. Over the past decade, kindergarten teachers were asked to "up the ante" in their classrooms, to expect five-year-old children (often turning six) to be taught in ways that resemble what one might see in a first- or second-grade classroom. Paper and pencil tasks took the place of play centers, and learning to read became a kindergarten expectation. As higher kindergarten expectations became prevalent, parents began to wonder why preschool teachers weren't implementing a more *academic* program as well. Public assumptions defined *academic* as less time devoted to play and socialization and more time in teacher-led activities related to learning the alphabet letters, letter sounds, and math concepts through formal, didactic instruction.

Developmentally Appropriate Practices and Academics

In its signature document defining the best practices for young children, the National Association for the Education of Young Children (NAEYC) cautions against inappropriate expectations for young children (Copple and Bredekamp 2009). Are academics an inappropriate expectation?

The critical answer to this question involves *how* those academics are presented to children. All developmentally appropriate programs should include stimulating learning opportunities for children in a variety of content areas. Teachers should be accountable for the skills and concepts young children gain in their classrooms. Children should not, however, be relegated to passive learning, with teachers acting as instructors, imparting knowledge to "empty vessels." Instead, children should actively learn academics with teachers acting as facilitators and guides more often than as instructors.

Quality preschool and kindergarten programs that include play and exploration *are* academic programs. They include carefully planned opportunities for children to learn more about the world around them, to develop skills and competencies, to understand concepts, and to gain knowledge. The academics of these programs are carefully embedded in active learning and play throughout the daily schedule. Situations are planned so children can figure things out for themselves. They are exposed to new materials and possibilities. They are supported and challenged by teachers who know the best ways to match learning activities to the traits of preschool and kindergarten children. Teachers in programs with young children with special needs adapt the learning goals to the developmental level at which the child is performing. For these children, age-appropriate learning goals may not be acceptable, but individualized learning goals are still incorporated into the curriculum for each child.

When teachers incorporate academics into the curriculum, they raise the level of accountability. When they incorporate learning goals in the planning and observation process, teachers remind themselves that indeed they are thinking first and foremost about learning.

It's important for teachers to communicate to others about their goals for children's learning. When they do, teachers help others witness how much they know about the children's growth and development and how hard they work to support and challenge each child. Chapters 2 and 3 show ways that teachers can use planning and reflection frameworks to document their attention to learning goals. Chapters 7 and 8 address many ways teachers can share learning goals with families and incorporate learning goals into the assessment process.

Learning in Daily Classroom Routines

Let's look more closely at the idea that curriculum happens throughout every minute of the preschool or kindergarten day. You may ask yourself, "How can learning be happening from the moment a child arrives until he leaves?" You may think, "I see learning when I lead small- or large-group time, but is learning really happening during the daily routines? Are children always learning as they play?"

Let's consider the daily routine of arrival time and analyze the learning it involves. As a child arrives, he makes a transition from the familiarity of home and family to the classroom. In the classroom, he must get along with twenty or so other children. He must follow the routines of the day and accept the guidance and authority of adults who are not his parents. As he arrives, he needs to be supported in this transition, welcomed warmly, given clear instructions for a familiar arrival routine, and given time to ease himself into the social group.

Many teachers plan several tasks for each child to do on arrival. After being warmly greeted by the teacher, the child is expected to put his backpack and coat in his cubby and to sign in, writing his name down at the sign-in table or moving his photo from the "At Home" column to the "At School" column on a magnetic board. He may also be asked to answer the "Question of the Day" by putting his name card under "Yes" or "No" in the pocket chart. Then he must choose from some table activities where hands-on materials are available (paper and instruments for writing or drawing; small manipulatives for constructing, such as Lego blocks; and playdough). He can talk with friends as he works at his chosen activity until all of his classmates have arrived and the group gathers for a morning meeting to plan for the day.

Now, let's look at the learning that occurs at arrival time.

- The child *speaks* with the teacher and *listens* to her warm words and directions for the arrival routines. Speaking and listening are important *language arts skills that build vocabulary and grammatical understanding* as well as relationships with others.
- He shows developing *independence* and *responsibility* (both important *approaches to learning*) when he puts away his backpack and coat.
- He uses his *writing skills (letter recognition, fine-motor control)* when he signs in by writing down his name, and his *sorting and categorizing skills* when he moves his photo on the magnetic board.
- He *reads* the question of the day (or a teacher reads it out loud to him as he *tracks along* with his eyes), *recognizes* his name card and the words "Yes" and "No," and *categorizes* his answer accordingly.
- He joins his friends at the tables and *interacts socially, sharing materials, taking turns, and talking with others, showing concern and care to members of his school community* (all important *social/ emotional skills* that lead to the development of citizens in a democratic society).

The learning goals identified above cover a range of domains including language arts, mathematics, approaches to learning, and social/emotional development. And all of them were addressed in a ten- to twenty-minute time period that occurs every day in a preschool or kindergarten classroom! With some thoughtful planning, teachers can embed academic learning goals in routine activities that happen every day in their classrooms.

Learning during Play

How can teachers make sure that learning occurs during play experiences as well? First they must organize a rich classroom environment. The classroom environment is the most important source for learning activities and must be organized and used in ways that make learning positive, engaging, active, and exciting. Then they must facilitate children's play experiences so that the play is high-level play that deeply engages children, rather than play that is chaotic and out of control. They may facilitate by providing certain materials—menus and other restaurant items, for example—or by asking children provocative questions—"What else do you think you could make with the blocks?" When the environment is well organized and teachers are involved with the children as they play, behavior problems are kept to a minimum, and learning occurs.

Effective preschool and kindergarten teachers organize the classroom environment—and they plan for play. They think carefully about each area of the classroom—blocks, dramatic play, sensory table, manipulatives, writing center, class library, art area—and identify learning goals related to what children will do in each area. These learning goals help teachers determine what materials are needed and how they can support the children's learning and development. Teachers review their plans for children's play every week and change the learning goals as needed.

Consider how to plan for play in one area of the classroom, the block area, let's say. Most preschool classrooms (and I hope most kindergarten classrooms!) have a large set of wooden blocks organized on shelves by shape and size. In addition, the area may include small cars, traffic signs, and people and animal figures too. Many learning goals are addressed as children play with these materials, including the following:

- *shape identification* as they use the different shaped blocks, match and compare them, determine that two triangles make a square, two squares a rectangle, and so on
- *measurement concepts* as they use long and short blocks and create taller structures or longer roads
- *sorting and categorizing* by shape and size
- *counting and understanding of quantity* as they figure out how many blocks are needed to complete a planned structure ("We need three more blocks for the bridge to reach the road.") or place one car on one block or a group of animal figures in a pen ("I have four horses in my barn.")
- *understanding of the properties of gravity, weight, balance, and momentum*

- *cooperation and communication with others* as they work together to complete a structure or road
- *creativity* as they represent their world and create symmetrical structures

When a teacher plans for play in the block area, she chooses one primary learning goal and records it on her plan. When she (and her colleagues in the classroom) interacts with the children who are playing in that area, she asks the children questions and makes suggestions related to the learning goal. She uses the learning goal as a guide to remind herself of the learning that is embedded in block play. With the learning goal in mind, she maintains a clear idea of what to watch for, what to suggest, and when to facilitate or help the children. She does not ignore the children at play or force the children to do only things that are related to the goal. If the children are interested in using the blocks in a different way from those suggested by the learning goal she identified, then she is ever ready to follow along. If the children do take their play in another direction, it's probable that she will be able to identify another goal (one likely present on the list above) in their play. Of course, if the children become rowdy or destructive, then she will step in, intervene, and redirect the play back to something more productive.

Lists of learning goals taken from early learning standards or assessment tools can be identified for each of the play areas in a classroom. Chapter 2 provides frameworks for play area planning goals, and chapter 3 explores in more depth embedding academic learning goals in play and daily routines. Chapter 4 focuses on planning and sustaining high-level play and includes the following:

- setting up the environment for play
- allowing ample time for high-level play to develop
- facilitating play

Six Elements of the Curriculum Process

In addition to integrating academic learning goals, there are six other elements related to the curriculum process. If one element in the process is missing, then the curriculum may be less successful for preschool and kindergarten children. The six elements are

1. A rich, well-organized classroom environment
2. Ample time for play and investigation with children making choices
3. Teachers scaffolding and assisting children as they play
4. More child-initiated activities than adult-led ones
5. Respectful, caring relationships with children and families
6. Integration of curriculum and authentic, observational assessment

Elements of the Curriculum Process

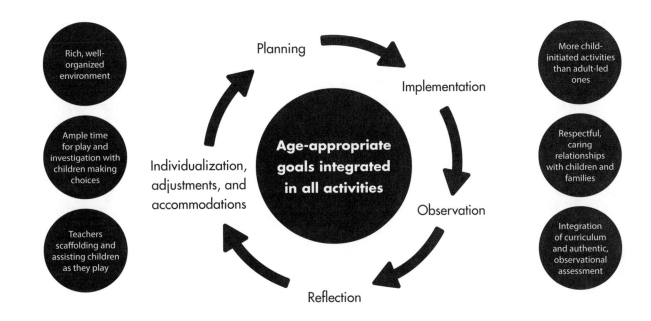

In chapter 2 you will find planning and reflection frameworks that incorporate all of these elements. These frameworks can help teachers make sure they address all of the aspects of the curriculum process. They can contribute to the supervision process as directors and principals work with teachers. And they can help teachers more effectively inform parents and administrators of the work they are doing with the children in their classrooms. When they are used, the frameworks may replace inappropriate expectations for paper-and-pencil tasks and instructional academics with a better understanding of how children learn through play and investigation with teacher support. The rest of the book analyzes each of the elements of the curriculum process in depth, but here is a brief look at each one.

A Rich, Well-Organized Classroom Environment

The classroom environment can provide learning opportunities, create a sense of community, and maintain a positive atmosphere where productive interactions occur among children and adults. Children take the lead in exploring the classroom. Teachers provide the structure for that exploration by the way they organize the areas of the classroom and the materials in those areas, and by the way they carefully plan for the use of those materials. Teachers plan for activities and experiences that will encourage children to use their skills and capabilities and challenge them to learn new concepts and try something that is just beyond their present level. Planning and organizing the environment are part of teaching. Interacting with the children within the classroom environment helps a teacher evaluate how effectively the environment is supporting children's learning and what changes might need to be made.

Mary B.: "I can still follow the child's lead and be planful."

The room arrangement and presentation of materials communicate important messages to the children. Those messages deeply affect behavior. If the classroom is messy and disorganized, children will probably not take good care of the materials. If the shelves are placed along the walls so that huge open spaces dominate the room, children may run and jump, actions much more suitable for outdoors. On the other hand, if materials are carefully organized and presented in a clear, appealing fashion, children may treat them with more care and put them away more easily at cleanup time. If shelving and tables are used to create specific learning areas throughout the room and placed in a way that breaks up running paths and creates intimate spaces for using certain materials, children will settle down and become engaged with activities for longer periods of time and with more productive ends.

When the environment is functioning as a key part of the curriculum, the room arrangement literally directs children toward the productive use of materials in specific areas. Noise levels are considered so that materials that tend toward greater physical and verbal involvement on the part of the children are placed near each other. Materials that tend toward quieter use are also grouped near each other.

Chapter 2 explores ways to use the frameworks to plan for the most effective use of the classroom environment. Chapter 4 discusses ways to set up the environment to encourage and sustain high-level play.

Ample Time for Play and Investigation with Children Making Choices

Supported by long-term research, recommendations from national organizations continue to emphasize the importance of play as a vehicle for learning (NAEYC and NAECS/SDE 2003, 6):

> Particularly for younger children, firsthand learning—through physical, mental, and social activity—is key. At every age from birth through age eight (and beyond), play can stimulate children's engagement, motivation, and lasting learning (Bodrova & Leong 2003). Learning is facilitated when children can "choose from a variety of activities, decide what type of products they want to create, and engage in important conversations with friends" (Espinosa 2002, 5).

For children to engage in high-level play, which is the kind of play that is deeply engaging and full of learning opportunities, they need plenty of time to get involved. They may need to look over the materials and possibilities available in the different areas of the classroom. They may observe other children to get ideas or to decide which group to join. Once they start to play, they need time to develop ideas, to talk with other children, and to try out different things. Providing ample time (at least forty-five minutes to one hour) for deep play to develop is an important element of effective curriculum planning.

Teachers recognize that offering choices leads to more participation and engagement in play. Children will stretch themselves and apply more of their skills and capabilities when the activity is one in which they are interested. Thus, it's important for teachers to let the children figure out how long they want to stay with specific activities. Timing the children and making them rotate to different areas does not allow them the opportunity to make a plan and stick with it through completion.

Teachers Scaffolding and Assisting Children as They Play

It is not enough to organize a classroom environment and allow ample time for the children to explore it. Teachers need to facilitate children's use of the environment. Teachers first build trusting, caring relationships with children. They then offer a wide range of opportunities within the environment. Some of those opportunities allow children to make choices and to follow their own or their peers' interests. Some of those opportunities are adult led or adult chosen. A careful balance with flexibility for individual differences is all-important.

As children play, teachers are watchful. They pay attention to what children are doing in the different areas and provide assistance. Perhaps different materials are needed. Perhaps a disagreement needs to be mediated. Perhaps higher-level play needs to be stimulated with a new idea or suggestion. Perhaps a child is attempting to do something that is just beyond her present capabilities. She needs the teacher to serve as a "scaffold," to provide just the right amount of assistance so that she can be successful.

As children play, teachers do not act as instructors. Instead, they interact with children as facilitators, guides, resource providers, and supporters. All of these are teaching roles that further curricular goals and enhance children's learning through play. Throughout these interactions, teachers observe children closely to determine each child's capabilities. In this way, teachers are ensuring that children's play experiences benefit the children. In high-level play, children are learning new skills and concepts and applying and adapting ones that are already established. The playtimes in preschool and kindergarten classrooms are not "free-for-alls." Rather, they are times when children can become deeply engaged, work alone or together, and interact with adults who provide new vocabulary, help them determine problem-solving strategies, and provoke their thinking. In chapter 4 the focus will be on teaching strategies that lead to and sustain high-level play experiences for children.

More Child-Initiated Activities Than Adult-Led Ones

As teachers facilitate play experiences, they may be following the child's lead in the activity. The child initiates the activity and directs her actions, and the teacher helps in whichever ways are beneficial. Teachers also plan and lead activities and experiences for the children. They may plan for daily large-group meetings and focused small-group activities. The balance between child-initiated and teacher-led activities is important. For young children, this balance should lean more heavily toward child direction than for older children. Early childhood educators continually decide in which instances they will follow the child's lead and in which moments they will be in a more directive role.

Effective preschool and kindergarten teachers make sure they have planned for every part of the day. The classroom organization and use of time are structured. Within this structure, however, teachers enable the children to make choices about which activities they will do and when, different ways in which they will use the materials, and with whom they will interact while they do so. Also, within this careful planning, a teacher provides some activities where she is the leader and initiator, not the child. The question to consider is: How much of children's explorations should be based on their choices and how much should be based on teacher suggestions or directions? Chapter 6 will focus on finding just the right balance between child-initiated and teacher-led activities in preschool and kindergarten classrooms so that children's productive exploration of the classroom can take place without chaos or anarchy. Ways to plan for effective teacher-led large- and small-group times will also be explored.

Respectful, Caring Relationships with Children and Families

When they begin their preschool or kindergarten experience, many children may be leaving their home environment for the first time. Warm relationships with caring adults at school will make this transition go more smoothly for children and enhance their overall experience. "From birth, a child's relationships and interactions with adults are critical determinants of development and learning" (NAEYC 2009, 17).

Teachers and children build strong, caring relationships through their daily interactions. Teachers get to know each child well. They express their faith in children's potential and their willingness to help them to grow and learn. The classroom environment is set up to encourage children to be active explorers yet provides structure and guidance for their exploration. Being an explorer means being a risk taker. Young children will not take risks in a classroom unless they feel safe and trusting. They turn to the adults in the environment to provide that safety and to earn their trust. When they establish a caring relationship with those adults, they will venture further, develop more independence, try new activities, and experiment with new peer relationships.

Building relationships with children is an ongoing task involving observation, intuition, and knowledge of age-appropriate behaviors and skills. It also involves getting to know each child's family. Asking questions about their cultural background, the members of the household, and the family's dreams and goals for the child can help teachers work together with family members to support the child more fully. Establishing relationships with each child's family members strengthens the relationship between teachers and child. All adults in the child's life are working together

Robin: "It's so important to build rapport with students, to reach children so that they get it."

in partnership to assure the child's optimum growth and development. Ways to get to know each child well and incorporate that knowledge into the frameworks will be discussed in chapter 5, and ways to build relationships and communicate with families in chapter 7.

Integration of Curriculum with Authentic, Observational Assessment

The integration of curriculum planning with assessment of children's learning is the key to good teaching. Therefore, implementing assessment processes that will help with planning is essential. Authentic, observational assessment is the recommended assessment practice in early childhood programs and is well grounded in research and theory. Teachers watch and listen as children participate in activities and experiences throughout the day. They document observations for the purpose of reflection and planning as well as to assess each child's capabilities and progress. They collect portfolio documentation to capture tangible evidence of children's progress and growth to share with families and to help with curricular planning.

> Policy makers, the early childhood profession, and other stakeholders in young children's lives have a shared responsibility to assess young children's strengths, progress, and needs, use assessment methods that are developmentally appropriate, culturally and linguistically responsive, tied to children's daily activities, supported by professional development, inclusive of families, and connected to specific, beneficial purposes: (1) making sound decisions about teaching and learning, (2) identifying significant concerns that may require focused intervention for individual children, and (3) helping programs improve their educational and developmental interventions. (NAEYC and NAECS/SDE 2003, 2)

Assessment does not stand apart from curriculum. As demonstrated in the planning/observation/individualization cycle, teachers include learning goals in all aspects of the day, identifying the ways they will incorporate them into play experiences, daily routines, and large- and small-group activities. Teachers' observations related to age-appropriate learning goals and their documentation of children's performance related to those learning goals are ongoing. Teachers' reflections on these observations inform the teaching process and assist teachers in determining the most effective curricular strategies. Chapter 8 focuses on the integration of curriculum planning and assessment.

Conclusion

Curriculum is *everything* that goes on in a program from the moment a child arrives until she leaves. Teachers plan, implement, observe, reflect, and make adjustments based on individual children's needs and the needs of the group. Curriculum is an ongoing process that requires teachers to think about child development, observe how the children in their classroom are learning and growing, and make hundreds of decisions about the best ways to help them reach their full potential.

Six elements of curriculum are embedded in the ongoing planning/observation/individualization process and contribute to its successful implementation. Some of these elements are unique to early childhood education. Preschool and kindergarten teachers know that young children learn differently than older children. These elements reflect that knowledge by emphasizing the importance of play, child initiation, and warm relationships with children and families. When these elements are not attended to in a classroom, teachers will see changes in the children's behavior and engagement: children may act out in frustration; behavior problems may occur frequently; and children may complain about activities, refuse to cooperate fully with teachers, and lose their enthusiasm for learning.

Joy should be a part of early childhood education. Young children's enthusiasm, curiosity, and exploratory nature should be celebrated and treasured. When curriculum is limited to a box, a book, or a set of materials, teachers may find that they are missing precious opportunities to enhance children's learning and nourish their joy. By looking at curriculum as everything that happens, by focusing on the planning/observation/individualization process, and by including the elements identified above, preschool and kindergarten teachers will be more in tune with the nature of young children and will find their curricular practices match the children's learning styles more closely. Through their observations, reflections, adjustments, and accommodations, teachers will make sure that joyful learning is happening throughout their program day. In the next chapter, we will look at frameworks for planning and reflection that capture the elements of quality preschool and kindergarten curriculum and help teachers record all that they do on behalf of children.

Sue: "The definition of curriculum to be all-inclusive to what happens all day long is so true, yet often overwhelming and hard to put into words. The process and essential elements make it seem less daunting or haphazard. The success of this curricular approach is a very responsive and personal curriculum tailored for the individuals and group at that time."

Lauren: "The planning/observation/individualization cycle gives weight to all of the hard work that teachers put into their teaching. It will help preschool and kindergarten teachers feel like professionals."

CHAPTER 2

Planning and Reflection Frameworks

. . . .

This book contains two primary frameworks that teachers can use to plan for play, observation, and learning: one for preschool classrooms and one for kindergarten classrooms. Both frameworks include as many of the recommended teaching approaches from high-quality early childhood curricula as possible. Later in this chapter, other frameworks are shared. You can find photocopy-ready templates of all these frameworks in appendix A, or you can download them at www.redleafpress.org.

Preschool and kindergarten classrooms have more in common than not, so the two frameworks are very similar. But because many kindergarten programs are full-day while many preschool programs are half-day, the kindergarten framework assumes that the classroom schedule allows for more attention to literacy activities and math, science, and playful explorations than the preschool framework. For now, let's consider the aspects that the frameworks for both ages have in common.

Both frameworks contain pages with a variety of labeled boxes where teachers can write plans. Each box has a specific purpose and has been chosen to allow teachers to keep track of the many ways they engage young children, support their learning, build trust and friendship with them, and continually challenge them to their fullest potential. Parts of these plans can be posted on a bulletin board or online for parents to see.

Both frameworks include a page with boxes to record plans for observations and modifications for individual children and boxes to reflect about the plan's results. This reflection page is for the teacher's (and perhaps administrator's) eyes only; it should not be shared with parents. In her reflection, the teacher may have noted something about an individual child. To respect and honor the child's privacy, the teacher does not post or share this page with families.

With this combination of pages for planning and reflection, the frameworks provide a record of the planning/observation/individualization cycle as it occurs.

Robin: "I think it's a great idea to have separate formats."

Lauren: "The setup of the lesson plan is user friendly. There is enough room in all of the boxes, and learning goals are the first thing that a teacher will focus on. This will help them to become more intentional and thoughtful with their weekly plans."

Sue: "The emphasis on planning lessons plus materials, vocabulary, questions, groupings, and prompts makes the whole of teaching more evident and intentional."

Preschool Weekly Planning and Reflection Framework

Program/School: _____   Date: _____   Teacher(s): _____

Ongoing Project (optional): _____

	Learning goal(s)	Additional materials or focus	Vocabulary words
BLOCKS			
DRAMATIC PLAY			
SENSORY TABLE			
ART			
MANIPULATIVES			
CLASS LIBRARY			
WRITING CENTER			
OTHER CENTER			

Preschool Weekly Planning and Reflection Framework

Preschool Weekly Planning and Reflection Framework

DATE:		MONDAY	TUESDAY	WEDNESDAY	THURSDAY	FRIDAY
Large group	Learning goal					
	Activity and teacher strategy					
Small group	Learning goal					
	Activity and teacher strategy					

Plans for Building Community and Relationships	Plans for Outdoor Explorations	Plans for Meals and Transitions

Preschool Weekly Planning and Reflection Framework

Preschool Weekly Planning and Reflection Framework
OBSERVATIONS, MODIFICATIONS, AND REFLECTIONS

FOCUSED OBSERVATIONS:	MODIFICATIONS FOR INDIVIDUAL CHILDREN:
REFLECTIONS: What worked? What didn't? What did you learn about individual children and group interests?	PLANS: Based on your reflections, what will you change for next week?

Preschool Weekly Planning and Reflection Framework

Kindergarten Weekly Planning and Reflection Framework
READERS AND WRITERS WORKSHOP

Program/School: _____   Date: _____   Teacher(s): _____

Ongoing Project (optional): _____

	Learning goal(s)	Additional materials or focus	Vocabulary words
LISTENING CENTER			
DRAMATIC PLAY			
JOURNALING CENTER			
ALPHABET CENTER			
FLANNEL BOARD/ POCKET CHARTS			
CLASS LIBRARY			
TEACHER-LED LITERACY ACTIVITY			
WRITING CENTER			
OTHER CENTER			

Kindergarten Weekly Planning and Reflection Framework

Kindergarten Weekly Planning and Reflection Framework

DATE:		MONDAY	TUESDAY	WEDNESDAY	THURSDAY	FRIDAY
Large group	Learning goal					
	Activity and teacher strategy					
Small group	Learning goal					
	Activity and teacher strategy					
Afternoon Story Time	Learning goal					
	Activity and teacher strategy					

Plans for Building Community and Relationships	Plans for Outdoor Explorations	Plans for Meals and Transitions

Kindergarten Weekly Planning and Reflection Framework

Kindergarten Weekly Planning and Reflection Framework
INVESTIGATION TIME

Program/School: _____ Date: _____ Teacher(s): _____

Ongoing Project (optional): _____

	Learning goal(s)	Additional materials or focus	Vocabulary words
BLOCKS			
MATH ACTIVITY			
SENSORY TABLE			
ART			
MANIPULATIVES			
SCIENCE EXPLORATION			
INFORMATIONAL READING			
MATH AND SCIENCE JOURNALING			
OTHER CENTER			

Kindergarten Weekly Planning and Reflection Framework

Kindergarten Weekly Planning and Reflection Framework
OBSERVATIONS, MODIFICATIONS, AND REFLECTIONS

FOCUSED OBSERVATIONS:	MODIFICATIONS FOR INDIVIDUAL CHILDREN:
REFLECTIONS: What worked? What didn't? What did you learn about individual children and group interests?	PLANS: Based on your reflections, what will you change for next week?

Kindergarten Weekly Planning and Reflection Framework

The preschool and kindergarten frameworks are for teachers to use when they think ahead to the next week in their classroom. The frameworks are designed to be completed on a weekly basis because young children don't need the whole classroom environment or their activity choices to change every day. Children appreciate the opportunity to try things again and again, practicing and refining their skills and knowledge and learning to deepen their involvement with various materials. Only the teacher-led groups, both large and small, are listed so that daily plans can be written (though they do not necessarily have to change daily).

The basic classroom environment is the centerpiece of both frameworks. This gives focus to the use of the environment and any changes to be made to it—for example, changes to specific learning goals, or to challenge the children's thinking, or to incorporate their ideas and interests into projects or long-term studies. This focus helps a teacher organize necessary materials ahead of time and consider special activities, such as stories, songs, fingerplays, science experiments, or project activities. Both frameworks include places to plan meals, transitions, and outdoor play so

Mary B.: "There's flexibility in the lesson plan framework."

Suzanne: "We are able to easily adjust our plans when necessary based on either the needs of the children or the needs of the day. We plan very deliberately the order in which we want to present materials and/or activities."

that teachers don't miss opportunities for learning in these daily routines. The frameworks also remind a teacher to make individual adjustments and to conduct focused observations.

However, the environment is meaningless without the people who function in it day in and day out. Teachers facilitate children's use of the environment. Teachers build relationships with young children and create a caring community in their classroom. The frameworks incorporate ways for teachers to include their relationship-building steps with children while they do their planning. They include recording individual adjustments within the curriculum as teachers learn more about each child's strengths, developmental challenges, and individual characteristics. And the frameworks provide a way for teachers to focus their observations of children in action in order to make modifications for individual children.

Now let's review each page of both frameworks. You will see that some pages are the same for preschool and kindergarten classrooms, and some are different. Later in the chapter, we will explore each page in more depth and consider some different sample plans.

Planning for Play Areas

Play is an important vehicle for learning in early childhood classrooms. The classroom environment can provide learning opportunities, create a sense of community, and maintain a positive atmosphere where productive interactions occur among children and adults. The first page of the preschool framework focuses on planning for children's exploration and play in designated areas of the classroom. It includes seven boxes identifying areas that should be available every day to children:

- blocks
- dramatic play
- sensory table
- art
- manipulatives
- class library
- writing center

One additional box is provided to identify an additional play area that a teacher may choose to provide for the week as well.

In each box teachers write three things:

1. One or more learning goals
2. Any additional materials they may want to add to the area or a focus they may want to emphasize as they interact with the children in that area
3. Vocabulary words that could be part of conversations with children as they play in that area

In addition, at the top of the page, a teacher may note an ongoing project that is occurring in the classroom.

Preschool Weekly Planning and Reflection Framework

Program/School: _____ Date: _____ Teacher(s): _____

Ongoing Project (optional): _____

	Learning goal(s)	Additional materials or focus	Vocabulary words
BLOCKS			
DRAMATIC PLAY			
SENSORY TABLE			
ART			
MANIPULATIVES			
CLASS LIBRARY			
WRITING CENTER			
OTHER CENTER			

First page, Preschool Weekly Planning and Reflection Framework

A full day in a kindergarten classroom allows children more time to explore and investigate the classroom and participate in focused literacy, math, and science activities. Therefore, the first and third pages of the kindergarten framework are structured similarly to the first page of the preschool framework but with important differences:

- the first page of the kindergarten framework contains boxes to write plans for playful and exploratory literacy experiences in a time of the day called "Readers and Writers Workshop"
- the third page of the kindergarten framework is called "Investigation Time" and contains boxes with many of the same play areas as the preschool framework but also additional areas that focus on math and science activities

Kindergarten Weekly Planning and Reflection Framework
READERS AND WRITERS WORKSHOP

Program/School: _____ Date: _____ Teacher(s): _____

Ongoing Project (optional): _____

	Learning goal(s)	Additional materials or focus	Vocabulary words
LISTENING CENTER			
DRAMATIC PLAY			
JOURNALING CENTER			
ALPHABET CENTER			
FLANNEL BOARD/ POCKET CHARTS			
CLASS LIBRARY			
TEACHER-LED LITERACY ACTIVITY			
WRITING CENTER			
OTHER CENTER			

First page, Kindergarten Weekly Planning and Reflection Framework

Like preschool teachers, kindergarten teachers write three things in
each box:

1. One or more learning goals
2. Any additional materials they may want to add to the area or
   a focus they may want to emphasize as they interact with the
   children in that area
3. Vocabulary words that could be part of conversations with children as they play in that area

When teachers are more aware of learning possibilities as children
play, they interact with children more intentionally to facilitate the learning. Whether you are planning for preschool or kindergarten children,
identifying learning goals for children's play experiences helps connect

Kindergarten Weekly Planning and Reflection Framework
INVESTIGATION TIME

Program/School: _____ Date: _____ Teacher(s): _____

Ongoing Project (optional): _____

	Learning goal(s)	Additional materials or focus	Vocabulary words
BLOCKS			
MATH ACTIVITY			
SENSORY TABLE			
ART			
MANIPULATIVES			
SCIENCE EXPLORATION			
INFORMATIONAL READING			
MATH AND SCIENCE JOURNALING			
OTHER CENTER			

Third page, Kindergarten Weekly Planning and Reflection Framework learning and play more clearly. Parents and administrators then can see the learning results of high-level play. Noting when materials are added or a different focus is emphasized helps teachers be thoughtful in following children's interests and bringing new challenges and experiences to them. Additionally, writing down vocabulary words that can be included in conversations reflects the importance of an extensive vocabulary in children's literacy development.

Planning for Group Times, Community Building, Outdoor Explorations, Meals, and Transitions

The second pages of the preschool and kindergarten frameworks are essentially the same. They both provide spaces for teachers to write plans for large- and small-group times and for community and relationship building, outdoor explorations, meals, and transitions. Large- and small-group times are organized so that daily plans can be written. Teachers often change the storybooks they read each day or the songs and fingerplays they sing and use. Goals for small-group times can also change daily, if desired. Thus, the framework lists the five days of the week for these group times. For large- and small-group times, the teacher writes a learning goal and the activity that she will lead with the group. She also identifies teaching strategies she will use to guide the children in the group experience. It is not necessary to change the plans each day for either large or small groups. A teacher uses her discretion to determine if she wants to plan different activities and goals for each day or use the same ones throughout the week. (A template for a Weekly Planning and Reflection Framework is included in appendix A or you can download it at www.redleafpress.org.) For a full day kindergarten (or preschool) many teachers lead an afternoon story time. A planning space has been included on the second page of the kindergarten plan for this activity.

In the three boxes at the bottom of the page, teachers can identify one or two ways to work with the group throughout the week on building community and relationships, plans for additional materials and activities outdoors, and strategies to enhance meals and transitions.

Preschool Weekly Planning and Reflection Framework

DATE:		MONDAY	TUESDAY	WEDNESDAY	THURSDAY	FRIDAY
Large group	Learning goal					
	Activity and teacher strategy					
Small group	Learning goal					
	Activity and teacher strategy					

Plans for Building Community and Relationships	Plans for Outdoor Explorations	Plans for Meals and Transitions

Second page, Preschool Weekly Planning and Reflection Framework

Observations, Modifications, and Reflections

The third page of the preschool framework is the same as the fourth page of the kindergarten framework. It includes boxes for planning and reflection. To assure that teachers plan for the observation of individual children and specific areas of the classroom, a box for focused observations is included. Here a teacher may write certain children's names or note that she is going to focus on all the children's fine-motor skills for the week. She and her coteachers may want to note the amount of participation in

Sue: "Reflection is the most challenging time piece—to have the time to record and reflect within a reasonable time span. This also made me think that when two people are working together, to have time to share observations, reflect together, and then make the adjustments is so important. All parties need to have input and understanding."

specific play areas or carefully observe children's interest and engagement at large-group time. Based on previous observations and reflection about what was seen and heard, teachers plan for modifications for individual children and note those on this page as well.

The last two boxes of this framework are for reflection and can be used on a daily or weekly basis. At the end of the half day or the full day, a teaching team may sit down for a few minutes to discuss how things went. The reflection questions can be used to focus the agenda of that brief discussion and serve as a recording tool. Or a teacher may use the reflection questions to review how the week has gone, events that occurred, and the children's responses to the activities before she begins planning for the next week.

Reflection is an important part of the planning process. By taking the time to think about the previous week and writing about what worked and

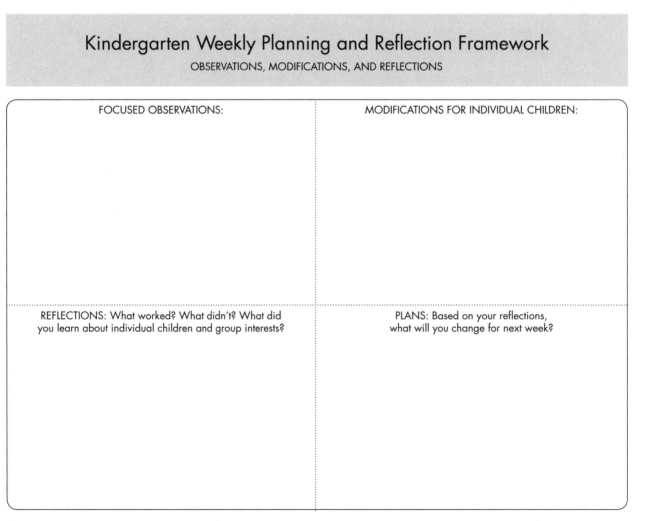

Kindergarten Weekly Planning and Reflection Framework
OBSERVATIONS, MODIFICATIONS, AND REFLECTIONS

FOCUSED OBSERVATIONS:	MODIFICATIONS FOR INDIVIDUAL CHILDREN:
REFLECTIONS: What worked? What didn't? What did you learn about individual children and group interests?	PLANS: Based on your reflections, what will you change for next week?

Third page, Preschool Weekly Planning and Reflection Framework/Fourth page, Kindergarten Weekly Planning and Reflection Framework

what did not both for individual children and the whole group, teachers formalize the reflection process. Their reflection becomes a written document of importance. This document can be helpful not only to future planning but also to demonstrate to supervisors the thoughtfulness and intentionality of what is occurring in the preschool or kindergarten classroom.

By combining the planning and reflection processes, teachers are more fully aware of children's needs. Each week connects to the next week, building on children's interests and capabilities. Assessment information gained through observing children is integrated into planning for the next set of activities. The curriculum flows more smoothly.

By using the planning and reflection framework, a teacher generates a written history of classroom life. These written records can provide direction and ideas for the next activities, projects, academic learning, and individual adjustments. They can provide the basis for family communication and for teaching team conversations. Administrators can review the planning and reflection frameworks and get accurate information for supervision and evaluation.

Let's look at each page of the two frameworks in depth and examine some examples of teachers' plans and reflections. Several completed plans are shown throughout the book. I share these plans with the hope that you will review them and figure out ways to plan for your program, whether you teach preschool or kindergarten. The plans were created by actual preschool and kindergarten teachers for their settings, where they know their children and their needs. The only people who can determine the best plans for a classroom are the teachers who work in that setting. You will fill out your own planning and reflection pages based on your knowledge of the materials you have access to, the amount of adult support you have, and the needs of your particular group of children. To create a truly individualized curriculum, you must consider all of these factors.

Plans for Play Areas in a Preschool Classroom

Preschool teachers provide the structure for children's play and exploration by the way they organize the areas of the classroom and the materials in those areas, and by the way they carefully plan for the use of those materials. Planning and organizing the environment are part of teaching.

Sarah: "A challenge that I personally experienced and I suspect other teachers have experienced as well, was training myself to be a reflective teacher, documenting in such a way that is clear and concise, and learning to trust that with goals in mind, I am working toward supporting the children in the best possible ways."

Lauren: "When using the lesson plan, it can be challenging to ensure that your additional materials and focus really do support the goal that has been identified. They have to be connected to each other in order to really give the teacher the opportunity to watch the work the children do with that goal in mind. I have found that it may be more beneficial if you begin by choosing a goal and then figure out how you can help that goal become alive by planning interactions, setting up an activity, or adding a new material."

Suzanne: "We select three goals for each planning period. We look for these goals in all centers of the room. Some may be more easily observed in a given activity we have planned, but in general, we don't assign specific goals to centers."

Interacting with the children within the classroom environment completes the teaching process.

The first step in planning for play is to identify learning goals for play experiences. In the eight boxes on the first page of the preschool framework, a teacher notes at least one learning goal for that play area for the week. Multiple learning goals across multiple domains can be addressed. For example, for children trying to put together the various manipulatives and puzzles you have in your manipulative area, your learning goal might be one from the physical domain, such as "develops hand-eye coordination." And for children constructing and building with the blocks in the block area, the learning goal you write on your plan might be from the scientific domain: "explores physical properties of weight and balance."

When you write down your learning goals for each play area, you keep yourself focused on the purposes for activities. This will then influence the ways you and your teaching colleagues interact with children to support learning and development. Each learning goal can then be directly correlated with expectations for children's performance and tied to assessment information. (See chapter 8 for more on tying these goals to various assessment tools.) You can identify different learning goals for each of the activities, or you can focus on three or four learning goals that cross over into multiple areas. You decide what's best for your program.

As the school year gets started, you do not have to jump right into an ongoing project or thematic study. Instead, it's best to focus on children exploring all of the play areas in the classroom. In this way the children can discover the range of materials available and try using those materials in the ways they were intended. On the next page is Celia's plan. She has identified the learning goals for her preschool classroom environment for one of the first weeks of the school year. Throughout this chapter, I will continue to show Celia's plan as she adds to it step by step.

Notice that in the field labeled "Ongoing Project," Celia wrote "Explore the classroom." Starting right in with a project or thematic study did not make sense to her. She felt it was more important that children explore the basic play areas of the classroom and try out the many possibilities in each of those areas in the first weeks. Later in this chapter, and more in depth in chapter 5, we will explore ways to determine and incorporate projects and studies in the environment.

Preschool Weekly Planning and Reflection Framework

Program/School: _Community Preschool_   Date: _9/12/11_   Teacher(s): _Celia_

Ongoing Project (optional): _Explore the classroom_

	Learning goal(s)	Additional materials or focus	Vocabulary words
BLOCKS	experimenting with balance and stability		balance, stable
DRAMATIC PLAY	understanding families		mother, father, sister, brother
SENSORY TABLE	measurement	water, measuring cups, and funnels	
ART	using tools to cut and write	markers, scissors, paper, and paste	
MANIPULATIVES	hand-eye coordination		
CLASS LIBRARY	knowledge of books and print		front, back, author, illustrator, title
WRITING CENTER	writing skills	stationery, pads, etc.	
OTHER CENTER	none		

Celia's completed first page

You can see that Celia identified a variety of learning goals that can be addressed as children play in the various parts of the classroom. Notice that the learning goals describe what the child will do with the materials in each area. *They do not tell what the teacher will do.* The learning goals focus on the children and give clear ideas for what teachers can watch for, suggest to the children, facilitate, or help the children do.

For most of the areas, Celia did not identify the materials involved, did she? When you use this kind of framework, listing materials is not always necessary. Instead, it assumes each area has been equipped with materials that are available to children most of the time, making it unnecessary to write them on the plan every week. Celia did not fill out the "Other Center" box either.

Celia only identified additional materials or a different focus for three of the play areas. She left the others blank. But as the school year progresses, she will include additional materials or different foci when appropriate. Celia did identify some vocabulary words that she and her teaching colleagues will use as they interact with children at play. She did not do so for all seven areas, however. She used her common sense to decide where the inclusion of new vocabulary words is important. When the project, materials, or focus change, she will note more vocabulary words on the framework.

The learning goals and materials on Celia's framework could continue for several weeks. When teachers select materials in each area, they choose ones that will be extensive and rich enough so the children will continue to explore the possibilities for using those materials over several weeks. The teacher's role is to encourage that exploration, to watch what the children repeat and practice, and to suggest different ways of using the materials. Later in this chapter we will look at reflecting about the environment to determine when to change learning goals and materials.

Plans for Ongoing Projects

What would a plan look like if an ongoing project was to be implemented? When a teacher does decide to focus curriculum around a topic, she may want to change some things in the classroom environment. Here's a story about implementing an ongoing project.

> Mrs. Chang started the school year in the same way that Celia did, keeping the focus on exploring the classroom. However, a bird began building a nest right outside the classroom window. The children started paying attention to the bird and watched her carefully prepare her nest. Mrs. Chang and her teaching assistant noted the children's interest in their weekly reflection discussion. They decided to follow up on the children's interests and provide some bird-related activities throughout the classroom.

In the following plan for the classroom environment, notice that some areas now focus on the topic of birds, whereas others do not.

Preschool Weekly Planning and Reflection Framework

Program/School: Learning Time Preschool   Date: 9/26/11   Teacher(s): Mrs. Chang and Mrs. Allen

Ongoing Project (optional): Birds and nests

	Learning goal(s)	Additional materials or focus	Vocabulary words
BLOCKS	understanding community (build roads and buildings)	traffic signs and maps, cars, and trucks	neighborhoods, roads, highways, bridges, stop signs
DRAMATIC PLAY	learning to play and get along with other children		
SENSORY TABLE	demonstrating curiosity and interest in new things	using sticks, twigs, strips of cloth to create nests	nests, scavenger, weave
ART	focusing attention and persisting in tasks	make feather collages or Popsicle stick birdhouses	feathers, soft, light
MANIPULATIVES	counting and quantity and geometry	count items and identify shapes and colors	numbers, shapes, and color words
CLASS LIBRARY	vocabulary development and demonstrating curiosity and interest in new things	study books and magazines about birds	cardinal, sparrow, robin, pheasant, duck, swan
WRITING CENTER	writing skills	use writing tools and alphabet stampers	
OTHER CENTER	listening	listen to bird calls on tape	

Mrs. Chang's focused curriculum plan

As you can see, Mrs. Chang changed only the areas of the environment that made sense to correlate to birds and nests. Teachers may rack their brains trying to figure out correlation to a topic for every area of the classroom, but many topics do not fit with every area. Some teachers then feel compelled to make new materials (such as bird matching games) to fit everything around a topic. This is not necessary!

When learning more about birds, changing the materials in the block area does not make sense. Changing art, library, and sensory table materials, however, does. The basic classroom environment does not need the extra layer of a topic in every area. Instead, think carefully about which areas lend themselves to helping the children explore a topic or engage in a project, and only make changes in those areas.

Of course, Mrs. Chang planned for other bird activities to happen in the classroom too, such as stories, songs, bird watching, walks outdoors, and so on. The second and third pages of her plans are included later in this chapter.

Planning for Literacy Play and Investigation in Kindergarten Classrooms

Many kindergarten programs across the country are full-day programs. Therefore, there are more opportunities to include times for exploration of the classroom environment in the schedule. Furthermore, in most kindergartens, the curriculum is more focused than preschool curriculum on developing children's literacy skills and their understanding of math and science concepts. Kindergartners are indeed ready to be more independent from their families, to attend for a full day with peers, and to begin to grasp more about reading, writing, math, and science. To address that readiness, the first page of the kindergarten framework is designated as a Readers and Writers Workshop, where teachers can plan opportunities for children to work on many aspects of literacy. And the third page is designated as Investigation Time, with play areas and math and science activities noted. The assumption is that a Readers and Writers Workshop will take place for forty-five minutes to one hour in the morning, and Investigation Time for the same time period in the afternoon. (A preschool program that is full day could adapt this framework.)

Let's look more closely at planning for a Readers and Writers Workshop.

You can see on the next page that eight of the boxes identify areas of the classroom set up to focus on the following literacy experiences:

- listening center
- dramatic play
- journaling center
- alphabet center
- flannel board or pocket charts
- class library
- teacher-led literacy activity
- writing center

Kindergarten Weekly Planning and Reflection Framework
READERS AND WRITERS WORKSHOP

Program/School: _____   Date: _____   Teacher(s): _____

Ongoing Project (optional): _____

	Learning goal(s)	Additional materials or focus	Vocabulary words
LISTENING CENTER			
DRAMATIC PLAY			
JOURNALING CENTER			
ALPHABET CENTER			
FLANNEL BOARD/ POCKET CHARTS			
CLASS LIBRARY			
TEACHER-LED LITERACY ACTIVITY			
WRITING CENTER			
OTHER CENTER			

First page, Kindergarten Weekly Planning and Reflection Framework

A teacher could always add another center in the ninth box (labeled "Other Center") if she desired. If she has an ongoing project or thematic focus going, then she could add that as well at the top of the page. Or if she is linking her literacy activities to books or stories from her school district's chosen reading series, she can note that at the top. Again, in all of the boxes, the teacher identifies one or more learning goals for each area, additional materials or focus that she might provide, and vocabulary words that could be developed in that activity. On the next page is Elena's plan for Readers and Writers Workshop in her kindergarten classroom.

Kindergarten Weekly Planning and Reflection Framework

READERS AND WRITERS WORKSHOP

Program/School: _Buckley Elementary_   Date: _10/3/11_   Teacher(s): _Elena Monroe_

Ongoing Project (optional): _____

	Learning goal(s)	Additional materials or focus	Vocabulary words
LISTENING CENTER	phonological awareness of sounds and syllables	tapes of rhyming books and nonsense rhymes	rhyme, syllables
DRAMATIC PLAY	speaking skills	encourage conversational turn-taking	conversation
JOURNALING CENTER	reading comprehension	write and draw about their favorite story	
ALPHABET CENTER	knowledge of books and print	go on letter hunts around the room; how many A's can you find?	
FLANNEL BOARD/ POCKET CHARTS	reading comprehension	retell "Old Lady Who Swallowed a Fly" with flannel board pieces	wiggled, jiggled
CLASS LIBRARY	reading comprehension	read stories and pick a favorite for journaling	
TEACHER-LED LITERACY ACTIVITY	reading comprehension	talk with children about favorite stories	beginning, middle, end
WRITING CENTER	phonological awareness of sounds and syllables		beginning sound, ending sound
OTHER CENTER			

Elena's Readers and Writers Workshop plan

Brenda: "Kindergarten teachers are being asked to stress early literacy skills. They may want to focus their Readers and Writers Workshop on featured stories or books for the week and then pull developmentally appropriate activities from their basal series."

Notice that Elena does not have a different goal for every literacy activity. Some goals are the same across centers. Many teachers focus on three or four goals per week during literacy activity time or during any play- or investigation time.

Now let's look more closely at planning for Investigation Time in a kindergarten classroom.

Kindergarten Weekly Planning and Reflection Framework
INVESTIGATION TIME

Program/School: _____   Date: _____   Teacher(s): _____

Ongoing Project (optional): _____

	Learning goal(s)	Additional materials or focus	Vocabulary words
BLOCKS			
MATH ACTIVITY			
SENSORY TABLE			
ART			
MANIPULATIVES			
SCIENCE EXPLORATION			
INFORMATIONAL READING			
MATH AND SCIENCE JOURNALING			
OTHER CENTER			

Third page, Kindergarten Weekly Planning and Reflection Framework

There are nine rows of boxes on this page. In the bottom row is a box labeled "Other Center." At the top is a place where a teacher can note if she has an ongoing project or thematic focus. The rest of the boxes on the page identify areas of the classroom set up for play or various math and science experiences:

- blocks
- math activity
- sensory table
- art
- manipulatives
- science exploration
- informational reading
- math and science journaling

As with the Readers and Writers Workshop page, in each box the teacher identifies one or more learning goals for each area, additional materials or focus that she might provide, and vocabulary words that could be developed in that activity. Here is Elena's plan for Investigation Time in her kindergarten classroom.

Kindergarten Weekly Planning and Reflection Framework
INVESTIGATION TIME

Program/School: _Buckley Elementary_   Date: _10/3/11_   Teacher(s): _Elena Monroe_

Ongoing Project (optional): _____

	Learning goal(s)	Additional materials or focus	Vocabulary words
BLOCKS	sorting and categorizing (ordering and patterning)	encourage block building with similar shapes	symmetry
MATH ACTIVITY	sorting and categorizing (ordering and patterning)	sort keys, screws, nuts, bolts, buttons, and seashells in sorting bins	categories, similarities, differences
SENSORY TABLE	experimenting and sorting and categorizing	sort objects by what sinks and what floats	sink, float
ART	experimenting	mix paint colors and see what happens	color words such as bright, dark, muddy, transparent, opaque
MANIPULATIVES	sorting and categorizing (ordering and patterning)	create patterns	AB, AB pattern
SCIENCE EXPLORATION	experimenting	use magnifying glasses to look at collections of keys, bolts, seashells, etc. from math activity	magnify
INFORMATIONAL READING	demonstrating curiosity and interest in new things	books on insects and spiders	webs, arachnids, six-legged vs. eight-legged
MATH AND SCIENCE JOURNALING	demonstrating curiosity and interest in new things	record results of sink/float activity and patterning in manipulatives	
OTHER CENTER			

Elena's plan for Investigation Time

You can see that Elena has limited the number of learning goals she is addressing during these activities. She has chosen three goals to work on with the children so that she and her teaching teammates can have a clear focus for the week. Teachers can decide to identify a different goal for each area or focus on a few each week.

Plans for Group Times

The second page of the framework is organized to include daily plans for both large and small groups. The daily schedule in preschool and kindergarten classrooms includes opportunities for children to work independently, play with other children, participate in routines like snack, outdoor time, and perhaps naptime, and join in large- and small-group experiences. Group times are generally times when the teacher, not the child, is the leader and the initiator.

In both preschool and kindergarten classrooms, many teachers include a variety of activities in their large-group gatherings. They may call the children together with songs and movement activities. They may help them settle down and build a sense of group cohesiveness by singing songs or chanting fingerplays. Once children are settled in, teachers may introduce topics for discussion, do a demonstration, or read a story. In some classrooms, teachers include daily routines such as taking attendance, identifying classroom helpers, looking at a calendar, and making plans for the day.

The space on the framework for large-group planning is not large enough to list everything that will occur at large-group time. The focus should be on the learning goal for the main activity and the teacher's strategies for facilitating that activity. It is assumed that the songs, movement activities, and daily routines will occur each day and that the activity (discussion, demonstration, or story) will change. The only caution is when a substitute teacher may need to use the framework in the teacher's absence. Explanations of daily routines at large-group time should be available to substitute teachers somewhere in a substitute teacher folder.

On the next page are Celia's plans for the week for large groups in her preschool classroom.

You can see that Celia addresses the same learning goal through different activities for most of the days. This is one way to plan for large-group times. You can also change the learning goal each day, change the activity, or repeat activities as well. If you wish to plan for the same activity across the week, use the framework provided for group-time weekly goals in appendix A or you can download it at www.redleafpress.org. Teachers have many choices when planning for large-group times with preschool and kindergarten children. In chapter 3, we will look at learning goals for large-group times, and in chapter 6, we will analyze large-group planning in more depth and discuss whether it is even necessary to plan a large-group time every day.

DATE: 9/12/11		MONDAY	TUESDAY	WEDNESDAY	THURSDAY	FRIDAY
Large group	Learning goal	vocabulary development (body parts)				
	Activity and teacher strategy	"Hokey Pokey" "Head, Shoulders, Knees, and Toes" Daily routines Build flannel board body with parts Read "Here Are My Hands"	Play "Knee to Knee" "Where Is Thumbkin?" Daily routines Read "Maisy Dresses Up"	Hap Palmer: "Shake Something" "Touch" Daily routines Body part mix-up with flannel board	"Hokey Pokey" Play "Knee to Knee" "Where Is Thumbkin?" Daily routines Read and act out "I Can Do That"	Hap Palmer: "Shake Something" "Touch" Daily routines Children choose story from three read this week

Celia's large-group plans

Teacher-Led Small-Group Time

Sometimes preschool and kindergarten teachers lead small-group activities. These may include work with specific skills, such as counting, writing, shape recognition, or sorting and classifying. They may include producing something, such as an "All About Me" book or artwork using coffee filters and food dye. For safety purposes, many teachers do science experiments or cooking activities in small groups where they can supervise the children closely. It's often easier to keep the children's attention in a small group. And since small-group times allow teachers to pay closer attention to individual children and focus on their growing skills and abilities, assessing their progress is more easily accomplished.

There is a caution about small-group planning: If done during play, the small-group activity should be a choice for children. This is a reminder so teachers do not forget the importance of children's engagement in high-level play. If children are interrupted when playing productively and told they are required to participate in a teacher-led small group, they are being told that their play is not important. This is not the message we want to give young children. Instead, we want to support and sustain their play experiences. Yet in some classrooms, it's hard to fit small-group times in the daily schedule, so using the playtime period seems to work best. In that case, *inviting* children to participate, rather than *requiring* them to, is recommended. Information about learning goals for small-group times will be shared in chapter 3, and about planning for effective small-group times in chapter 6.

On the framework is a box to list plans for teacher-led small groups. Again, the focus is on the learning goal for the small-group activity and the teacher strategies for facilitating that activity.

If you wish to plan for the same activity for your small-group gatherings across the week, a format has been provided for group-time weekly goals in appendix A or you can download it at www.redleafpress.org. Here are the learning goals, activities, and teacher strategies for small-group times that Elena wrote on her plan for her kindergartners.

Small group	Learning goal	writing skills, phonological awareness, and knowledge of print	writing skills, phonological awareness, and knowledge of print	phonological awareness	writing skills	writing skills, phonological awareness, and knowledge of print
	Activity and teacher strategy	Do a name study and have children practice writing own name	Have them choose a friend's name, analyze it, sound it out, and write it	Find items in the room that begin with the same letter as their name and a friend's name	Practice writing names and key words on blackboard slates or whiteboards	Figure out a different way to do a name study and practice writing own name

Elena's small-group plans

Afternoon Story Time

Many kindergarten teachers bring children in after lunch and recess and settle them down with quiet time during which the teacher reads a story (perhaps an ongoing chapter book, favorite storybook, or something that correlates with an ongoing project or thematic study) or children look quietly at books by themselves. This allows them to transition back into the classroom. A space is provided on page 2 of the kindergarten plan to identify goals and strategies for this activity.

Plans for Building Community and Relationships, Outdoor Explorations, Meals, and Transitions

Building respectful, caring relationships with children and their families is an important element of the curriculum process. By writing plans to build these relationships on the framework, teachers avoid leaving this task to chance. They think about relationships with children and implement steps to strengthen those relationships. In this way, preschool and kindergarten teachers create a sense of community where teachers and parents are working together on behalf of the children's best interests, and children are learning to be respectful and caring of each other. The following are some of the many possibilities for teacher actions for this part of the framework:

- welcome a child by name with a warm smile
- greet and chat with family members at pickup and drop-off times
- give an individual child positive feedback ("Wow! Look at all the colors you used!" "You jumped really high!"), or compliment the group ("We sure did a good job at cleanup time today!")
- have favorite group songs and fingerplays for gathering children together
- encourage children to recognize acts of kindness by their classmates

Here is Celia's plan for building community and relationships. We will explore more of these possibilities in depth in chapters 5 and 7.

Plans for Building Community and Relationships

Introduce "More We Are Together" as gathering song.
Help children learn routines with lots of reminders and consistent patterns of activities.

Celia's community- and relationship-building plans

Quality early childhood programs offer outdoor physical activity on a daily basis (weather permitting, of course). Young children's growing bodies are developing muscle control and need to expend energy and experience fresh air and the delights of nature. Teachers should include recess or outdoor time whenever weather permits.

The frameworks offer a box for teachers to record their plans for outdoor explorations. Children truly benefit when teachers think about what outdoor opportunities to provide. Planning for outdoor opportunities may also help teachers feel that outdoor time is more purposeful and less chaotic.

Planning outdoor time does not mean that this activity should be totally teacher directed. Freedom to run until their lungs ache from the fresh, cool air flowing through them is important for young children. Using muscles in new ways and taking risks in climbing or swinging cannot be taught. Sitting under a tree and watching the clouds go by through the leaves or observing the ants around their hole is a precious individual moment with nature in which no one, not even a teacher, should intervene.

However, planning to bring different play materials outdoors or to play a special game can add to children's outdoor experiences. The many possible materials and activities to write on this part of the framework include

- streamers or scarves for feeling/seeing the wind at work
- binoculars for watching birds or clouds
- reading under a tree (sitting on a blanket or plastic mat)
- painting outdoors; using the easel

Here are Elena's plans for outdoor explorations. Ideas for incorporating learning goals in outdoor play will be explored in chapter 3.

Plans for Outdoor Explorations

Collect leaves and seeds for sorting and categorizing.

Elena's outdoor exploration plans

Meals and transitions are times that can be ripe with opportunities for teachers to learn more about the children, to talk with them, and to teach them. Meals and transitions are not "throwaway" times because learning goals can be embedded into these daily occurrences. Mealtimes provide marvelous possibilities for back and forth conversation. When teachers sit with children during snack, breakfast, or lunch, the atmosphere can be much like that of a family seated at the kitchen table. Encouraging children to talk, pour their own water or milk, and clean up their own place setting and trash are all ways teachers can help children build their language, self-help skills, and independence.

Transitions between activities can be difficult for young children. The children may be anxious to get going on their chosen play activity. Or they may have trouble waiting patiently for their turn to wash hands. It's much wiser for preschool and kindergarten teachers to use songs, fingerplays, games, and routines to help children through transition times. Teachers can use songs and chants that incorporate children's names (such as "Willoughby, Wallaby") to dismiss children from group time to the play areas or to hand washing. Asking children to pretend to be butterflies as they move down the hallway to the large-motor room or the cafeteria will encourage them to walk quietly past other classrooms.

Planning for ways to enhance meals and to ease transitions will help teachers take advantage of every minute of their day with the children. This kind of intentionality can lead to children's better behavior and also prepares teachers for their own role during all parts of the day.

Here are Celia's plans for meals and transitions. In chapter 3 we will show ways to incorporate learning goals in meals and transition times.

Plans for Meals and Transitions

Talk with children at snack about textures of food— crunchy, soft, chewy.
Teach children "Willoughby, Wallaby" as dismissal song for transitions.

Celia's plans for meals and transitions

Mrs. Chang also planned for large and small groups and the other areas on the second page of the planning and reflection framework. Some of her plans included attention to the bird project, and others did not. Again, she decided where it made most sense to incorporate this topic (see the following page).

Plans for Focused Observations

On the third page of the preschool framework and the fourth page of the kindergarten framework, teachers can note a focus for observing children throughout the week. Every day, teachers watch children in action, noticing what they are interested in, what they like and dislike, and what is hard or easy for them to do. These observations help teachers assess children's development formally and informally, thinking carefully about what the next step might be for each child.

The framework includes a box labeled "Focused Observations." If your focus will be to watch specific children, here's where that list of names can be written. If your focus will be to pay attention to specific classroom areas

Preschool Weekly Planning and Reflection Framework

DATE: 8/29/12		MONDAY	TUESDAY	WEDNESDAY	THURSDAY	FRIDAY
Large group	Learning goal	reading comprehension	balance and coordination	demonstrating curiosity and interest in new things	balance and coordination	reading comprehension
	Activity and teacher strategy	Daily routines Read *Are You My Mother?*	Daily routines Play movement game "Go In and Out My Window"	Daily routines Read *Chickens Aren't the Only Ones*	Daily routines Songs: "Way Up in the Sky" and "Here's a Baby Bird"	Daily routines Read *The Best Nest*
Small group	Learning goal	fine-motor skills	→			
	Activity and teacher strategy	Cutting pictures out of magazines, picking up buttons and toothpicks with tweezers, and using hole punchers	→			

Plans for Building Community and Relationships	Plans for Outdoor Explorations	Plans for Meals and Transitions
Invite any family bird experts to come in and share with us about birding.	Look for birds with binoculars; listen for their songs and calls.	Talk with children about birds they have seen in their yards or other places. Pretend to fly to different activities (slowly, of course).

Mrs. Chang's completed second page

or activities, you will note that here. And if your focus will be to observe for a specific developmental domain for assessment purposes, you will note that in this box.

Sometimes teachers divide up the children in the classroom and focus their observations on the same group of children over time, perhaps with attention to specific learning goals each week. The teachers' goals for observation can correlate with the learning goals identified for each of the play areas. That way, the planning and observation processes are working in harmony.

Alternatively, each teacher may focus instead on a specific area of the classroom. They may pay attention to the identified learning goal as well as the number of children engaged in that area. They may want to see who tends to play together or when and where behavior problems seem to erupt. You and your colleagues will need to communicate clearly about this aspect of your teaching. Focusing observations for assessment purposes will be explored more in chapter 8.

Here is Celia's plan for focused observations. Note that since it is one of the first weeks of the year, her plan is more general than it will be as she gets to know the children better.

FOCUSED OBSERVATIONS:

Celia: William, Luis, Stephanie, Gregory, Michelle, Anna, Cullen, Marin, Luz

Linda: Tony, Alicia, Alberto, Jonathan, Marissa, Megan, James, Lindsey, Nicolas

Celia's plans for focused observations

Plans for Modifications for Individual Children

As teachers get to know each child well, they figure out ways to modify the curriculum so that each child can be successful. Teachers pay close attention to initial signals the child sends out about her personality, her approach to learning, her social comfort levels, and her relationships with her family members. When a teacher senses that a child withdraws any time she is touched, the teacher is careful not to touch the child unnecessarily. When a teacher sees a child inappropriately approaching other children to play, she makes an effort to provide assistance and modeling for that child, stepping in at just the right time and giving the child words to say, "Can I play too?"

This is truly individualizing the curriculum. A rich classroom environment can provide opportunities for individual children. A teacher's careful planning of how to support the child in those opportunities, or to

Suzanne: "In our planning meetings, each observation is discussed. Notes are made on individual needs. Based on observations, we adjust our plan for the following week. We either pull activities and/or ideas forward or develop new activities based on our observations and the needs of the children."

change the possibilities, is where individualization occurs. No longer are you thinking of activities for all the children. Now, within those activities, you're thinking about each individual child. In the box labeled "Modifications for Individual Children," teachers write down the changes they will make to existing activities to help specific children be successful. This attention to individual children helps strengthen the children's sense of trust. They recognize that their teachers care deeply about them.

Here is Elena's plan for modifications for individual children.

MODIFICATIONS FOR INDIVIDUAL CHILDREN:

Put out alphabet matching game (lower to upper case) as a challenge for all children but especially for Rebecca, Jason and Heather.

Give Jarrett a special assignment to measure the classroom, doorways, tables, etc. with unifix cubes.

Provide emotional support for Stephanie for her fear of loud noises.

Watch for best seating at group times for Grecia and Ricardo—perhaps they should be separate from each other?

Elena's plan for modifications for individual children

Reflections

Reflection is an ongoing process. As teachers implement their plans and observe the children, they reflect on what happens each day in the classroom: what worked, what didn't work, what proved especially engaging for children, and when children were bored or restless. They consider what they are learning about individual children and the group as a whole. They assess their own planning and preparation. They do this internally and sometimes make immediate modifications and adjustments. Or they may write down a thought that they want to remember when planning for the next week.

With the planning and reflection framework, teachers can formalize and record their reflection process. They can set aside a time to quietly reflect and record their thoughts by themselves, or they can reflect with colleagues in team meetings. Reflection can happen at the end of the day

Lauren: "I really like the reflection page. I believe that this is a very important part of supporting teachers in improving their teaching practices and interactions with children."

or at the end of the week. The questions provided on the planning and reflection framework can guide these reflection times.

- What worked?
- What didn't?
- What did you learn about individual children and group interests?

As teachers consider these questions, they can record key points on the framework. Some key points may be noted on the first or second page. For example, if the materials and choices offered in some of the play areas worked well, they may just note a smiling face in that section of the form. If a large- or small-group activity went particularly well, they may do the same. Other significant thoughts can be written in the Reflections box. These might include

- individual children's responses to activities or difficulties with concepts
- a record of spontaneous changes the teaching team made in the room arrangement or in planned events as the week went on
- whole group responses to activities (such as too many wiggles at story time or lack of interest in the sensory table)
- how children demonstrated their learning of various concepts and skills (Are they ready for greater challenges in some areas, or do they need more time to practice specific skills or explore certain concepts?)

In addition, noting the results of activities coordinated with an ongoing project or study can help determine the next steps in continuing children's engagement with that project.

Here are Celia's reflections after one of her first weeks of the school year.

> REFLECTIONS: What worked? What didn't? What did you learn about individual children and group interests?
>
> Art and Lego blocks at manipulatives worked best this week. Children wandered in and out of dramatic play. Blocks needed help getting started. Very few interested in the writing center.
>
> Jonathan, Tony, and Stephanie stayed a long time at sensory table each day. Marissa and Alberto did so at the library.
>
> Group time should be shorter for now—too early in year for long time sitting.

Celia's reflections

Plans for Changes for Next Week

As the reflection process goes on, planning can occur as well. Teachers can jot down ideas for possible new activities for the next week from ideas that were generated by the children. They can give themselves written reminders to keep specific materials available in the next week or to make sure to change something. It is not necessary to change the plans for all of the areas or activities—it is only necessary to do so for the ones that were not successful. Using the planning and reflection framework will help determine what aspects of the curriculum need changes.

Many of Celia's reflections from the first week showed her that no changes were needed in the plans for most of the play areas. However, she and her colleagues did note that most of the children were not choosing the writing center or library. In addition, Celia's team determined that they needed to shorten the length of the large-group activity and to make the small-group activity more hands-on for the children. And they discussed modifications for some of the children. Here is Celia's plan for changes for the next week based on her reflections from above.

PLANS: Based on your reflections,
what will you change for next week?

Only change writing center—make "All About Me" books with
Linda helping children in this area.

Add more books to library each day as we read them and
encourage children to look at pictures and print in stories
we've read in large group.

Shorter circle times.

Celia's plans for changes

Sarah: "It can be a challenge to use the framework as your plan for the week rather than for each day. You realize that not all areas of the plan need to change daily or even each week. Instead, goals can be extended as the children work toward meeting them."

You can see that Celia and her teammates decided to change the plans for two play areas: class library and writing center. In addition, they discussed the need for more adult leadership and interaction in those areas. They decided that in the next week, one of them would go to the library to read with the children. They also noted that making the "All About Me" books in the writing center required adult supervision. Through clear communication in their reflection process, they planned for one of the team to be assigned to that area each day. These notes and assignments will be written on the framework for the next week to help everyone involved remember their specific duties for the day or week.

Determining when to change materials and activities in the play environment will be explored in depth in chapter 4, and reflecting and planning for individual children's needs in chapter 5.

Throughout this chapter we have also looked at Mrs. Chang's planning and reflection framework with a focus on the bird making the nest outside the window of the classroom. On the next page is her completed third page of the preschool framework. You will see that her focused observations and modifications for individual children do not reflect that topic. However, she and her assistant made reflection notes and plans for changes for the next week that included more bird activities. Throughout the coming weeks, these teachers will continue to watch the children's interest to determine if there is sufficient engagement in the topic to continue it in further weeks and in more depth.

Preschool Weekly Planning and Reflection Framework
OBSERVATIONS, MODIFICATIONS, AND REFLECTIONS

FOCUSED OBSERVATIONS:	MODIFICATIONS FOR INDIVIDUAL CHILDREN:
Mrs. Chang—focus on cooking activity and observe for scientific observation and analysis and predictions. Mrs. Allen—float and observe all areas, helping where needed.	Do hand over hand for children who cannot write their names at sign-in yet. Offer some play coaching with the blocks and dramatic play for those children having a hard time getting going there.
REFLECTIONS: What worked? What didn't? What did you learn about individual children and group interests?	PLANS: Based on your reflections, what will you change for next week?
Name recognition improving. Cooking activity took too long—too much adult involvement rather than kids. Some throwing of sand at sand table again—supervise more closely? Good response to movement activities by most children—except Josie. Should we let her watch until she's ready? Great interest in bird building a nest outside of the classroom—Jennifer and Harland checked on it every day. Should we add bird activities for next week?	Keep up with name cards and name games. No cooking this week. Supervise sand table instead. Let Josie watch when we dance—in fact, give all children the choice. They can be the audience for "Dancing with the Stars." ☺ Let's do a project on birds—add bird activities to some areas of the classroom and group times.

Mrs. Chang's completed third page

Other Models for Planning and Reflection Frameworks

There are other models for planning and reflection that you may want to review. The New Mexico PreK Program has adopted a formal lesson plan (adapted from my original *Focused Early Learning* framework and from which the frameworks in this book have been adapted). You can find that format at www.newmexicoprek.org (scroll down and click on materials). The implementation of this framework has been an overall success. Here are two stories about the use of the New Mexico PreK Lesson Planning Framework:

There have been many positive results that have come from the implementation of the pre-K lesson plan. One that immediately comes to mind is from discussion with one of the teachers. Through our conversation about how the lesson plan is working for her in the classroom, we came to the conclusion that the lesson plan is evidence of the important work that she is doing with the children every day. She said that the lesson plan is backing up her job. We discussed how, if an administrator were ever to come in and question an activity that she was doing, that she would be able to refer them to the lesson plan. There they could see exactly what the goal of the activity was and why she chose to do it with the children. The lesson plan really helped her to see the value of all the decisions that she makes in the classroom on a daily basis. (submitted by Lauren Michael, PreK Training and Development Consultant)

———————

I hear teachers saying such things as "I can see the learning," "I understand the importance of goals and am able to support the children," and "I use this lesson plan to demonstrate the importance of what we are working on to parents and administrators." One of my favorite things about the PreK lesson plan is that it helps teachers to see that it is through direct experiences and play that children learn best!! (submitted by Sarah Simms, PreK Consultant Program Manager)

In Connecticut, a Preschool Assessment Framework has been developed and includes a Learning Activities Planning Form, a Brainstorming Web (including teaching strategies, activities, and materials), and a Weekly Calendar. These can all be found on pages 11, 12, and 14 in the manual at the following website: www.sde.ct.gov/sde/lib/sde/PDF/DEPS/Early/Preschool_Assessment_Framework.pdf.

Here is a testimonial from the director of a preschool program in Connecticut:

We describe our process slightly differently: planning includes individualizing for children; implementation and observation go hand in hand; and reflection includes assessment. Planning, implementation, assessment, and back to planning. And it works. It provides insight into each of the children in your care and also insight into your own professional practice. It provides a beautiful, ongoing story of the child in the classroom, documenting areas of strength and areas of challenge. Then, each child can receive attention in the planning process and the design of strategies to assist his progress. And teachers can create a record of the child's response to strategies as well (adding to your knowledge of what works for this particular child and what doesn't), so the process of his learning and growth is illuminated. (Submitted by Kathy Stewart, preschool director)

Creating Your Own Planning and Reflection Framework

Preschool and kindergarten teachers are unique individuals—just like the children they teach. Their teaching styles vary. The emphasis they place on their classroom activities reflects their special talents and interests, background, and experience. To recognize that uniqueness, this book also includes the same framework design for both planning and reflection with some blank boxes (see appendix A or go to www.redleafpress.org). Fill in the ways you integrate curricular approaches in your classroom. You may wish to use some from the frameworks provided here and add your own. Some teachers have added "Classroom Rituals," whereas others have added "Music" or "Puppets."

Kindergarten teachers may feel the need to add more specific literacy, math, and science activities or to include computers and special activities, like gym and art. They may want to structure small groups in a different manner. Or some report that they are required to use literacy or math approaches outlined in teacher guides that accompany reading series or math manipulatives. If that's the case for you, then use whatever parts of the planning and reflection frameworks presented in this book that will work for you.

The framework design presented here is by no means all-inclusive. Please take ownership of the framework and make it work for you.

Some programs require teachers to post their weekly plans for parents and family members, as well as supervisors, to review. As I stated earlier, the framework includes some information that might be considered confidential or inappropriate for such posting. Because of that, focused observations, modifications for individual children, reflections, and plans for next week have all been organized to appear on the last page of both the preschool and kindergarten frameworks. Teachers who wish to post their

Robin: "Themes, goals and vocabulary can easily be transferred from the curricular programs that my district requires I use. The part that seems most helpful (especially when working in teams) is the reflection and modification sections."

Sue: "The challenge I have felt is adapting the 'box' of materials (the math program or reading series that is set up lesson by lesson) to meet the curriculum goals and needs of the children."

plans may want to make a photocopy and post only the first pages (two for preschool, three for kindergarten) instead of the whole framework.

The frameworks shared in this book are meant to be used by preschool and kindergarten teachers as well as family child care providers who work with these age groups. However, I have been approached by infant/toddler specialists asking if there is some way to adapt them for those age groups. I welcome you to consider doing so in ways that meet the needs of the youngest children in your care. Kacey Deverell, an early childhood mentor with the State of Indiana, designed a format that she shares with early childhood professionals who work with infants and toddlers, and generously shared it with me for this book. You can find an adapted version of her format in appendix A or at www.redleafpress.org.

Conclusion

In the following chapters, I will continue the discussion about the planning/observation/individualization cycle and guide teachers through the process of using the framework for both planning and reflection. Each chapter will include sample plans and reflections from preschool and kindergarten teachers around the country for you to review. Suggestions, information, and recommendations will help you integrate the planning and reflection process with the actual implementation of an integrated preschool and kindergarten curriculum.

In the next chapter, the focus will be on embedding learning goals and academics in play, daily routines, and teacher-led group activities.

CHAPTER 3

Embedding Learning Goals and Academics in Play, Daily Routines, and Teacher-Led Group Activities

As I showed in chapter 1, learning goals are at the core of the curriculum process. The learning goals will be different for preschool and kindergarten children. Yet they can be approached in similar ways for both age groups.

In high-quality preschool programs, teachers set goals to support the development of each child. Those goals will encompass what traditionally might be seen as academic domains—language arts and literacy, mathematics, social studies, and science. Teachers will plan activities in which children

- learn about books and reading
- develop writing skills
- learn to count, match, sort, measure, and work with shapes
- understand more about how members of a community work together
- explore various aspects of nature and scientific phenomena

Rather than rely on group work only to achieve these goals, teachers embed them in everyday activities in the classroom. Science exploration occurs as children play at the sensory table. Reading stories is a part of almost every large-group time. Books are available for children to look through and listen to in the class library daily. Math activities are provided through manipulatives and block exploration but also occur in classroom routines such as taking attendance or setting the table for snack.

In kindergarten classrooms, academic learning goals may be even more evident. Teachers may plan for playful and exploratory activities that focus on literacy (as in a Readers and Writers Workshop) and hands-on

Mary B.: "If I know I need to record some data on specific children, I'll use the goal to focus what I'm doing with the children. But in the beginning of the year, I'm more open to multiple goals."

math activities. More small-group work may be planned to address specific goals and give children time to practice skills they are learning. In kindergarten classrooms, teachers can also embed learning goals in play experiences and daily routines.

There is potential for learning goals to be addressed in all aspects of a high-quality early childhood program. What's needed then is teacher intentionality.

By taking the following steps, teachers can raise their own awareness and attention to academic learning as well as communicate about it with others. Preschool and kindergarten teachers can

- plan to address learning goals in all activities and record those goals on a planning and reflection framework such as the ones found in this book in chapter 2 and appendix A
- share those plans in parent newsletters and on bulletin boards or online class pages to inform parents (and administrators) about the embedded goals
- facilitate children's experiences as plans are implemented, so that learning goals are met
- observe and document what children do, say, create, and build, and share that documentation on bulletin boards, in newsletters, in online postings, and in assessment portfolios
- reflect on what's been observed to plan for and better match the learning trajectories of each child

These actions allow family members, supervisors, and community members to plainly see that "embedding" does not mean "hoping academics will occur." Instead, the teacher clearly addresses the learning goals of various activities and notes them on the weekly plan. She plans for ways to make learning evident to all.

The *How* of Academics

There has been much confusion about the issue of academics for young children. When early childhood programs describe their curricula as "play based," many people outside the field interpret that to mean that learning is not part of the curriculum. Academics are indeed incorporated into play-based preschool and kindergarten programs. It's *how* academics are

Laura: "The integration of academic learning goals and the planning of a rich, well-organized classroom environment are all tied together."

Mary M.: "Teachers have reported much success with choosing specific developmental foci for children in the classroom learning areas. By writing these learning goals on the lesson plan, teachers ensure that their teaching is intentional and that all developmental areas are covered."

addressed in the program that many people do not understand. Teachers skillfully weave in the goals and objectives of traditional academic domains as they build on what the children can do and challenge them to try new things. Academic learning can be playful and exploratory.

In play-based programs, children are invited to contribute their own ideas, use their own problem-solving strategies, and pursue their own interests. Teachers recognize that they must have expectations and standards in their programs. However, they also know the nature of learning at this age. Just because teachers use play as a way to build children's success does not make the curriculum less rigorous or less academic. It means that it is appropriate for the children.

As discussed in chapter 1, kindergarten teachers have been put under tremendous pressure in recent years to teach five- and six-year-olds in ways that are more appropriate for older elementary-age children. In many kindergarten classrooms, young learners are asked to sit at tables or desks for long periods of time doing paper-and-pencil tasks that are repetitive and drill oriented—and behavior problems often develop. Some children have trouble controlling their physical energy, sitting still, listening, and attending. Kindergarten children are much more successful when the same skills are embedded in playful and exploratory activities.

Here are two stories that illustrate contrasting approaches to teaching the same skills to kindergarten children. Both stories show ways that teachers addressed the same learning goal: writing basic sight words.

The Workbook Approach

In her kindergarten program, Lucy is required to use a workbook tied to the language arts textbooks that the school district adopted. In this workbook, a basic set of sight words is identified for the kindergarten children to learn to read and write. The list includes words such as the, and, is, he, and she. Lucy has all of her children sit at their assigned seats at tables and write the sight words several times in their workbooks. They are to write between the lines with spaces in between the words. They are required to stay at their tables until everyone's work is completed. Children work quietly with little conversation. Those that finish before others often have a hard time sitting still while waiting for all to complete the activity. When dismissed, they anxiously rush off to the play areas or more hands-on choices available in the classroom.

Sarah: "Some of the teachers with whom I have worked have found it difficult to plan with goals in mind versus thinking only of the activities and projects that they commonly planned for in the past. But with time and practice they were able to focus on goals and use the plan as evidence of learning."

Robin: "One thing I do is to share my learning goals with my students."

The Journal Approach

Amanda has planned for journal writing to occur every day in her kindergarten program. Children are free to write about whatever they want. Sometimes they begin by drawing a picture. Amanda walks around and asks children to tell her about the drawing and makes suggestions about what they might write. Based on these discussions with children, she has created lists of words that have meaning to them. As they suggest the words they want to know, she writes them on a sentence strip and places them on a bulletin board so they can be easily seen. Children return to the bulletin board again and again, finding the words they want to copy into their journals. They may call out to Amanda or to other children to be reminded of what some of the words are. Much conversation goes back and forth among teacher and children. Journal writing may go on for twenty to thirty minutes. New words are added daily. And these kindergarten children are recognizing and writing words like tyrannosaurus, bulldozer, butterfly, transformers, *and* princess *in addition to words such as* the, and, he, *and* she.

Both teachers are working hard with their children to meet reasonable, age-appropriate expectations. Yet *how* they plan and implement activities to meet those expectations is different, isn't it? Kindergarten classrooms should still look very much like preschool ones. Curricular approaches that embrace play and exploration with attention to learning goals work better with five- and six-year-olds than ones that require lots of sitting, listening, and working on skills that are not meaningful and interesting to children. The learning goals are the difference between preschool and kindergarten curriculum—not the approaches.

Identifying Learning Goals for Play Areas

To help counteract the misinterpretation about academic learning for young children, I suggest that early childhood professionals consider describing the embedded academics in their programs using terminology that sounds like it came from a university course catalog. For example, in any quality early childhood classroom structured for exploration of a rich classroom environment, children are exposed to the concepts of physics, chemistry, meteorology, biology, botany, and anatomy. When children build and construct with blocks in the block area, they are routinely experimenting with gravity and balance, force and mass, friction, and momentum—all physical forces studied in physics. When children cook with teachers and observe changes to ingredients as they are mixed and heated, they are exploring the principles of chemistry. Daily weather observations are common in most early childhood classrooms, and seasonal changes are experienced during outdoor time and neighborhood walks. Biology and botany are included in studies of animals and plants. Children care for classroom pets and plants, visit farms and zoos, and learn more about insects and spiders. They may plant a center garden or flowerbed.

Human anatomy is always included in any classroom of young children because their own bodies fascinate them. Teachers recognize this fascination and plan activities that capture the children's interest. They help children learn more about health and nutrition, the importance of exercise, and the functions of various body parts and organs.

Using the university course catalog terms of physics and anatomy can help parents and community members recognize that the concepts of many scientific disciplines are included in the early childhood curriculum. Lectures followed by paperwork, quizzes, and tests are not the ways in which these concepts are taught to young children. Instead, they are included in an exploratory, active learning environment through a variety of hands-on activities.

General Concepts for Language Arts, Math, Social Studies, and Science

Here are lists of general skills that are embedded in quality early childhood curricula from the core academic areas of language arts, math, social studies, and science. The terms for these general skills may not sound like they come from a university course catalog, but you may recognize them as ones commonly used in the elementary grades. These skills will serve children well as they mature into older grades and are ready to combine more skills and understand more abstract concepts. By no means are these lists complete. What would you add?

Language Arts
- listening skills
- reading comprehension

- phonological awareness of sounds and syllables
- speaking skills
- vocabulary development
- knowledge of books and print
- writing skills

Math
- sorting and categorizing (ordering and patterning)
- counting and quantity
- geometry and spatial relationships
- problem solving
- measurement
- representing mathematical information

Social Studies
- understanding families
- getting along with others
- understanding community

Science
- developing observation and analysis skills
- making scientific predictions
- experimenting

In addition, children's social/emotional skills and approaches to learning are also important at this age. To be contributing members of society and effective learners throughout their lives, children need these domains to be nurtured by preschool and kindergarten teachers. Let's consider some general social/emotional skills and approaches to learning domains.

Social/Emotional
- learning to play and get along with other children
- listening to and following the guidance of teachers
- expressing emotions appropriately
- developing self-regulation

Approaches to Learning
- demonstrating curiosity and interest in new things

- showing initiative
- focusing attention and persisting in tasks

And many sets of standards or assessment criteria include physical development as a domain as well. Here are some general sets of physical skills:

Gross-Motor Development
- showing balance and control
- exhibiting body coordination in walking, running, jumping, and climbing stairs

Fine-Motor Development
- demonstrating hand-eye coordination
- using tools to write and cut
- using self-help skills, such as buttoning and zipping

State early learning and kindergarten standards, assessment tool criteria, and the new national Common Core Standards can be resources to look to for defining the more specific ways that children demonstrate the general skill areas listed above. Of course, kindergarten expectations will be higher than those for preschoolers. For example, kindergarten children can be expected to listen and follow more lengthy oral directions than preschoolers. And kindergartners generally show more independence as they work and play in the classroom community. The capability for writing and recognizing letters and words is far greater for five- and six-year-olds than for three- and four-year-olds.

Learning goals from all of the domains identified above can be written on the planning pages in the play areas of the frameworks. In this book, I will use the lists above as the basis for discussions about learning goals and will trust that each teacher will turn to the appropriate resources when identifying the learning goals for her planning purposes.

We already looked at the possible learning goals for the block area in chapter 1. Let's look at a different play area—dramatic play—and identify possible learning goals from the list above that could be addressed as children pretend to cook, care for babies, and take care of household chores. There are many more specific goals that could be appropriate. Feel free to add more in your own mind. (In appendix B you will find possible learning goals identified for all seven of the play areas on the preschool framework.)

Rosemary: "Someone suggested creating signs near each center. They write goals on sentence strips and Velcro them to the sign to remind not just the parents but the teacher what the focus was. Identifying the goal as sorting and classifying may help the teacher add one or two more questions or vocabulary words to an activity in which children are engaged already."

Dramatic Play

- language arts: listening, speaking, vocabulary development, knowledge of books and print (as in reading to baby dolls or looking at grocery circulars), and writing (as in making grocery lists or writing letters)
- math: sorting and categorizing (as in putting the dishes away), counting and quantity, and measurement
- social studies: understanding families (as in imitating family roles), getting along with others, and understanding community (as in playing restaurant, grocery store, hospital, etc.)
- social/emotional: learning to play and get along with other children, expressing emotions appropriately, and developing self-regulation
- approaches to learning: demonstrating curiosity and interest in new things, showing initiative, and focusing attention on and persisting in tasks
- gross-motor development: showing balance and control and exhibiting body coordination in walking, running, jumping, and climbing stairs
- fine-motor development: demonstrating hand-eye coordination, using tools to write and cut, and using self-help skills, such as buttoning and zipping

Do you notice that learning goals from almost all of the domains can be addressed in the dramatic play area? As you look at the lists of goals for the other play areas in appendix B, you will see the same. Play areas are rich in possibilities for children to learn. Choosing learning goals for play should not be a difficult task.

Choosing exactly what learning goals to consider and what specific academic activities to plan will be determined during the reflection process. As you reflect back on the week and what you saw in the classroom, you will ask yourself questions like the following to help you focus on the children's academic skills:

- What do the children already know and do related to reading, writing, math, science, and the other domains?
- What is the level at which they can demonstrate with some adult help a concept or a skill that they haven't quite mastered yet? (Vygotsky [1978] called this the "zone of proximal development.")

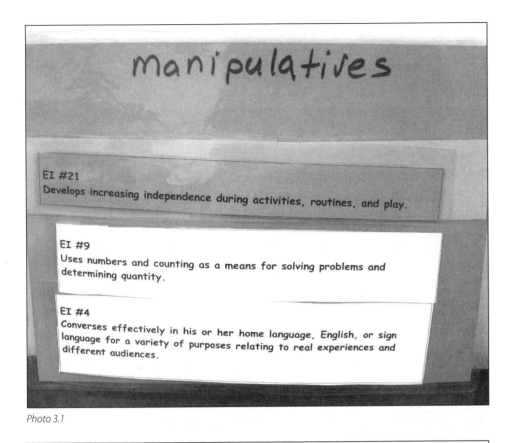

manipulatives

EI #21
Develops increasing independence during activities, routines, and play.

EI #9
Uses numbers and counting as a means for solving problems and determining quantity.

EI #4
Converses effectively in his or her home language, English, or sign language for a variety of purposes relating to real experiences and different audiences.

Photo 3.1

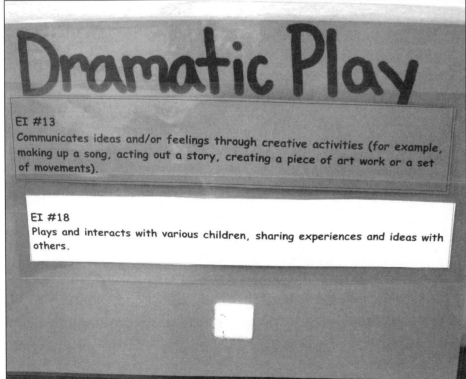

Dramatic Play

EI #13
Communicates ideas and/or feelings through creative activities (for example, making up a song, acting out a story, creating a piece of art work or a set of movements).

EI #18
Plays and interacts with various children, sharing experiences and ideas with others.

Photo 3.2

Kathy: "Every two weeks during planning, the teaching team chooses three relevant learning goals from the Connecticut Preschool Assessment Framework. They are placed in the center of our planning form. As the team considers experiences that could be explored in the centers, they do so with the three learning goals in mind. Then we are focused on and managing observations for these three goals over a two-week period. Several activities have been planned for the children that will assist them in each learning goal."

Then you will observe the children in action and record these observations on the reflection page of the framework.

When you are ready to plan for the next week, those observations will guide you in choosing materials and activities to extend the children's academic learning. For example, if your preschool children are routinely counting up to five objects using one-to-one correspondence, it may be time to introduce activities where they can count ten objects. If kindergarten children are figuring out different ways of grouping objects to make five (such as one and four or two and three), it may be time to introduce grouping objects to make six or more. If preschool children are capable of writing their first names, it may be time to introduce name cards with their last names on them. If kindergarten children are noticing that some words start with capital letters, it may be time to teach them more about capitalization and proper nouns. Teachers include the academic areas in their reflections and then plan academic learning activities according to the children's successes in the classroom.

Just Identifying Goals Is Not Enough

As I stated earlier in this chapter, there is *potential* for learning goals to be addressed in all aspects of a high-quality early childhood program, but teachers are the key to making sure that happens. When a teacher identifies a learning goal for a play area, what she is really doing is giving herself (and her teaching colleagues) an assignment: as children play in that area, the adults will interact with them around the learning goal. The learning goal guides adult interactions with children, influencing any of the following:

- supportive comments that might be made
- open-ended questions that could be asked
- skills that might be modeled or demonstrated
- vocabulary that could be used
- new ideas or possibilities that might be offered
- challenges that could be presented to provoke deeper involvement or more critical thinking and problem solving
- additional materials that might be provided
- documentation that could be recorded (observation notes, photos, work samples)

These teacher actions are possibilities. They depend on what the children are doing. The emphasis is on being responsive to children, observing and listening to determine the best way to interact with this child (or this group of children) at this time.

The intention of identifying learning goals is not to force children to play in ways that address the goal. It is to introduce the key concepts, skills, and vocabulary related to that goal in a way that builds on what children are already doing and enhances and sustains their engagement in the play area.

Many teachers introduce materials available in the different play areas to the children and then invite them to choose where they will play first. This is an excellent time to introduce the learning goals planned for the area as well. If your goal for the sensory table area is measurement, you might say,

> *"Today, at the sensory table, we're going to practice measuring water with measuring cups and spoons. We have all sorts of different sizes of cups. You can see how many little cups it takes to fill up a big cup or how many teaspoons it takes to fill one-half of a pitcher."*

Once the materials and learning goal have been introduced, adults interact with children at the sensory table around measurement. The conversation might go something like this:

> *"Wow, look at all the different sizes of cups and spoons we have here. Oh, Joey, you have two little cups. Do they fit inside one another? They do. How about that? Let's see what it says on them. Oh, this one says it's one-fourth cup, and this one is one-half cup. I wonder how many of the smaller cups would fit into the bigger one. Can you try filling the one-fourth cup with water and pouring it into the one-half cup? I knew you could figure it out!"*

This conversation included supportive comments, open-ended questions, vocabulary, and challenges, didn't it? This is teacher intentionality in action—expertly weaving in academic learning goals as children play and explore.

However, this conversation required Joey's interest and participation. What if he had come over to the sensory table, picked up the cups of water,

Sue: "One of my concerns about learning goals in centers is how do you support these goals without forcing the children to do something that is not their intention? While you can look for different learning goals within what the children are doing, how do you provide experiences with the goals you need to cover?"

Mary M.: "Some teachers struggle to remain flexible during lesson plan implementation. For example, if a teacher plans to focus on measuring skills in the block area for a particular week (long, short, etc.), but the children are more interested in driving cars and trucks over and around the blocks, she may feel she has to push her own measurement agenda. With such a focus on intentionality in teaching, it is sometimes difficult for teachers to let go of a planned activity. The experienced teacher accepts the children's interest in the cars and trucks and adjusts her plan to scaffold learning based on that. Perhaps the focus in the block area changes to one of comparing the speed of different toy vehicles as they travel down a ramp built from blocks (which is actually a form of measurement!). Maybe cooperative play and problem solving become the focus as children try to work together to build structures and share the cars and trucks. Measurement can be worked on another day or in another classroom area."

and asked if he could use the water wheel? Maybe he said, "I want to see how fast the wheel can go around." The adult involved could say, "No, Joey, we're not doing the water wheel this week. We're doing measurement. That's our goal." But Joey's interest may be lost at that point—and to what end? How about getting the water wheel and working with him as he pours water from the different size cups? You might be able to relate what he is doing back to the measurement goal (the smaller cups pour less water, and therefore the wheel turns more slowly). However, what's most important is to follow up on Joey's interest and sustain his engagement. As long as what he is doing is not destructive, chaotic, or simplistic and repetitive, it can be supported by some teacher flexibility and quick-thinking adjustments. Joey's interest is more oriented to a learning goal around observation and experimentation with cause and effect (in the science domain).

There is no reason to demand that children stop what they are doing when they take activities in different directions than the identified goal. If they are still engaged productively, the new goal (and direction) can be supported and noted on the reflection part of the framework.

Changing the Learning Goals for the Play Areas

When do you change the learning goals for the play areas? It may be when the children use the materials in different ways, as Joey did above. Or there will be times when *you* want to emphasize different learning goals with the same materials. (In the next chapter, we will explore when to change materials.) In reflection, you may decide that the initial learning goals from earlier plans are being met by most of the children. Or you may determine that children's interest is waning in activities related to that goal. Perhaps the learning goal is too challenging at this point in time. Then you will note your reflections about either the children's accomplishment of the goals or their lack of interest and plan for changes for the next week. Here are Genevieve's reflections and plans for changes after she implemented the same learning goals for three weeks.

REFLECTIONS: What worked? What didn't? What did you learn about individual children and group interests?	PLANS: Based on your reflections, what will you change for next week?
The children have started exploring most of the areas and using them successfully, meeting our goals. They're engaged most of the time.	Change goals for play areas but not necessarily materials.
	More adult help at cleanup time.
Cleanup time is chaotic still. Help children put away paints, etc.	When coming in from outdoors, put on a dancing record and have part of the class dance and sing while part washes hands—then switch.
Coming in from outdoors was a tough transition this week.	
Jared needs more one-to-one with an adult. Maria is so quiet.	Genevieve: have Jared be her "special friend." Pair Maria with Sophie and Alicia—they're more outgoing.
Noah and Taylor seem to be pairing up as friends.	

Genevieve's reflections and plans for changes

Based on her thoughts about the children's accomplishments over those three weeks, Genevieve decided not to change anything in the materials available or the choices possible. Instead, she kept the exact same materials and focus and identified different learning goals for each area in her plan for the play areas in week 4.

The new learning goals caused Genevieve and her colleagues to implement different ideas for facilitating the children's use of the materials. Their focus in their interactions with the children helped them observe and learn more about the ways children demonstrated the new goals. The teachers' focus changed. But that new focus did not require new materials or a different room arrangement. It only required a different point of view for the adults in the room. Changing the learning goals can be a way to make sure that each play area is being used to its fullest potential by the children.

Embedding Learning Goals and Academics in Daily Routines

We know that academic learning can be embedded in children's play experiences, but where else do these academics occur in a preschool or kindergarten classroom? If there are no lectures, if the approach emphasizes children as active learners, then how can we be sure that academic learning is addressed throughout the time children are in our classrooms? Daily routines in our classrooms can be rich in learning possibilities if teachers are intentional and plan for them to be so.

Sue: "Thinking about goals is important in daily routines. There are embedded skills that need to progress throughout the year and not remain stagnant. They can be addressed at these routine times."

In all programs for young children, daily routines can incorporate reading, math, social studies, and science. The following daily schedule of a typical preschool classroom is listed alongside possible academic goals for each part of the day. The goals are written in the language of both a university course catalogue and the general skills listed previously to help others see how learning is at the core of everything teachers do with preschoolers.

....

Sample Daily Schedule for a Preschool Half Day

8:00–8:25 a.m. Arrival Time
The children put away their backpacks and coats and go to tables where hands-on materials are available (paper and instruments for writing or drawing, such as markers or pencils; small manipulatives for constructing, such as Lego building blocks; and playdough).

Academics: speaking, vocabulary development, writing, getting along with others, taking care of our community (namely, the classroom), fine-motor skills

8:25–8:45 a.m. Large-Group Time
The children join in movement games, songs, and fingerplays, then listen to discussions and stories before planning for the day.

Academics: listening, reading comprehension, phonological awareness (such as rhyming songs), counting and quantity (such as counting when taking attendance), observing and predicting (when watching a science demonstration), getting along with others, listening and following the guidance of teachers, using balance and coordination (in movement activities)

8:45–10:00 a.m. Work or Activity Time
The children choose among a variety of play areas and may be invited to join in a small-group activity led by a teacher for approximately ten to fifteen minutes of this time.

Academics: physics (balance, gravity, mass, force), measurement, and problem solving at the block area; chemistry in the cooking activity (teacher-led small group); knowledge of books and print at the class library; understanding families, speaking, and self-regulation at dramatic play; sorting and categorizing at manipulatives; throughout all, fine-motor skills and social/emotional skills as well as approaches to learning are used as well

10:00–10:15 a.m. Cleanup Time
The children help clean up the entire classroom.

Academics: sorting and categorizing, counting and quantity (the children place items back in their baskets and on shelves); understanding community (the children work together for a common end); social/emotional skills in working with others and demonstrating self-regulation

10:15–10:30 a.m. Snacktime
The children converse and eat snack.

Academics: speaking, vocabulary development (words about health and nutrition), getting along with others (waiting for turns), fine-motor skills (pouring, using utensils), understanding community (setting the table and cleaning up)

10:30–11:00 a.m. Outdoors
The children engage in a variety of large-muscle activities, outdoors if weather permits.

Academics: botany and meteorology (explore plants and weather outdoors), gross motor (run, jump, and play), counting and quantity (wait for turns on the bikes or swings), getting along with others, showing curiosity and initiative

11:00–11:15 a.m. Prepare to Go Home
Get materials, backpacks, coats, and so forth. Review the day's activities and make plans for tomorrow.

Academics: our community (cleanup), listening and comprehension (review and plan), self-help skills

11:15 a.m. Dismissal

....

And here is a sample full-day kindergarten schedule analyzed for embedded academic learning throughout the day.

....

Sample Daily Schedule for a Full-Day Kindergarten

8:00–8:25 a.m. Arrival Time
Children put away their backpacks and coats and go to tables where hands-on materials are available (greetings and conversation; writing and drawing; small manipulatives for constructing, such as Lego building blocks; and playdough).

Academics: speaking, vocabulary development, writing, getting along with others, taking care of our community (namely, the classroom), fine-motor skills

8:25–8:50 a.m. Large-Group Time
Children join in movement games, songs, and fingerplays, then listen to discussions and stories before planning for the day.

Academics: listening, reading comprehension, phonological awareness (such as rhyming songs), counting and quantity (such as counting when taking attendance), observing and predicting (when watching a science demonstration), getting along with others, listening and following the guidance of teachers, using balance and coordination (in movement activities)

8:50–10:15 a.m. Readers and Writers Workshop

The children choose among a variety of literacy activities (listening to books on tape, writing and drawing in their journals, playing roles in dramatic play, using flannel boards and pocket charts to tell stories, writing letters to classmates and family members). The children may be invited to join in a small-group activity led by a teacher for approximately ten to fifteen minutes of this time.

Academics: listening, vocabulary development, reading comprehension, phonological awareness (such as rhyming songs), letter and word identification, writing, fine-motor skills, and learning more about our families, speaking, and self-regulation at dramatic play

10:15–10:30 a.m. Cleanup Time

The children help clean up the entire classroom.

Academics: sorting and categorizing, counting and quantity (the children place items back in their baskets and on shelves), understanding community (the children work together for a common end), social/emotional skills in working with others and demonstrating self-regulation

10:30–10:45 a.m. Snacktime

The children converse and eat snack.

Academics: speaking, vocabulary development (words about health and nutrition), getting along with others (waiting for turns), fine-motor skills (pouring, using utensils), understanding community (setting the table and cleaning up)

10:45–11:30 a.m. Special Activities

Children engage in gym, music, library, or other special activities.

Academics: Many domains and skills will be addressed by these activities.

11:30 a.m. Lunch

The children converse and eat.

12:00 p.m. Recess.

12:30 p.m. Large- or Small-Group Story Reading and Quiet Time

The children listen to teachers read stories in large or small groups.

Academics: listening, reading comprehension, vocabulary development, self-regulation (quieting oneself down)

1:00 p.m. Investigation Time

The children choose among a variety of math, science, and play activities (sorting, classifying and counting manipulatives, creating shapes with small and large blocks, measuring items in the room, engaging in an ongoing science experiment, caring for pets, writing in math and/or science journals, reading nonfiction books about nature and other topics, playing at the sensory table, making creations in the art area) and may be invited to join in a small-group activity led by a teacher for approximately ten to fifteen minutes of this time.

Academics: experimenting with balance, gravity, mass, force, shapes, measurement, and problem solving (blocks); listening; knowledge of books and print; writing; sorting, categorizing, and counting (manipulatives); investigating with senses; fine-motor (art, journaling, manipulatives); and social/emotional skills and approaches to learning (throughout all areas)

2:00 p.m. Cleanup Time

The children help clean up the entire classroom. (with the same academics embedded as in the morning cleanup)

2:15 p.m. Prepare to Go Home

Get materials, backpacks, coats, and so forth. Review the day's activities and make plans for tomorrow.

2:30 p.m. Dismissal

....

Consider analyzing the daily schedule of your preschool or kindergarten program. Academic learning can happen at all times of the day!

Academic Learning and Daily Routines

Let's look more closely at ways teachers can embed academic learning into daily routines. Again, teachers play a key role in making sure that happens. With some careful planning, they can infuse daily routines with predictable rituals that incorporate learning goals. When they do, they engage children's brains in higher-level cognitive thinking. Children focus on the challenge presented and complete the task at hand more smoothly. This is true for daily routines as well as for transitions between activities.

Teachers need to plan for ways to address learning goals at these times. In their planning conversations, they should ask themselves the following questions:

- What will need to be set up ahead of time for this daily routine?
- Will there be expectations that need to be communicated to the children?
- What teacher actions will need to be planned?
- How will we interact with the children during the routine?

Let's look at the daily routines included on the second page of the planning and reflection framework (meals, transitions, and outdoor explorations) and consider some ways that you could plan for learning goals to enhance these routines.

Meals

Teachers can enhance the snack or mealtime experience for children and weave in the learning goals identified in the two daily schedules above in a variety of ways.

- *To meet the goal of speaking*, teachers set up meals and snacktimes to occur at tables where children and teachers are seated so they can easily converse with each other. To facilitate such conversations, teachers sit *with* the children during the meal or snack for as much of the time as possible. They are not setting up other areas of the classroom or talking among themselves.
- *To meet the goal of vocabulary development*, teachers engage in naturally flowing conversations with the children, introducing new words as it seems appropriate. Questions such as "What are some foods you eat at home that make you healthy?" or "What's your favorite vegetable?" can spark interesting discussions that inform teachers and develop vocabulary. Discussions can include reviewing what children have done at school that day or what they plan to do after they finish eating. The sky's the limit as far as conversation topics!
- *To meet the goal of getting along with others (waiting for turns)*, teachers can encourage waiting for items to be passed, using "Please" and "Thank you," and keeping hands to selves. Recognizing when children are being kind and thoughtful encourages them to continue. "Wow, Phillip, I see that you passed the water pitcher to Juanito. Thank you for doing that!"
- *To meet the goal of fine-motor skill development (such as pouring or using utensils)*, teachers provide small pitchers and plastic

utensils that children can handle easily. They communicate the expectation that children serve themselves, and they are ready to step in and offer assistance if a child needs help pouring the juice or spooning fruit onto his plate. Again, they recognize children's growing fine-motor skills and independence with positive comments. Putting lines on cups (say two-thirds of the way to the top) will help children fill their drinks up without spilling. And cutting fruit pieces ahead of time will help them serve themselves and eat more neatly.

- *To meet the goal of community (setting the table and cleaning up)*, teachers invite children to help prepare the tables for meals or snacktime. A few children per day can be designated to take on that task. And every child is expected to clean up his own place when finished eating. Scraping dishes, pouring out extra drinks, and throwing away trash are all chores that young children can perform. They develop a sense of responsibility and contribute to the classroom community. Again, recognizing their actions will encourage them to continue doing them each day.

Transitions

Transitions are a part of every day in a program for young children. Teachers have to help the group move from one activity to another. Unfortunately young children do not always transition easily. They may be deeply engrossed in what they are doing at a play area when cleanup time is announced and be reluctant to stop what they are doing. Or they may be very excited to get outdoors and run to the door to be first in line. Teachers can help children be more successful at these times by being intentional and planning ahead for transitions. Again, planning some learning goals and thinking through the planning questions listed previously will make transitions a valuable time in your curriculum and help them go more smoothly.

Let's look at lining up children to go outdoors (or wherever) from this perspective. Lining up is a chore for young children and should not dominate their time! Young children are not patient, so waiting for everyone to get in line is difficult. They do not like standing close to others; it feels to them like their personal space is being invaded. So how can a teacher make the best of this situation and still add learning goals? First, simply consider whether it's really necessary for all the children to line up at the same time. If you have a teaching colleague, then remember the adage "divide and conquer." Young children will handle a smaller group much better. Wait time will be shortened, and you all will get outside (or wherever you are going) much faster.

In addition, adding some learning opportunities to the task of lining up children will help engage their brains and move the task along more successfully. Here are some ways that teachers have incorporated goals into lining up children.

Shape, Color, Letter, and Number Recognition

Leslie cut out large shapes from different colored construction paper. She affixed them to the floor with clear contact paper in the area that goes from the door into the classroom alongside the cubby area. She left plenty of space between each shape to prevent children from feeling too crowded as they lined up. Now, she uses the shapes and colors as ways to engage children as they're getting in line: "Be ready to tell me what shape you're standing on when I call your name," or "Can you tell me the color of your shape when I call your name?" Sometimes she dismisses children to go line up by showing them a card with the colored shape or by saying, "Jeremy, please stand on the blue square. Sasha, please stand on the red triangle." As children are consistently successful in recognizing shapes and colors, she complicates the task by giving descriptions rather than names: "Maria, I'm thinking of a shape that has three corners and is the same color as a stop sign. Please go stand on that shape." Or she might say, "Abdo, please stand on the shape that rhymes with the words *mellow* and *where*." Leslie continues to complicate the task throughout the year by writing a letter or a numeral on each of the shapes. Then, she can incorporate letter and number recognition into lining up as well.

Sorting, Categorizing, Counting, and Comparing

Knowing that children love to be first in line and will sometimes clamber over each other to be in that position, Brian has given responsibilities to the role of line leader that go beyond standing at the head of the line. When a child is assigned the role of line leader on the helper chart, Brian reminds them that they have to organize the group into two lines. "How will you sort our group today?" he asks. Children are familiar with different ways to sort because Brian and his colleagues have demonstrated this for the children. Sometimes, they play the "people sorting" game. Brian says, "I'm looking for anyone who is wearing tie shoes. Please come and stand in front of the group." Then, he has the seated group count how many children have on shoes that tie. He may have that group remain standing while he calls for anyone who is wearing shoes with buckles. Again, he has the seated group count how many children have on shoes with buckles. He has the two lines stand next to each other, child by child, so that the length of each line can easily be seen and compared. He does the same thing with lining up. The line leader calls out two categories by which children line up (boys and girls, belts and no belts, Velcro on their shoes and no Velcro, etc.). Then, the line leader counts each line out loud, compares which is longer, and off the group goes (outdoors or wherever).

Pretending

Sylvia has found great success in getting children lined up and to the next activity by suggesting that they pretend. She knows that when children pretend to take on a role, they have greater self-regulation than when they do not. She takes advantage of that when she has to transition children and get them someplace else. Here are some of the ways she has had them pretend:

- chewing a big wad of bubble gum in their mouths
- holding a bubble in their mouths
- tiptoeing on a narrow, high wire as in the circus
- flying quietly and gently like butterflies, like a leaf falling off a tree, like a petal dropping off a flower
- being a cat quietly stalking a mouse
- being fish swimming in the sea

It is not necessary that children line up for every transition throughout the day. In fact, avoiding lining up as much as possible will help the day go much more smoothly. Many teachers have children move from one activity to another (say from large-group time to washing hands and going to the snack table) by using songs, chants, or movement activities. One teacher remains with the large group. She dismisses only a few children at a time so that no long lines can form at the sink, where the other teacher is supervising. In this way, the children who remain in the large group are engaged through the song. The teacher who is leading the song pays attention to when it's time to send more children to the sink and snack tables. In this way, the transition moves quickly and keeps the interest of the children.

And many of the songs and chants used as transition tools have other benefits as well. Learning goals such as hearing and discriminating rhymes and sounds and color identification can be addressed, as well as waiting one's turn and following teacher guidance. At the end of this chapter are some songs and chants that can be used for transitioning children from one activity to another. Here is one of them:

> ### Willoughby Wallaby Woo
> Willoughby, wallaby wee, an elephant sat on me!
> Willoughby, wallaby woo, an elephant sat on you!
> Willoughby, wallaby w_____ (substitute child's name starting with a *w* sound).
> An elephant sat on _____ (child's name).

As in the song above, a child's name is used in each one of the songs and chants provided at the end of this chapter. By using the child's name, she is alerted that it's her turn to head to the sink or to choose a play area. There are many great songbooks, CDs, and resources that teachers can turn to for effective transition activities. Noting plans for transitions on the framework will help teachers remember how important it is to help children be successful during these difficult times of the day.

Outdoor Explorations

Quality early childhood programs offer outdoor physical activity on a daily basis (weather permitting, of course). Young children's growing bodies are developing muscle control and need to expend energy and experience fresh air and the delights of nature. Teachers should include recess or outdoor time whenever weather permits.

Thinking about and planning for children to expend physical energy outdoors (or in the classroom on rainy days) is an important task that will enhance an early childhood classroom. Outdoor opportunities provide multiple benefits to the children and can make the time more purposeful and less chaotic. Preschool and kindergarten teachers' jobs will be much easier and successful in the long run if they think about ways for children to engage in purposeful activities outdoors as they run off energy and enjoy fresh air. Flexibility and responsiveness are necessary as well. How many times have teachers talked about how "squirrelly" their children were today? Or asked, "Is it a full moon? My kids sure are acting crazy!"

When a teacher plans for outdoor time, she may focus mostly on learning goals related to gross-motor development: children running, jumping, climbing, hiding, swinging, digging, and taking advantage of the basic equipment, space, and freedom in the outdoor area. Most programs' outdoor areas contain at least some running space and climbing equipment. If teachers introduce new equipment, materials, or activities periodically, they can make every outdoor time an adventure. With changing possibilities, children may try more new things or stay interested longer. And many more academic learning goals can be addressed. Teachers are providing a sense of some structure to a time that is ripe with freedom for exploration and physical expression.

Here are some ideas for equipment, materials, and activities that can be added to the outdoor area and recorded on the framework. Possible learning goals (beyond gross-motor development) are identified for many of the suggestions. By no means is this list of possibilities all-inclusive. What else has worked successfully for you?

Robin: "I find outdoors provides a fun time to bond with kids over activities that they are more comfortable with. I can also work with students who need to build strength because they spend so much time in front of the television or computer screen."

Equipment
- bikes, wagons, and carts
- climbing tunnel
- large exercise ball
- balls in different sizes, targets (comparing sizes, distances)
- woodworking bench (fine-motor skills)
- sand/water table (sensory exploration)
- gardening tools (exploring nature, developing responsibility for a class garden)

Materials
- streamers or scarves for feeling/seeing the wind at work (sensory exploration)
- bubbles (sensory exploration, fine-motor skills)
- spray bottles filled with water for painting the pavement or walls (fine-motor skills; painting letters, numbers, and names on the pavement)
- paintbrushes and buckets of water for painting (same as above)
- magnifying glasses and books about insects (vocabulary development, studying the natural world)
- sidewalk chalk (letter, number, and name writing; fine-motor skills)
- small cars and trucks for the sandbox

- jump ropes
- plastic-can stilts
- hoops of various sizes
- binoculars for watching birds or clouds
- tape recorder for taping bird songs or outdoor noises
- dress-up clothes for dramatic play (avoid long skirts and high-heel shoes)

Activities
- read under a tree (sit on a blanket or plastic mat) (interest in books, reading comprehension)
- wash the baby dolls or dishes in the water table
- wash the classroom chairs and tables (responsibility, working together)
- paint outdoors; use the easel or tape butcher paper to the building or fence
- carefully observe ice cubes as they melt (making predictions)
- adopt a tree; check on it regularly in each season
- go on a nature scavenger hunt: collect leaves (different colors, shapes), nuts, rocks, and feathers (sensory exploration, sorting, and categorizing)
- count and categorize the trucks that drive by (how many cement trucks? dump trucks? tow trucks?) (counting, understanding quantities, sorting and categorizing)
- do texture rubbings with crayons; use paper, pavement, cement, fence, wall, slide, and so on
- organize a driver's license bureau for all bike riders; have "police officers" enforce traffic rules, check licenses, and give tickets (self-regulation in playing roles, speaking, vocabulary development)
- do an obstacle course: climb up the slide and go down the slide, run over to the sandbox, walk around the edge, jump through the hoop, and give me a hug (listening and following directions)
- organize group games: Red Light, Green Light; Duck-Duck-Goose; Mother, May I?
- run relay races; add variations such as running, jumping, walking like various animals

- play catch and rolling games
- have a picnic—eat snack outside!

The possibilities are endless, aren't they? The suggested equipment, materials, and activities listed above are offered in addition to the basic setup of your outdoor area.

Embedding Learning Goals and Academics in Teacher-Led Group Activities

At large- and small-group times, children are usually expected to participate in a group activity that is chosen and directed by the teacher. Teachers often have an easy time identifying learning goals for group times, and during those times teachers feel more like they are teaching by instructing and directing. However, with young children, these teaching times need to be limited and offered in conjunction with many opportunities for children to take the lead, exploring their own interests with teachers acting as guides and facilitators. Chapter 6 provides more information about planning for effective large- and small-group times and balancing them with child-initiated activities. For now, let's consider the ways learning goals can be incorporated into them.

Large-Group Times

For large-group times, children often sit on the floor in a circle formation. Most teachers incorporate some daily rituals that involve gathering children together through movement games and songs, helping them get settled down and ready to listen, and giving them opportunities to participate in discussions about the day. Here are learning goals that can be addressed through those rituals:

- listening and following the guidance of teachers
- getting along with others (building group cohesiveness, turn taking)
- phonics/awareness of sounds (such as rhyming songs)
- counting and quantity (such as counting when taking attendance)
- using balance and coordination (in movement activities)

On the second page of the framework, teachers write at least one learning goal for large-group time. Some days, the rituals of large-group time may be all that are included at that time. Then a teacher would write one of the learning goals listed above on the plan. Other days, the teacher may read a story, lead a discussion about a topic, or demonstrate something. The children are expected to listen, take turns, participate by raising their hand, and wait to be called upon to make comments or ask questions. Instead of writing any of the learning goals addressed in the rituals above, a teacher would identify one that is related to the special activity. Here are some learning goals that could be addressed when reading a story, doing a science experiment, demonstrating a new game, or writing a group description of a recent field trip:

- listening and speaking
- vocabulary development
- reading comprehension and knowledge of books and print (when listening to a story)
- observing and predicting (when watching a science demonstration)
- developing self-regulation
- showing curiosity and interest in new things
- understanding the writing process (when writing a group description of the field trip)
- math goals of counting, quantity, numeral and shape recognition, sorting, or measurement (if a math game is demonstrated)

There are many possibilities for learning goals at large-group time, aren't there? Again, it's most important for teachers to remember that large-group time is not equivalent to lecture time. Paying attention to the interest and engagement of the children is essential; they will not benefit if they are bored and anxious to get on to more active parts of the day. Again, chapter 6 gives many more ideas for planning an engaging and effective large-group time.

Small-Group Times

Many teachers plan to work with children in small groups so that they can pay more individualized attention to each child, observe each closely, and make notes about capabilities and challenges. A small group usually occurs with one teacher and six to eight children seated around a table or gathered in a small area on the floor. As in large groups, the teacher is the focus. She determines the activity and expects the children to listen to her directions and to participate alongside their peers. Small-group times often involve hands-on activities. Compared to large-group time, there may be less time spent listening quietly or waiting one's turn, which allows some children to shine during group time. It's important to give children as many opportunities to be successful as possible.

Keeping the purpose of small group clear and establishing time limits ensures that the children gain from the experience rather than just pass time. If a specific project, such as an experiment or cooking, is involved, the small-group time can last until the project is completed. If the activity involves working with specific skills, the teacher can be sensitive to how long the children stay interested and actively engaged.

Remember, if small-group time is to take place during the time children are engaged in play areas, then it should be a choice, not a requirement, for children. In fact, small-group activities could be planned to take place in the play areas. A teacher could decide to offer support and guidance as children play a board game, work with puzzles or manipulatives, engage in sensory exploration with sand or water, or pretend in the dramatic play area. In chapter 6, more ideas for effective small-group planning will be shared. For now, let's look more closely at addressing learning goals during small-group time.

On the second page of the framework, there is a box to list plans for teacher-led small groups. No matter what specific focus or activity is planned, some learning goals are embedded in the gathering together of a small group of children. These include the following:

- listening and speaking
- getting along with others
- following the guidance of teachers
- expressing emotions appropriately
- developing self-regulation
- demonstrating curiosity and interest in new things
- showing initiative
- persisting and solving problems

A teacher could write any of these goals for small-group time. But more likely she will choose to focus the activity on one or two specific learning goals related to literacy, math, science, or fine-motor development. Then she will plan an interesting and engaging way for children to work on that learning goal in the small-group setting. For example, if the learning goal is for children to practice the math skills of sorting and classifying, a teacher may want to provide many different small manipulatives that will encourage the children to demonstrate sorting and classifying skills in a variety of ways, such as colored tiles on colored plates, stringing beads and string, bottle caps and buttons. The learning goal written on the plan would read "sorting/classifying different objects in multiple ways." The variety of materials provided keeps the children's interest in the small-group activity for a longer period. This helps develop children's attention spans and gives them the opportunity to work more fully with the concept at hand. In the process, the teacher gains more information about how each child understands the concepts involved.

Here are a few ideas for small-group activities that are interesting and engaging to children (more will be shared in chapter 6). Possible primary learning goals are identified for each.

Read a Story

Reading a story in a small group helps a teacher assess whether each child is listening and following along. More questions and comments can be shared so that the reading experience is truly interactive. Having multiple copies of the book allows children to reread, tell the story in their own words, look at the pictures, make predictions, and begin to recognize familiar words and decode others. You can complicate the experience by inviting the children to act out the story, paying close attention to the sequence of events or changing the outcome in some way. Learning goals could include listening, speaking, vocabulary development, reading comprehension, awareness of sounds, and persistence.

Write and Draw

Inviting children to write and draw at small-group time helps a teacher get a better sense of how each child is developing in the literacy and fine-motor domains. Encouraging conversation about their drawing and helping them write down words in phonetic language as well as with proper spelling will further children's engagement. Then, inviting them to share their writing with each other gives them an audience and more purpose to the task. Learning goals could include listening, speaking, vocabulary development, understanding of print, recognition of letters and words, awareness of sounds, persistence, and grasp and control of a writing tool.

Shopping the Room with Number Cards

A fun way to engage children in counting objects is to suggest that they go "shopping" in the classroom. Each child in the small group receives a card with a numeral on it (representing quantities that are determined by how high they can count), and a grocery bag, basket, or cart. They are instructed to go shopping for that many items and return to the group area to share what they bought. The task can be complicated by asking children to record what they bought by drawing that many items on their paper. Learning goals could include listening, speaking, awareness of counting and quantity, mathematical problem solving, representing mathematical information, and grasp and control of a writing tool.

Conclusion

There is tremendous potential for addressing learning goals in all parts of the day of a preschool or kindergarten program. It's up to the teachers to make sure that it happens. They plan for learning goals at play areas, in daily routines, and at large- and small-group times. They note those on the framework and communicate with others about them. The learning goals do not magically appear. Teacher intentionality makes the difference.

In the next chapter, we will look in depth at teacher intentionality as children play. We will analyze the many ways that preschool and kindergarten teachers can ensure that children's play experiences are rich, rewarding, and full of learning.

Transition Songs, Chants, and Fingerplays

Calling to and Sending Away

Willoughby Wallaby Woo
Willoughby, wallaby wee, an elephant sat on me!
Willoughby, wallaby woo, an elephant sat on you!
Willoughby, wallaby w_____ (substitute child's name starting with a w sound).
An elephant sat on _____ (child's name).

Hicklety Picklety Bumblebee
Hicklety Picklety bumblebee, who can say their name for me?
_____ (child says name)!
Clap it! _____ (child's name)!
Shout it! _____ (child's name)!
Whisper it! _____ (child's name)!

Paw Paw Patch

Where oh where is little _____ *(child's name)*?
Where oh where is little _____ *(child's name)*?
Where oh where is little _____ *(child's name)*?
Way down yonder in the paw paw patch.
Picking up paw paws and putting them in *(her/his)* pocket.
Picking up paw paws and putting them in *(her/his)* pocket.
Picking up paw paws and putting them in *(her/his)* pocket.
Way down yonder in the paw paw patch.

Rich and Chocolaty

We love _____, she's rich and chocolaty.
Her mother *(or grandma, or uncle, or foster dad)* puts her in her milk for extra energy!

Chickee Chickee

Hey there _____ you're a real cool cat.
You've got a lot of this and a lot of that.
We all think that you are really neat.
So come on down and do the Chickee Chickee beat.
Hands up Chickee Chickee, Chickee Chickee.
Hands down Chickee Chickee, Chickee Chickee.
Boom Boom *(punch the air)* Chickee Chickee, Chickee Chickee.
Turn around Chickee Chickee, Chickee Chickee.

The More We Get Together

Oh the more we get together, together, together,
The more we get together, the happier we'll be.
There's _____, and _____, and _____, and _____.
Oh the more we get together, the happier we'll be.

If You Have on Red

If you have on red, stand up quick.
If you have on red, stand up quick.
If you have on red, stand up quick.
And take a bow *(or go wash your hands, or go get your coat on, or go choose your center, and so on)*.

CHAPTER 4

Planning and Sustaining High-Level Play in Preschool and Kindergarten

This is an exciting time to be an early educator who believes strongly that play is important. Professional organizations from a variety of fields have released position papers stating the importance of play in children's lives. And new research has shown the connection between play and learning. The third edition of *Developmentally Appropriate Practice in Early Childhood Programs*, published by the National Association for the Education of Young Children, makes many references to such research. Studies, such as those described in the following quotes, have shown that children's participation in interesting and challenging play experiences has a direct connection to their later academic achievement (Copple and Bredekamp 2009, 131–32):

> A study of children from around the world . . . showed that when preschool experiences at age four included lots of child-initiated, free-choice activities supported by a variety of equipment and materials—the kinds of environments that support play—these children had better cognitive (and language) performance at age seven than their peers (Montie, Xiang, & Schweinhart 2006).

> Other research shows that pretend play strengthens cognitive capacities, including sustained attention, memory, logical reasoning, language and literacy skills, imagination, creativity, understanding of emotions, and the ability to reflect on one's own thinking, inhibit impulses, control one's behavior, and take another person's perspective (Kavanaugh & Engel 1998; Bergen & Mauer 2000; Elias & Berk 2002; Lindsey & Colwell 2003; Ruff & Capozzoli 2003; Berk 2006b).

Making a Strong Case for the Value of Play

Early educators are not the only ones emphasizing the importance of high-quality play experiences for children. Experts from many other fields have published statements and made recommendations about the value of play for children's health and well-being. I share these quotes with you here so that you know about the strong support for play and can use this information to explain to others why you incorporate play into your preschool and kindergarten curriculum.

> Theorists . . . suggest that the absence of play is an obstacle to the development of healthy and creative individuals. Psychoanalysts believe that play is necessary for mastering emotional traumas or disturbances; psychosocialists believe it is necessary for ego mastery and learning to live with everyday experiences; constructivists believe it is necessary for cognitive growth; maturationists believe it is necessary for competence building and for socializing functions in all cultures of the world; and neuroscientists believe it is necessary for emotional and physical health, motivation, and love of learning. (Isenberg and Quisenberry 2002, 33)

In their clinical report on play released in 2007, the American Academy of Pediatrics states, "Play is essential to development because it contributes to the cognitive, physical, social, and emotional well-being of children and youth" (Ginsburg 2007, 182). They identify a variety of factors that have reduced children's opportunities to engage in child-driven play and raise concerns about overly scheduled and hurried family lifestyles and mistaken overemphasis on academics and enrichment activities in the early years of children's lives.

> In contrast to passive entertainment, play builds active, healthy bodies. In fact, it has been suggested that encouraging unstructured play may be an exceptional way to increase physical activity levels in children, which is one important strategy in the resolution of the obesity epidemic. Perhaps above all, play is a simple joy that is a cherished part of childhood. (Ginsburg 2007, 183)

Psychiatrists and psychologists have raised concerns about rising stress and anxiety levels in children, saying that "limiting free play in kids may result in a generation of anxious, unhappy and socially maladjusted adults"

(Wenner 2009, 24). Furthermore, in a front page article in *USA Today*, it was noted that there is a rise in serious bullying behaviors in adolescents. Some psychologists are concerned that one cause may be "less playtime in kindergarten and pre-school" where children learn to get along with other children through play experiences (Hampson 2010).

Evolutionary biologists see play as necessary to learn how to cope with the unexpected, saying that "play encourages flexibility and creativity that may, in the future, be advantageous in unexpected situations or new environments. . . . Animals that are not alert and watchful are at risk of being attacked by predators" (Wenner 2009, 29).

In their report, *Crisis in the Kindergarten: Why Children Need to Play in School*, the Alliance for Childhood released a passionate plea connecting play to democratic citizenship:

> We believe that the stifling of play has dire consequences—not only for children but for the future of our nation. . . . No human being can achieve his full potential if his creativity is stunted in childhood. And no nation can thrive in the 21st century without a highly creative and innovative workforce. Nor will democracy survive without citizens who can form their own independent thoughts and act on them. (Miller and Almon 2009, 8, 59)

The social skills children develop as they try to sustain rewarding play with others are indeed building their citizenship skills. They will work at problem solving and compromise because play is rewarding in and of itself.

> A wonderful cycle of learning is driven by the pleasure in play. A child is curious; she explores and discovers. The discovery brings pleasure; the pleasure leads to repetition and practice. Practice brings mastery; mastery brings the pleasure and confidence to once again act on curiosity. All learning—emotional, social, motor and cognitive—is accelerated and facilitated by repetition fueled by the pleasure of play. (Perry, Hogan, and Marlin 2000)

Stuart Brown makes the connection between play, innovation, and corporate profitability: "The genius of play is that, in playing, we create imaginative new cognitive combinations. And in creating those novel combinations, we find what works" (2009, 37). He consults with Fortune

500 companies around the world, helping them bring playfulness into the workplace. Brown says, "Nations that remain economically strong are those that can create intellectual property—and the ability to innovate comes out of an ability to play" (200). He concludes

> Play is how we are made, how we develop and adjust to change. It can foster innovation and lead to multibillion-dollar fortunes. But in the end the most significant aspect of play is that it allows us to express our joy and connect most deeply with the best in ourselves, and in others. (218)

Play in the Preschool and Kindergarten Curriculum

In recent years, many teachers have reported a true loss of joy in their classrooms. Some preschool and kindergarten teachers have experienced pressure to reduce the time allotted to play in their programs and to replace that time with more formal instruction. They then found it harder to engage the children's interest and sustain instructional activities. More behavior problems developed, and teachers heard children say "I'm bored" more frequently than ever before. These teachers miss seeing the high motivation children show when they play. They know that children can experience much joy and benefit when play experiences are rich and interesting.

Yet they also recognize that not all children's play is productive. Sometimes energy levels get out of control. Other times safety issues arise. Adults are important guides as children play. They help make sure the play experience is one that benefits children's development, furthers their learning, and is rich and interesting as well. This takes planning.

It's important to take the research that connects learning and play and make it clear in our curricular practices. As the previous chapter shows, writing learning goals for play areas helps others see that play can involve learning. Being clear about teacher strategies to facilitate play helps keep the play and learning connected. In this chapter, we will look at three ways teachers can plan for and sustain high-level play in their classrooms. They can

- set up the environment for play and make changes as appropriate
- allow ample time for high-level play to develop
- act as play facilitators

Setting Up the Environment for Play

We have already discussed the importance of a well-organized environment that contains many rich possibilities for children's exploration and play. Because it is well organized, children have a clear understanding of where materials can be found (and will be put away) and how they can be used. The environment communicates structure.

In the classroom, each learning area is distinctively set up as a separate space. Shelving and tables help delineate that space. Baskets, bins, and tubs help organize a variety of materials. Shelves are labeled with photos, pictures, and/or words. Order is communicated clearly to children by this arrangement. As children are using materials and putting them away by themselves, they develop independence and a sense of responsibility.

Teachers know that the room arrangement and presentation of materials can deeply affect children's behavior. They consider traffic flow and noise levels. If the children's work is constantly interrupted when other children pass by, they will become frustrated and may strike out at others. However, if traffic flow is directed by organizing the classroom in such a way that shelves and tables block any running paths and protect areas for block building or dramatic play, the children will feel their work is important and protected. The arrangement of furniture and shelves directs children toward the productive use of materials in specific areas. Noise levels are considered so that materials that tend toward greater physical and verbal involvement are placed near each other. Materials that tend toward quieter use are also grouped together.

Consider the classroom arrangement in the diagram on the following page. Do you see the organization strategies in use here? Do you see any potential problems with traffic flow? How would you rearrange this classroom? Now think about your own classroom arrangement, and ask yourself the same questions.

Every teacher's classroom space is different in the square footage, the arrangement of windows and doors, the availability of electrical outlets, and the accessibility to sinks and restrooms. No classroom arrangement in a book will match your own. However, basic room organization that helps children function as independently as possible can be accomplished.

Materials in the Environment

Most teachers set up each area in the classroom with a set of basic materials. These basic materials are available to children most of the time.

Sue: "I like the idea of planning for play, not only planning materials, but questions, challenges, or a new way to use the materials that would help elevate the level of play."

Robin: "I place the art and science centers near a water source for easy clean up."

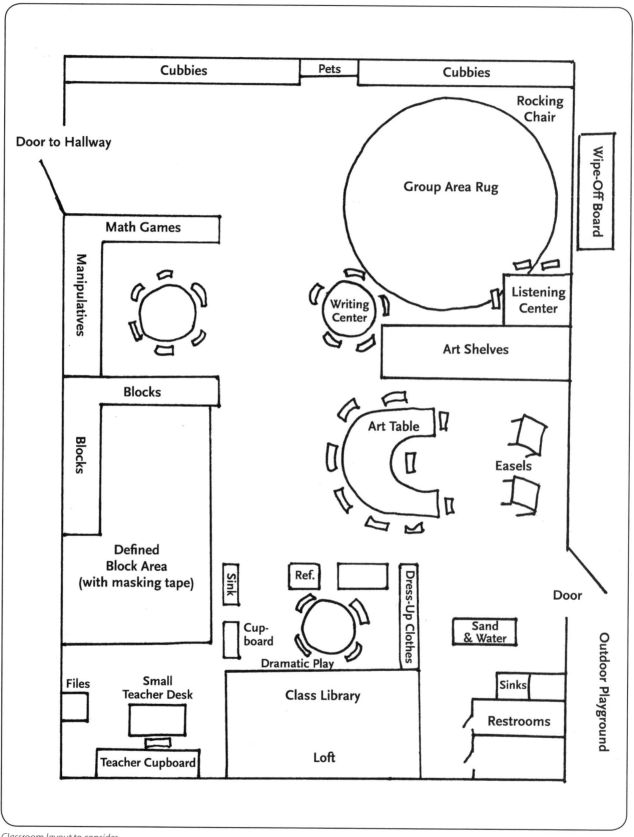

Classroom layout to consider

There is no need to change materials daily or weekly. In fact, the basic set may remain intact for a good part of the year. Additional materials may be added to complicate play experiences or to lead the children into new play possibilities. All materials are attractively displayed and organized on shelves and in bins, tubs, or baskets. Here's a very basic list of suggested materials to start with for each of the seven areas identified on the first page of the preschool planning and reflection framework (and on pages one and three of the kindergarten framework). You may recall that you can find these frameworks in chapter 2 or in appendix A of this book.

- Block area: wooden unit blocks; cardboard blocks; small colored blocks; animal and people figures; cars, trucks, and other vehicles; traffic signs and roadways
- Dramatic play: play house equipment (including a table and chairs, play refrigerator, stove, cupboards and sink with play dishes, pots, pans, utensils, and silverware); baby dolls representing multiple races with baby blankets, clothes, baby beds, and strollers; dress-up clothes and hats
- Sensory table: a table with a tub (or a large plastic tub set on the floor) at which children can work with sand, water, or other materials; utensils to work with, such as shovels, scoopers, measuring cups, pitchers, water wheels, etc.
- Art: a paint easel (or designated space on the wall) for large sheets of paper to be affixed where children can paint with brushes and tempera or watercolor paints or can draw with markers or crayons; a variety of papers, scissors, paste, glue sticks, crayons, markers, tape, collage materials (such as feathers, pompoms, glitter, twigs, sequins, etc.) from which children can choose for their creations
- Manipulatives: shelves with bins and baskets of interlocking materials (such as Lego blocks or bristle blocks), and items for sorting and categorizing (such as colored bears, vehicles, animal figures, buttons, beads, keys, and small colored blocks); puzzles with varying numbers of pieces and levels of difficulty
- Class library: fiction and nonfiction picture books; class-made books; class photo albums (such as "Our Families," or photos of a recent field trip); listening headphones and books on tape

- Writing center: a variety of writing utensils (pencils, pens, markers, crayons) and papers (lined and unlined, stationery, cards, forms, checks); name cards (one for each child); picture dictionaries; word lists

There are some wonderful resources to consider for guidance in organizing the environment and materials. Here's a short list:

The Creative Curriculum for Preschool, fourth edition, by Diane Trister Dodge, Laura Colker, and Cate Heroman

Creating Inclusive Classrooms by Ellen R. Daniels and Kay Stafford

Reflecting Children's Lives: A Handbook for Planning Child-Centered Curriculum, second edition, by Deb Curtis and Margie Carter

The Inclusive Early Childhood Classroom: Easy Ways to Adapt Learning Centers for All Children by Patti Gould and Joyce Sullivan

Big as Life: The Everyday Inclusive Curriculum by Stacey York

Designs for Living and Learning: Transforming Early Childhood Environments by Deb Curtis and Margie Carter

Classroom Routines That Really Work for PreK and Kindergarten by Kathleen Hayes and Renneé Creange

Each of these books includes extensive lists of materials to put into learning areas and ways to organize the classroom itself.

Many teachers who use these resources to help them set up the classroom environment report that behavior problems dramatically lessen. The children's use of materials becomes more productive. They stay with activities longer. They participate more willingly in cleanup. Teachers are no longer running interference or playing "referee" as frequently as before. Chaos does not reign. Instead, the classroom has a busy hum of activity. Teachers find more opportunities to interact with the children and observe them at work. Many teachers say they can relax and enjoy their time with the children much more fully.

Continually Evaluating the Environment

A teacher carefully plans the basic environment. She recognizes the importance of communicating order, structure, and extensive possibilities for the productive use of materials. She also continually evaluates the classroom environment to see how it is working. In reflection discussions, she and her colleagues discuss how effectively the setup is contributing to the children's comfort, risk taking, and learning.

One way to evaluate the effectiveness of a classroom environment is to get down on your knees and look at the room from a child's perspective. As adults, our height puts us at a disadvantage in seeing exactly how obstacles and traffic patterns are laid out from a child's perspective.

Here is one teacher's story that illustrates another way to evaluate the environment and determine if changes are needed.

Carole kept a pad of sticky notes and a pen in her pocket. As she interacted with the children throughout her preschool classroom, she paid attention to times when she noted boredom or poor behavior. She placed a sticky note somewhere in that area of the classroom, out of reach of the children. At the end of the week, she and her teaching assistant, Armando, noted where the sticky notes were located and took time to carefully examine that area of the classroom. They asked themselves important questions such as:

- *Are new materials needed here?*
- *Is the furniture arranged in ways that are conducive to traffic flow and personal space?*
- *Is more adult presence necessary?*
- *Should the number of children in that area be limited or extended?*

They made changes as they answered those questions, then observed closely to see the resulting behaviors and engagement with the materials in those areas. For example, one week, Carole and Armando noted lots of yelling and fighting among the children in the block area. Lots of sticky notes ended up on the wall above the block area. The next week, they both watched carefully and realized that a traffic path went right through the rug area where many of the block constructions were being built. As the children walked by on their way to other classroom areas, they inadvertently knocked against the constructions, causing them to fall, much to the dismay of the builders. Carole and Armando rearranged the shelving in the block area to eliminate this traffic path and rerouted it around the shelves to protect the block constructions.

In *Reflecting Children's Lives*, Deb Curtis and Margie Carter suggest additional characteristics that help to create an environment where both teachers and children love to spend time. Curtis and Carter (2011, 34–35) argue that teachers should look at the way their room is organized and materials presented while contemplating the following checklist:

- Materials are visible, accessible, aesthetically organized, and attractive to children.
- Diverse textures, shapes, and elements of the natural world are present to invite exploration and discovery.
- The space is flexible, allowing for expansion when many children are working in the same area. There are minimal restrictions to moving in and out of areas.
- In addition to specialized toys, such as pretend food, wooden blocks, and Lego building blocks, there is an ample supply of "loose parts"—open-ended materials such as large pieces of fabric, corks, tubes, and plastic rings.
- Children's lives and interests are represented throughout the room.

Considering these suggestions can help us continually evaluate the effectiveness of our classroom environment.

When to Make Changes in Play Areas and Materials

The selection of basic materials in each area should be extensive and rich enough so the children will continue to explore the possibilities for using those materials. A teacher need not be concerned with constant rearrangement or change. Children appreciate consistency. They relish practicing things over and over again, which is how mastery is attained. If the original materials provided in an area include a range of possibilities, the children should be able to return again and again and become engaged in productive and creative use of those materials. The role of the teacher is to encourage exploration, watch what the children repeat and practice, and suggest different ways of using the materials. Since there are many possibilities present, the plans for the materials in the areas do not need to change every day or every week. As I showed in chapter 3, a teacher may change the learning goals but not necessarily the materials. This is one way to plan for play.

However, when a teacher sees boredom or poor behavior or wants to follow an interest or a topic of study, she should introduce new materials and activities. The following circumstances warrant a change in materials:

- The children are ignoring a particular area.
- The children are bored with what's available (they may say they are bored; they may appear bored in their interactions; or they may change the area themselves, bringing new materials or doing different things with those materials).
- The children's behavior is not productive or positive in an area.
- The materials could be changed to support an interest of the children, a developmental need, or a topic of study or project that has emerged in the classroom.

In reflective conversations, teachers discuss and make note of these circumstances and plan for changes for the next week. Below is Keisha's third page of her planning and reflection framework for her preschool classroom, where she and her colleagues reflected on the previous week and considered plans for the following one. On the next page you will see her specific plans for the play areas. You can see the direct connection between her reflections and the changes made to materials available for the next week.

Suzanne: "I find that varying the environment and materials presented is important. Both children and teachers gain fresh perspectives when changes are made. Materials can be presented for the children to explore and then rotated out. When the same materials are brought back weeks later, the children have gained new knowledge and are able to explore the returned materials on the next level."

REFLECTIONS: What worked? What didn't? What did you learn about individual children and group interests?	PLANS: Based on your reflections, what will you change for next week?
We had lots of involvement in blocks, and once we helped get play started, dramatic play was very popular and engaging. Need more cleanup at sensory table. Art and manipulatives had only a couple of takers each day.	Add small brooms and dustpans to sensory area so children can clean up sand as they go.
Jose, Maria, and Thomas were counting up to five and six objects.	Try more enticing activities at art and manipulatives.
Ashley and Corrine are very creative painters—lots of colors.	Put out counting activities for Jose, Maria, and Thomas.
Joshua asked to read stories three days in a row.	See if Joshua can get more readers in the class library.

Keisha's reflections   *Keisha's plans*

Preschool Weekly Planning and Reflection Framework

Program/School: _Children's Growing Place_　　Date: _11/14/11_　　Teacher(s): _Keisha Johnson and Darius Romano_

Ongoing Project (optional): _Exploring the classroom_

	Learning goal(s)	Additional materials or focus	Vocabulary words
BLOCKS	mathematical problem solving		
DRAMATIC PLAY	developing self-regulation		
SENSORY TABLE	understanding community (to help cleanup)	whisk brooms and dustpans for sweeping up sand	responsibility
ART	demonstrating hand-eye coordination	marble painting	rolling, angles, color mixing, designs
MANIPULATIVES	representing mathematical information	challenge children to represent quantities with manipulatives (2 and 2 make 4)	equations, equals, addition, subtraction
CLASS LIBRARY	showing initiative	encourage children to join Joshua in listening to stories	
WRITING CENTER	knowledge of books and print	add name cards and encourage name writing	
OTHER CENTER	none		

Keisha's plan for the next week

Sometimes, changing the learning goals means changing or adding materials. If a teacher has identified awareness of community as a goal for the block area, she will want to add books with photos of different kinds of buildings in the community (such as grocery stores, fire stations, schools, etc.). She may also add a map of the town for children to study as they lay out the blocks to make streets and neighborhoods. If she has identified shape recognition at the art area, she will want to add precut shapes for collage making and shape puzzle pieces for tracing. On the plan, the teacher writes the learning goal and lists only the materials added. On the next page is the first page of Marcus's plan for his play areas. You can see that some of the learning goals he has chosen necessitate a change or addition to materials.

Preschool Weekly Planning and Reflection Framework

Program/School: Rainbow Preschool   Date: December 12, 2011   Teacher(s): Marcus

Ongoing Project (optional): role playing

	Learning goal(s)	Additional materials or focus	Vocabulary words
BLOCKS	writing skills	add paper, markers, tape and name cards for making signs in block area	architect
DRAMATIC PLAY	writing skills	add pads and pencils for grocery lists, telephone messages, etc.	message, list
SENSORY TABLE	hand-eye coordination	add tongs and ping pong balls and ask children to pick up balls and place in a bucket	
ART	using tools to cut	add plastic scissors, playdough, cookie cutters, and rollers	
MANIPULATIVES	showing initiative	as children create with manipulatives, ask them to draw what they have done, and take their dictation	
CLASS LIBRARY	listening skills	set up headphones for listening to books on tape	
WRITING CENTER	understanding families	encourage children to draw their families; provide word cards for them to copy "Mom," "Dad," and other family members' names	parents, sister, brother, family
OTHER CENTER	speaking	play with puppets and make up stories and puppet plays	

Marcus's first page

If an ongoing project has developed in the classroom (as the bird's nest did in Mrs. Chang's in chapter 2), materials may need to change in some areas as well. But sometimes a teacher may choose a learning goal that has many possibilities for application in more than one play area. In that case, the learning goal may be identified as the ongoing project throughout the classroom. She may change materials in some of the areas to help bring about children's engagement related to that goal.

On the next page is an example of a plan for Investigation Time in a kindergarten classroom where measurement was the ongoing project and learning goal for multiple centers. Notice the ways the teacher used different materials in specific areas to bring about that goal (she did not try to do so for all areas, however, just where it made sense to her). We will

Kindergarten Weekly Planning and Reflection Framework

INVESTIGATION TIME

Program/School: __Blair Elementary__   Date: __11/12-16/12__   Teacher(s): __mrs. Sampa__

Ongoing Project (optional): __measurement__

	Learning goal(s)	Additional materials or focus	Vocabulary words
BLOCKS	measurement	provide tape measures, yard sticks, and rulers; encourage children to measure their constructions	taller, shorter, longer
MATH ACTIVITY	measurement, focused attention	measure the classroom with yarn as long as your leg, your arm, your thumb, your foot, etc.	compare
SENSORY TABLE	measurement, scientific exploration	add a weighing scale and weigh rocks and stones; identify which are heavier or lighter	heavy, light, weight
ART	measurement, creativity	provide paper strips cut at different lengths and encourage conversation about the lengths used in a child's collage	longest, medium, shortest
MANIPULATIVES	measurement, counting, and quantity	measure table with linking cubes or links; measure other items with manipulatives	
SCIENCE EXPLORATION	measurement, prediction	predict which rock will be the heaviest and which the lightest	
INFORMATIONAL READING	measurement, story retelling	reread Inch by Inch, Caps for Sale, and Ten Apples Up on Top	
MATH AND SCIENCE JOURNALING	measurement, fine-motor	write and draw about what you measured	
OTHER CENTER			

Example of plan for Investigation Time in a kindergarten classroom

look more in-depth at planning ongoing projects in response to children's interests in chapter 5.

Once in a while it may seem that everyone in the classroom could use a dose of new possibilities. Maybe several areas appear to be boring to the children. Or perhaps lots of behavior problems are arising throughout the classroom. It may then be time to add materials in all of the areas in the environment. Six weeks into the preschool year, Luis sat down with his teaching assistants, Sandra and Suzie, to reflect on the previous week in their classroom and to plan for the next one. In their discussion, Luis and his teammates all agreed that the children needed some new activities and materials. They were seeing more wandering behavior and less purposeful exploration. Luis wrote their comments on the reflection portion of the framework for week 6, which you will find on the next page. They all determined that sweeping changes were needed throughout the classroom. Luis was not convinced that it was time to introduce a project or study. However, he and his colleagues decided to add some new materials to various areas. In other areas, they merely changed the ways they would suggest the children use the existing materials. Still, their plan (on the next page) reflects the developmental goals they have in mind as the children try out these new plans.

REFLECTIONS: What worked? What didn't? What did you learn about individual children and group interests?	PLANS: Based on your reflections, what will you change for next week?
Rough play and disagreements in block area; not much interest in manipulatives, art, or sensory table. Lots of wandering and disengagement. Lani, Frederick, and Alyssa played extensively with stuffed animals, taking care of them. Katie can retell the whole story of *Jump, Frog, Jump*.	New materials and goals are needed! Maybe start a project on veterinarians?

Luis's reflections and plans

Notice that in his reflections and plans, Luis is responding to the children's expressed interest in dramatic play with the stuffed animals. Maybe the veterinarian's office will develop into a full-fledged topic of study after the implementation of the plan for week 7.

A strong word of caution is needed at this point: Do not feel it is necessary to change all areas of the classroom regularly! Children relish repetition, familiarity, and consistency. They can go more in-depth with activities, develop and refine skills, and complicate their own interactions with materials if they have the opportunity to visit areas again and again. Many teachers create far more work for themselves by assuming they must change their environment daily or weekly. Instead, pay close attention to the children, and only change those areas that need changing. A plan like Luis's, where sweeping changes are made, will only be necessary once in awhile. It will be more common to change only a couple of areas per week.

Allowing Ample Time for High-Level Play to Develop

The research and recommendations I cited earlier make a connection between *high-level play* and learning, not just *any* play. Preschoolers and kindergartners can sometimes get loud and silly as they play. Safety can become a concern, and teachers have to step in and intervene to get play

Mary B.: "I plan for one hour of self-selection playtime in my preschool classroom. I don't work with a clock. If a child is still working on something, I follow the flow of his or her interest as much as I can."

Preschool Weekly Planning and Reflection Framework

Program/School: __Little Friends__   Date: __11/28/11__   Teacher(s): __Luis, Suzie, and Sandra__

Ongoing Project (optional): __Veterinarian's office?__

	Learning goal(s)	Additional materials or focus	Vocabulary words
BLOCKS	making scientific predictions	construct ramps for cars and trucks; predict which will go fastest and farthest; measure with stopwatch and tape measures	speed, incline, distance
DRAMATIC PLAY	vocabulary development	more stuffed animals and medical equipment	veterinarian, animal hospital
SENSORY TABLE	focusing attention and persisting in tasks	use sense of touch, hiding and finding various items in sand	archaeologist
ART	experimenting	make tissue-paper collages	
MANIPULATIVES	sorting and categorizing		
CLASS LIBRARY	listening skills	listen to tapes of familiar stories, following along in books	
WRITING CENTER	using tools to write and cut	copy own name and those of classmates	
OTHER CENTER	sorting and categorizing	make a graph of pets owned by everyone in class	

Luis's plan for week 7

Sue: "The challenge to providing adequate time to develop play is giving children opportunities so that you can document their learning during this time. The temptation is to say, 'You can play when you finish ____,' which does not value the play activity in which they are engaged."

back on track so that children are playing purposefully, in complex play that engages their full attention. This is the kind of play that is rich in benefits for children's development:

This is play that is so all-engaging that the children stand tall in confidence, using skills in a variety of ways and symbolically representing what they know and are learning about the world. This is the play that the developmental theorist Lev Vygotsky refers to when he says: "In play a child is always above his average age, above his daily behavior; in play it is as though he were a head taller than himself." (Gronlund 2010, 11)

In my book *Developmentally Appropriate Play: Guiding Young Children to a Higher Level* (2010), I analyze levels of play in depth and give many ideas and strategies for enhancing and sustaining children's engagement in high-level play. One of the most critical strategies is to provide ample time for such play to develop (Copple and Bredekamp 2009, 127):

> Preschoolers cannot become socially competent without many extended times to interact with one another. This requires teachers to plan the preschool day so that there are blocks of time available for children to play and work together. Rather than such times being a reward for those who complete seatwork, these times should be considered absolutely essential developmental investments (Bodrova & Leong 2007).

Kindergartners need ample time for play as well. Children need time to figure out where they will play, with whom they will play, and what they will do in the play area. Sometimes they approach the area slowly, watching to see who is there and what they are doing. They may watch for a while before getting involved themselves, either sitting alongside another child doing puzzles or engaging with friends in a dramatic play scenario. Once they do get involved, they often go deeper into the play experience. They may take on the challenge of a more difficult puzzle or come up with the idea of making their own tickets as they play at riding a train with friends. By allowing for at least forty-five minutes to one hour of playtime, teachers are giving children plenty of time to get started and then develop higher-level play.

During this time, teachers can enhance the level of engagement as well by honoring what children are doing. Teachers try not to interrupt but rather interact in supportive ways. If they do have to interrupt to make an announcement or remind children of something, they do so respectfully. Their goal is to facilitate children's growing attention spans so that their play becomes richer and more rewarding, ripe with learning opportunities.

The preschool and kindergarten classrooms of today are filled with children of diverse backgrounds, whether differing linguistically, culturally, or experientially. They need unhurried time to learn about each other, to figure out ways to enter play, and to socialize and communicate with other children in the process. . . . "But to

Suzanne: "Time is so crucial! So often I find the children are really beginning to explore something in depth when it comes time to clean up. I've learned how important it is to adjust our 'teacher' schedule and allow the children to continue what they are doing. The learning and/or socializing that is happening can be so much more valuable than keeping exactly to the schedule. Going back the next day frequently doesn't have the same value as those moments when the lightbulb first goes off!"

Laura: "I have seen the most growth in this area where teachers are really seeing the deep learning happening when there is ample time for play. They are gathering rich observations and a truer picture of what each child is learning and is capable of."

do so, they require time, space, interactional partners, engaging objects, and observant teachers who both further and document the communicative strengths revealed and nurtured by play" (Genishi and Dyson 2009, 64). Time to get deeply involved is truly a gift teachers can give to young children. (Gronlund 2010, 61)

Acting as Play Facilitators

As children play, teachers are facilitators, scaffolding and assisting children, stepping in and out of children's play. They are engaged in a delicate dance where their goal is for children to take the lead more often than the adult. Therefore, teachers must be watchful, observing children carefully to determine when is the best time to get involved with them as they play, and what the best strategies might be to enhance what they are doing. Once they are involved, they have to determine how long to stay and when it is time to step out again. This is truly the art of teaching young children.

There are many roles that teachers can take on to facilitate high-level play:

- They can be enthusiastic cheerleaders.
- They can be questioning, challenging, or provoking.
- They can be mediators or equipment suppliers.
- They can be a quiet presence nearby, observing, listening, and therefore ready to step in when children invite them or need them.

Notice that none of these roles involve taking over children's play. As long as the play is productive, engaging, and at a high level, the play belongs to the children. Adults respect that ownership and are available to support the children's success.

Timing is important when making comments or asking questions as children play. Well-timed questions can encourage children to think, problem solve, try a different approach, incorporate symbolic materials, or develop new play themes. If done well, children show greater interest in their play. Poorly timed questioning, however, can turn children off. It's an interruption. It stops the flow of the play and makes it less fun and enjoyable.

Open-ended questions and comments are more supportive than ones that have a right answer (closed-ended). Imagine children playing with colored cubes and the teacher asks questions such as: What color is this one? How many red ones do you have? If you put two red ones and three

Rosemary: "Ample time for play is important and including forty-five to sixty minutes emphasizes that importance. This can also be one of the most stressful times for teachers who are not sure of their role during play. For teachers who are more accustomed to teacher-led activities, letting go of that control can be difficult. They may not feel they are doing a good job until they understand how much children learn through high-level play."

Laura: "I see more teachers using scaffolding and assisting children as they play. The challenges are that teachers can sometimes interrupt play and cause a negative effect."

yellow ones together, how many would that be? The children will feel like they are being tested rather than encouraged to follow their own ideas for using the blocks. Instead, imagine the following scenario:

Tony is standing next to a table that is set against a wall. He is playing with small, colored cubes, all the same size. Tony stacks them up. He has no problem getting three to stay up but finds the stack is a little wobbly as he carefully adds the fourth and fifth. Finally, the sixth makes the stack topple. And he starts again. His teacher, Luz, comes by and sits quietly in an empty chair at the table. As the stack topples, Tony looks at her and says, "Oh, man!" She smiles at Tony and asks, "What do you think you could do to make it stay up? Is there any way you can do that with that many blocks?" Tony says, "Maybe I can stack them against the wall." He tries that and successfully stacks many more blocks. "Wow, that's really a tall stack you have there. You figured out how to make that work. Now, I wonder what else you'll try," Luz says. Tony starts placing stacks next to each other for support, building walls instead of just stacks. Luz suggests that they take a photograph of what he has built. Tony agrees. Then, she asks him to tell her about what he has done. As she writes down his comments, she says, "We'll put this up on the parent bulletin board so that your Mom and Dad will know what you did at school today." She adds the following learning goals to the documentation: problem solving, persistence, and hand-eye coordination.

Luz did not interrupt Tony's play, did she? Instead, she sat quietly, waiting for his inclusion of her. Her questions were open-ended ones. They also presented a challenge to Tony. When he rose to the challenge and was successful, she continued to validate what he had done by offering to document it and share the documentation with others. That's play facilitation in action!

Could she also have asked how many blocks were in his stacks? Could she have asked him to compare the heights of his stacks as he built the wall? Could she have talked with him about the colors? Yes, she could have. Closed-ended questions can be a part of interacting with children if they flow naturally within the conversation. Again, the factor of timing is important, and reading the child's response to such questions is as well. If a question seems to turn him off, other comments and questions might keep him more engaged.

Teachers use a variety of strategies when facilitating children's play. Sometimes they combine strategies. Other times they use only one. The following is a list of teacher strategies adapted from the third edition of *Developmentally Appropriate Practice* (Copple and Bredekamp 2009, 36–37).

- Acknowledge what the children are doing or saying.
- Encourage their efforts.
- Give specific feedback.
- Model attitudes, problem solving, and behavior toward others.
- Demonstrate the correct way to do something.
- Create or add challenge.
- Ask questions that provoke children's thinking.
- Offer assistance.
- Provide information.
- Give directions.

Here are comments from *Developmentally Appropriate Play* that illustrate what a teacher might say if using that strategy as she is supporting children's play (Gronlund 2010, 68–69).

- Acknowledge: *"Wow, I see that you all built a garage for your trucks. It's got very high walls. You stacked lots of long blocks up to make those walls."*
- Encourage: *"Your grocery store sure is a busy place. You have customers who are shopping and a cashier at the checkout. Oh, and you're stocking the shelves!"*
- Give feedback: *"You have spent a long time on your Lego construction. I see you put wheels on your vehicle, and you have some people riding in it. Where are they going?"*
- Model: *"Sometimes, I can't figure out what to make with my playdough. So, I just roll it and roll it, and pound it, and feel it with my fingers. I don't always have to make something, do I?"*
- Demonstrate: *"If you want the water wheel to go around when you pour the water into it, you have to pull open the latch at the bottom like this. There! Then, it works."*
- Create or add challenge: *"I wonder if you could build something with all of the blocks?"*
- Ask questions: *"What do you think would happen if we put water on the sand? How would it change? Would we need some different tools to work with it?"*

- Offer assistance: *"Would you like some help getting the marble run to stop toppling over? Maybe if we made stronger foundations with some of the pieces, it would stay up. I'll help you do that."*
- Provide information: *"You made an ambulance with your Duplos. Remember when we saw the ambulance that came to our school? The EMTs had a special bed on wheels, didn't they? That was called a stretcher."*
- Give directions: *"We have lots of art materials for you to play and create with at the art table. You may use glue or paste to make whatever kind of collage you can think of."*

Some of these strategies will match better to one learning goal over another. Some will match better to one child's personality or learning style over another. The only way to know if a teaching strategy is the right one is to try it. Then, you can reflect on its success or lack thereof, and try a different approach next time.

Scaffolding

An important teaching approach to remember is scaffolding: providing support that helps a child do something that she cannot quite do on her own. Like a construction scaffold, the help is temporary. As the child gains in confidence and skills, the adult removes the support and celebrates the child's independent actions:

> As a child begins a new challenge, he may need some support from the teacher to enable him to manage it. A skilled teacher doesn't overdo the help. The aim is to provide the least amount of support that the child needs to do something he cannot quite do on his own.... As the child begins to acquire the new skill or understanding, the teacher gradually reduces her support. (Copple and Bredekamp 2009, 39)

Scaffolding is applied when the child is functioning in what is called the zone of proximal development, or ZPD. *Zone of proximal development* is a term coined by Lev Vygotsky (1978), the developmental theorist. He defined the ZPD as what the child is learning to do with support. Sometimes that support comes from the teacher, and sometimes from another child who has the competence to act as a scaffold for the child.

For individual children, teachers pay close attention
to the child's ZPD

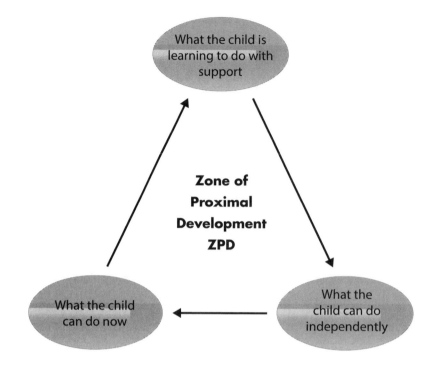

To be effective play facilitators, teachers pay attention both to what a child is capable of doing now and to what he is trying to do without success. This is the planning/observation/individualization cycle that makes up the curriculum process. When a teacher sees what the child is struggling with or attempting, she provides support so that he can be successful. And she removes that support once he can do the new task independently. But she is ever ready to step back in if needed.

In play, many children do not have the skills to get high-level play started or to sustain it—they may be easily distracted by other things going on in the room. They may not know how to approach a group of children at play and join in. If teachers are observant, they can provide assistance to each child in their ZPD so that the play experience is more rewarding for them:

Reaching the higher levels of play may require much adult assistance for some children. In addition, Vygotsky viewed play itself as a zone of proximal development or "a self-help tool that enables children to achieve higher levels of cognitive functioning" (Roskos and Christie 2004, 113). (Gronlund 2010, 26)

Once teachers coach children in some strategies for ignoring distractions or joining in play experiences, they may see those children get deeply engaged in play on their own. Here's an example of a teacher coaching a child in joining others at play:

> *Over several days, I observed Justin watch other children playing in the block area. More than once, with no warning, he would wander over to where they were and knock down their complex structure that they had been building. Each time, I intervened, leading a discussion between the boys and trying to encourage Justin to play cooperatively with the boys. While they expressed willingness to do so, Justin shook his head "No" and went off to another area. One day, I asked him if he wanted to play with me in the block area. He immediately responded with an emphatic "Yes!" For several days, we worked together building structures alongside of other players. As we played, the other boys came and joined us. I modeled ways to work cooperatively with them and, over time, I was able to sit quietly nearby and not be very involved.*

Suzanne: "One of the challenges I find is knowing when to step in and help them to the next level and when to let them muddle through a little."

A teacher's task is to determine the level of challenge in which each child can cognitively engage but not find overwhelming. This takes knowing each child well and seeing what activities and pairings with other children seem to work best for him or her to get into "the flow" of the play:

> When children are engaged in high-level play, one sees the all-engaging attention that children devote to a complex play experience. They are like athletes "in the zone" or as Mihaly Csikszentmihalyi (1997, 31–32) suggests, they are engaged in a "flow experience." He defines *flow* as: "When a person's entire being is stretched in the full functioning of body and mind, whatever one does becomes worth doing for its own sake. In the harmonious focusing of physical and psychic energy, life finally comes into its own." Even preschoolers and kindergartners can stretch in the full functioning of body and mind when an experience is worth doing, and high-level play can provide just such an experience. (Gronlund 2010, 25)

Conclusion

Our goal is for each child to be stretched to the fullest. Play is a marvelous vehicle for doing so for young children. And teachers are key in facilitating children's play if that play is to be the kind that research shows has so many benefits.

In the next chapter we will look more closely at ways to individualize curriculum and determine each child's ZPD. We will explore adaptations, accommodations, and strategies that will help each child learn and grow to his fullest potential.

CHAPTER 5

Individualization and Differentiation: Each Child Is Different

. . . .

Each child is different. Preschool and kindergarten teachers learn to recognize each child's strengths and areas of challenge, to know more about personality traits, talents, and interests, and to celebrate the child's growth and progress with his family. Building respectful, caring relationships with each child and family is one of the six essential elements of curriculum. These relationships help teachers know each child better, understand the familial and cultural context in which the child is being raised, and work in partnership with the family for the benefit of the child.

Each teacher has to earn the trust of the parents and the children. The parents have to learn to trust that their child will be well supervised and kept safe. They have to have a sense of what is going on each day in the classroom so they can relax and know their child is being supported as a learner and unique individual. And the child has to learn to trust her teacher. When a strong sense of trust is established, she will be more confident about trying new things, taking risks, showing what she is successful at, and trying things that are more challenging. Teachers have to work hard to earn the trust of children and families and to build strong relationships with them so they can individualize the curriculum and offer differentiated learning opportunities for each child.

In the next chapter we will explore ways to effectively communicate with families. For now, we will focus on four ways that teachers can work on individualization and differentiation for each child in the curriculum:

1. By planning for community and relationship building
2. By getting to know each child well

Lauren: "One of the greatest gifts of using a planning/ observation process in our classroom was how it helped me to really know the children in my classroom. By observing them at different times throughout the day, you not only learn about how best to scaffold them to the next skill level, but you also learn about their likes and dislikes, sense of humor and learning style."

3. By planning modifications, adjustments, and accommodations for individual children
4. By planning ongoing projects based on children's interests

When implementing good preschool and kindergarten curriculum, the task of individualizing is not left to chance. Instead, it is included on the weekly planning and reflection sheets. Teachers emphasize its importance by thinking about relationships with the children in advance, implementing steps to strengthen those relationships, and reflecting on what happens with the children each week in the classroom. And they write it all down.

On the second page of both the preschool and kindergarten frameworks, there is a box labeled "Plans for Building Community and Relationships." Here, a teacher writes down specific actions she plans to take in relationship building with the whole group as well as with individual children. On the last page of both frameworks, another box, labeled "Modifications for Individual Children," also involves this attention to individual children. Here, a teacher writes what changes to existing activities will be made to help specific children be successful. This attention to individual children helps strengthen their sense of trust. They recognize that their teachers care deeply about them.

Planning for Community and Relationship Building

Erik Erikson (1950), the developmental theorist, identified progressive stages in child development. Up to age three, he said, the child's primary task is to develop trust in others and autonomy for herself. The three- to five-year-old's task is to engage in initiative: trying things out, creating, and representing experience. The six- to eight-year-old's task is to engage in industry: using ever-growing skills toward an end and developing competence.

The development of trust precedes autonomy. It precedes initiative. It precedes industry. So, even for preschool children, who are in the stage of initiative, and kindergarten children, moving toward the stage of industry, trust must be developed in every new setting and relationship. For this reason, teachers work hard to assure children of their best intentions for them. They write plans for building a sense of community in the classroom and a strong relationship with each child.

There are many actions that preschool and kindergarten teachers can take to build a sense of community with the children in their classroom. Here are some ideas. By no means is the list complete. What else would you add? Teachers can

- welcome children and family members to the classroom
- greet and chat with family members at pickup and drop-off times
- have arrival rituals and routines for all children to help make the transition between home and school go smoothly
- have class songs, chants, and games (such as "The More We Are Together" or "All My Friends Are Here with Me") as rituals to gather the group together
- play name games (such as Who Stole the Cookie from the Cookie Jar?) so that children learn each other's names
- have ways of participating in group meetings that give each child a chance to talk and help them to listen and respect the time for others to speak (the speaker holds a talking stick or a special stuffed animal and then passes it on)
- have signals for getting children's attention when announcements need to be made (clapping a pattern that they repeat; ringing soft, pleasant chimes)
- involve children in problem-solving issues in the classroom ("Boys and girls, I've noticed that some people are not helping at cleanup time. Let's come up with some ideas for making cleanup go more quickly with everyone helping.")
- pay attention to which activities become the favorites with the group and enjoy them again and again ("I know this is one of your favorite things to do—so today we're going to _____ again!")
- adopt a tree outdoors as the class tree and do careful observations of how it changes through the seasons
- adopt another class as reading buddies or playground buddies
- have class pets and plants and rotate their care among the group
- make many kinds of class books that reflect the experiences of the group (such as a book about the children's families, or books that document field trips or special visitors, or rewritten favorite stories so that each child has a page)
- have ways to recognize and celebrate helpful, kind behavior (such as a Kindness Jar where children's names are placed)

Robin: "This is such an important aspect to emphasize: building relationships."

Sarah: "I have found that the children respond so positively to this process because the relationship is much richer and so are the interactions. Therefore, there is more trust, support, and awareness which in turn support the emotional intelligence of the children as well."

- set up a routine for solving conflicts (such as a Peace Table) and train children in conflict resolution strategies
- have dismissal routines and rituals (hugs, high fives, good-bye songs, or books)

These community-building activities go on throughout the year. On the framework, a teacher may write down one or two steps she is going to take to build community with all of the children for the week. As time goes on and these activities continue, the group develops a sense of identity, and close bonds are formed.

Building strong relationships with individual children is an essential task that also involves many possibilities. Assuring a child that he can trust his teacher takes up much of the first days in a classroom for young children. Teachers do this by warmly welcoming each child. They carefully learn each child's name and use it frequently. They pay close attention to initial signals the child sends out about her personality, her approach to learning, her social comfort levels, and her relationship with her family members.

The following list identifies some possibilities for steps to relationship building that might be included in a teacher's plan. Again, by no means is this list complete. Can you think of more ideas? The possibilities are endless, aren't they?

Possibilities for Steps to Relationship Building
- Welcome a child by name with a warm smile.
- Touch a child (rub a back or arm, give a hug).
- Look a child in the eye (wink, smile, or laugh).
- Sit with a child (seek out a child at circle time or activity time)
- Invite a child to sit on your lap.
- Use a child's home language or provide materials in that language.
- Respect a child's personality (avoid pushing a quiet child to speak; avoid touching a child who is sensitive to touch).
- Ask to play or work alongside a child (imitate his interactions with materials).
- Let a child take the lead (go first, answer a question, give an idea).
- Ask a child to be a special helper.

- Give a child positive feedback ("Wow! Look at all the colors you used!" "You jumped really high!").
- Set limits with a child ("No, I will not let you hurt yourself. That jumping platform is too high. Let's make it a little smaller and put a mat underneath.").
- Allow a child to have some quiet, private time.
- Recognize that a child has lots of physical energy to spend ("Let's get out the hoops and build a hopping path.").

As teachers get to know individual children's personalities and approaches to learning, the plans written in the "Building Community and Relationships" section may name specific children. Because this second page of the framework may be posted for parents and others to see, it's important that anything written in this part of the plan be positive and general. More specific modifications for individual children will be written on the last page of the planning and reflection framework, for the teacher's eyes only. Here are some examples of teachers' plans for "Building Community and Relationships" in their classroom.

Plans for Building Community and Relationships

Show children where their cubbies and personal art galleries are located. Give them a name card and help them sign in each day.

Plans for Building Community and Relationships

Invite families to send in 4–5 family photos. Make a "Class Family Photo Album" to be placed in the classroom library.

> ## Plans for Building Community and Relationships
>
> *At large-group time this week, introduce class songbook and review respecting others' feelings and property. Talk about this throughout each day as well.*

Many other possibilities will arise as you get to know the children in your program better. Do not feel limited to the list above. Be open to all of the possibilities to relate to the children in your care.

Getting to Know Each Child Well: The Individual Child Information Record

Teachers get to know each child well so that they can plan learning opportunities that match the capabilities and needs of each one. The Individual Child Information Record—which appears on the next page, in photocopy-ready form in appendix C, and online at www.redleafpress.org—has been designed as a tool on which teachers can record information about a child that can affect his success in an early childhood program. The record design gives a broad picture of the child's overall development. Therefore, it does not need to be used daily or weekly. It includes spaces for a teacher to write down the following information as she gets to know the child:

- culture
- life experiences
- family
- developmental strengths
- emerging developmental areas
- physical needs and health issues
- emotional makeup
- approaches to learning and responses to challenges
- interests
- learning style

Individual Child Information Record

Child: _____   Date: _____

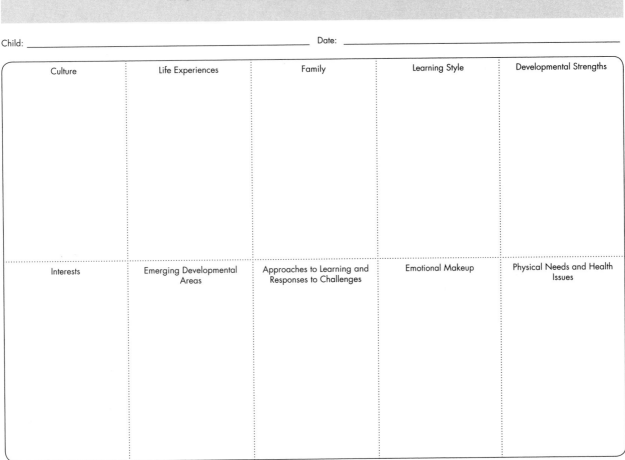

Culture	Life Experiences	Family	Learning Style	Developmental Strengths
Interests	Emerging Developmental Areas	Approaches to Learning and Responses to Challenges	Emotional Makeup	Physical Needs and Health Issues

As a teacher gets to know a child, she fills in information she gains on the record. Some teachers use it three times a year when they are meeting with family members: first in a get-acquainted or intake meeting; second and third in preparation for family-teacher conferences. It's an ongoing process so that by the end of the program year, all areas have been completed to provide a full and rich picture of this young individual.

Some of the information on the record is obtained in initial interviews with the family. Many programs have intake sheets that are filled out by family members as part of the registration process. Some programs interview the parents as the children are registered or at an initial home or classroom visit. In either case, many of the items on the Individual Child Information Record can be addressed at that time. Getting to know a child's family is a way of building a relationship with both the child and the family. Becoming familiar with a child's cultural background can help build the relationship. If the child's family speaks a language other than English, communicating in the home language can help immensely in building a positive relationship. Using a few words, providing books or posters in the child's language, or showing cultural aspects familiar to that child can be helpful.

Teachers have found that showing the information record to the parents in the first meeting lets them know that they will be working hard to find out exactly who their child is and the best ways to make the preschool or kindergarten experience successful for him. Families have a wealth of information to help give teachers a sense of the child. The record provides a way to invite their input and structure the conversation at this important getting-acquainted time.

Other parts of the record will become evident as the child attends regularly and teachers get to know him. All of the teachers involved should continually discuss what they are learning about this child and reflect on the categories listed on the record. Many preschool programs identify one teacher as the primary caregiver for each child. She may be the one who is responsible for recording on the form the information about the child gained from the family and from reflections of the teaching staff. At the very least, it's a good idea to assign one person as the primary record keeper for each child. This ensures that this important job will be accomplished.

On the following page are two examples of Individual Child Information Records filled out in the intake process with families.

Revisiting the Individual Child Information Record before each family-teacher conference allows the teacher to review the family's comments at the beginning of the year and compare what she has learned about the child over several months in the classroom. She can corroborate what the parents told her and add information. The Individual Child Information Record can guide the writing of a summary report about the child's progress and the next steps planned to stimulate and enhance this child's development. It can then be included when conferencing with the family.

On the following pages you will see examples of the completed Individual Child Information Records for Colin and Maribela from intake with additional comments from the teacher added before the first family-teacher conference. In addition, you will find examples of those same information records with the end-of-year comments from the teacher before the final family-teacher conference.

Individual Child Information Record

Child: Colin   Date: *Intake 9/7/11

Culture	Life Experiences	Family	Learning Style	Developmental Strengths
* Caucasian with Swedish and English background.	* Traveled, been to museums, zoo, etc.	* Mom, Dad, baby sister (Gwen).		* Loves being read to—listens to several books in a row.

Interests	Emerging Developmental Areas	Approaches to Learning and Responses to Challenges	Emotional Makeup	Physical Needs and Health Issues
* Cars, trucks, superheroes, music.	* Not very interested in alphabet.		* Gets frustrated—throws things.	* Lots of ear infections—tubes in ears. Sleeps, eats well.

Colin's record at intake

Individual Child Information Record

Child: Maribela   Date: *Intake 9/5/11

Culture	Life Experiences	Family	Learning Style	Developmental Strengths
* Mexican—moved here last month.	* Came from rural Mexico—still stays very close to family members.	* Mother, Father, Grandma, older brother (Carlos), twin younger sisters (Maria and Theresa).		

Interests	Emerging Developmental Areas	Approaches to Learning and Responses to Challenges	Emotional Makeup	Physical Needs and Health Issues
* Likes to dance—helps Mom with twins.	* English language still very limited.	* She likes to learn new things.	* Very calm and happy child.	* Prone to asthma attacks.

Maribela's record at intake

Individual Child Information Record

Child: _Colin_   Date: _*Intake 9/7/11, °Conference 11/3/11_

Culture	Life Experiences	Family	Learning Style	Developmental Strengths
* Caucasian with Swedish and English background.	* Traveled, been to museums, zoo, etc. ° Went to Toronto with his family—told us all about it.	* Mom, Dad, baby sister (Gwen). ° Loves his baby sister!	° Prefers physical movement, hands-on trial and error himself.	* Loves being read to—listens to several books in a row. ° Can tell whole stories; great block and Lego builder.

Interests	Emerging Developmental Areas	Approaches to Learning and Responses to Challenges	Emotional Makeup	Physical Needs and Health Issues
* Cars, trucks, superheroes, music. ° Dinosaurs, whales.	* Not very interested in alphabet. ° Writes part of his name.	° Likes to do his own thing rather than join group but is productively engaged.	* Gets frustrated—throws things. ° Very independent.	* Lots of ear infections—tubes in ears. Sleeps, eats well. ° Hearing?

Colin's record at first conference

Individual Child Information Record

Child: _Maribela_   Date: _*Intake 9/5/11, °Conference 11/2/11_

Culture	Life Experiences	Family	Learning Style	Developmental Strengths
* Mexican—moved here last month. ° Family has shared foods with class.	* Came from rural Mexico—still stays very close to family members. ° School friends are developing.	* Mother, Father, Grandma, older brother (Carlos), twin younger sisters (Maria and Theresa). ° Uncle came from Mexico.	° Takes things in, listens, observes first, then tries on her own.	° Fine-motor skills, general coordination, Spanish vocabulary and language usage.

Interests	Emerging Developmental Areas	Approaches to Learning and Responses to Challenges	Emotional Makeup	Physical Needs and Health Issues
* Likes to dance—helps Mom with twins. ° Becoming more interested in books and dramatic play.	* English language still very limited. ° Some English words now; separating from Mom better.	* She likes to learn new things. ° Yes, curious; not easily frustrated.	* Very calm and happy child. ° Goes with flow of classroom, just a few special friends.	* Prone to asthma attacks. ° We'll watch for cold weather activities for her.

Maribela's record at first conference

Individual Child Information Record

Child: __Colin__   Date: *Intake 9/7/11, ° Conference 11/3/11, Δ End of year 5/4/12

Culture	Life Experiences	Family	Learning Style	Developmental Strengths
* Caucasian with Swedish and English background.	* Traveled, been to museums, zoo, etc. ° Went to Toronto with his family—told us all about it.	* Mom, Dad, baby sister (Gwen). ° Loves his baby sister! Δ Grandma and Grandpa visited this spring.	° Prefers physical movement, hands-on trial and error himself. Δ Loses himself in building manipulatives—more listening skills evident.	* Loves being read to—listens to several books in a row. ° Can tell whole stories; great block and Lego builder. Δ Really can concentrate; gets along with others.

Interests	Emerging Developmental Areas	Approaches to Learning and Responses to Challenges	Emotional Makeup	Physical Needs and Health Issues
* Cars, trucks, superheroes, music. ° Dinosaurs, whales. Δ Building buses, RVs, trucks with Lego blocks—very intricate designs.	* Not very interested in alphabet. ° Writes part of his name. Δ Writes name with difficulty—fine-motor problems? Recognizes some letters.	° Likes to do his own thing rather than join group but is productively engaged. Δ Wants to do things right—so gets frustrated.	* Gets frustrated—throws things. ° Very independent. Δ Independence is a strength at times, a hindrance at others.	* Lots of ear infections—tubes in ears. Sleeps, eats well. ° Hearing? Δ Hearing tested—no problems.

Colin's record at final conference

Individual Child Information Record

Child: __Maribela__   Date: * Intake 9/5/11, ° Conference 11/2/11, Δ End of year 5/5/12

Culture	Life Experiences	Family	Learning Style	Developmental Strengths
* Mexican—moved here last month. ° Family has shared foods with class. Δ Went to Mexico in February...showed us pictures.	* Came from rural Mexico—still stays very close to family members. ° School friends are developing.	* Mother, Father, Grandma, older brother (Carlos), twin younger sisters (Maria and Theresa). ° Uncle came from Mexico.	° Takes things in, listens, observes first, then tries on her own. Δ Much more adventuresome—independent, confident learner.	° Fine-motor skills, general coordination, Spanish vocabulary and language usage. Δ Interest in books, reading, words, social skills.

Interests	Emerging Developmental Areas	Approaches to Learning and Responses to Challenges	Emotional Makeup	Physical Needs and Health Issues
* Likes to dance—helps Mom with twins. ° Becoming more interested in books and dramatic play. Δ Creative art; long dramatic play episodes show her loving family.	* English language still very limited. ° Some English words now; separating from Mom better. Δ Lots of English vocabulary, reading some words in Spanish and English.	* She likes to learn new things. ° Yes, curious; not easily frustrated. Δ She'll try anything!	* Very calm and happy child. ° Goes with flow of classroom, just a few special friends. Δ Becoming more of a leader.	* Prone to asthma attacks. ° We'll watch for cold weather activities for her. Δ Asthma improved in spring.

Maribela's record at final conference

Notice how much more complete the information is. These teachers really know their children, don't they?

The information written on the final child record is the result of a full year of careful planning and reflection. The planning and reflection frameworks help teachers represent the integration of the very best curricular approaches they are using every day in the classroom to address the needs and learning traits of children. An incredible number of accommodations for individual children occur in the life of a successful preschool or kindergarten classroom. The frameworks, in combination with the Individual Child Information Record, will help teachers develop an ongoing record of the ways they integrate their own knowledge of child development with the specific needs and interests of the children they teach.

Planning for Modifications, Adjustments, and Accommodations for Individual Children

Making adjustments in the classroom with a specific child in mind is another way to build relationships with the children. In the box labeled "Modifications for Individual Children," on the last page of both the preschool and kindergarten frameworks, a teacher writes the changes to existing activities that will be made to help specific children be successful. This is truly individualizing the curriculum. You may plan for modifications for an individual child in the classroom environment, changing the materials or activities that are available. You will also plan for ways to support the child in the opportunities that the environment provides. This is where individualization occurs. No longer are you thinking of activities for *all* the children. Now, within those activities, you're thinking about *each individual child*.

As you get to know a child, you will ask yourself questions about her success in the classroom, such as:

- Are there materials that she chooses more often than others? Why?
- Are those materials appropriate at her level of capability?
- Are they at the level where she is practicing and almost mastering them?
- When and with what materials does she need assistance?
- Does she avoid materials? Why?

- Do those materials require the use of skills she hasn't yet acquired?

Knowledge of a child's personality and dispositions to learning determines the modifications you will make. Several of the suggestions in the list of steps for relationship building from earlier in this chapter could be used as individual modifications as well. For example, if you learn that a child is routinely a leader in the classroom, you might want to offer a number of leadership opportunities. You also may want to help this child learn to work cooperatively with other children and may set up some situations where she is the follower rather than the leader. For a child who does not take the lead very often, you may want to set up nonthreatening opportunities for him to shine in front of the group once in a while.

A child with great curiosity needs opportunities to investigate. A child who does not try new things naturally may need new activities brought to her. All of these individual adjustments can be written on the framework. The following list, again, is not all-inclusive but gives some possibilities. What else would you add?

Individual Modifications, Adjustments, and Accommodations

- Offer materials that are more successful for the child.
- Offer materials that are more challenging for the child.
- Help the child ask another child to play or to use his words to express his feelings.
- Help the child join another group already engaged in play or work.
- Provide language modeling for a child ("Can I play with you?" "No, I don't like that.").
- Offer opportunities for leadership.
- Pair up specific children to support and help each other.
- Bring new materials or activities to a more reticent or set-in-his-ways child.
- Challenge an inquisitive child to investigate something more fully.
- Recognize a child's sensorimotor responses (for example, avoid forcing a reluctant child to fingerpaint with her hands; rather, accommodate by giving her sticks to paint with, while allowing a child who loves the feel of paint to paint away).

Robin: "I sometimes play a game or review learning skills and strategies with a student who may need a different approach or more repetition."

Rosemary: "A lot of differentiation occurs in small groups, as well."

- Prevent behavior problems by anticipating trouble (avoid letting two specific children sit together; sit with a child at circle time, rub his back, or provide a lap for comfort and self-control).
- Help a child cope with difficult situations (comfort a frightened child in a thunderstorm or during a fire drill; talk about sadness at the death of a classroom pet).

REFLECTIONS: What worked? What didn't? What did you learn about individual children and group interests?

Great dramatic play this week! Camping activities were a hit.

Group time is really hard for Aiden—should he have a separate activity?

Austin and David have delayed language responses yet seem to understand most questions and comments directed toward them. If you stay with them, they will eventually respond.

Josephine's and Marie's reflections from the previous week

MODIFICATIONS FOR INDIVIDUAL CHILDREN:

Encourage Hillary, Mason, and Edward to invite more children into the camping dramatic play.

Offer some quiet table activities for Aiden during group time.

Both Josephine and Marie will allow extra time for Austin and David to respond and will set up opportunities for them to point or touch and speak whenever possible.

Josephine's and Marie's modifications for individual children for this week

REFLECTIONS: What worked? What didn't? What did you learn about individual children and group interests?

Many more participated in camping—let's start documenting what they do with photos and their dictations.

Aiden worked quietly with playdough during group time—keep offering him this option.

Austin and David did better with the physical aspect of pointing and touching. Talk with speech therapist to help language responses.

Should we consider a communication board?

Josephine's and Marie's reflections from this week

Some weeks the individual adjustments you plan are a result of observations of children from the previous week. So often the reflection process will help guide planning for individual modifications. Then in reflection the following week you will evaluate how successful those adjustments were. Getting to know each child well and helping and supporting her to be successful in the classroom are ongoing processes that can be documented clearly both for planning and reflection purposes.

The "Focused Observations" section of the frameworks is another place where individual attention will be paid to the children. Coordinating this assessment piece with the steps to relationship building and the individual adjustments will help ensure that each child's development is being analyzed and supported. The documentation can then be used as assessment information in observations and portfolios. I will discuss more fully the observation and assessment process in chapter 8.

Here are examples of how teachers Josephine and Marie planned for the "Modifications for Individual Children" section of the frameworks. A reflection form from a previous week, a plan for an individual adjustment for the child, and a reflection form with the results of the adjustment are included so the full cycle can clearly be seen.

Modifications and accommodations are a central part of teaching children with identified special needs. Here is a specially designed format on which a teacher could record individual adjustments for up to sixteen children at a time.

Individual Adjustments

For week of: _____ Teacher: _____

Child's Name	Planned Adjustment	Child's Name	Planned Adjustment

Individual Adjustments form

This Individual Adjustments form can be used for children with IEPs as well as for typically developing children. You can find a photocopy-ready version of this form in appendix C and online at www.redleafpress.org. On the next page is an example of a completed form for a kindergarten class.

Individual Adjustments

For week of: _November 12, 2012_   Teacher: _Mrs. Wagner_

Child's Name	Planned Adjustment	Child's Name	Planned Adjustment
Aubra	Provide a reading buddy (Soledad?) at the Readers and Writers Workshop	Peng	Pair him with Davis and adult to help him negotiate play/investigation more successfully
Benjamin	Look for more challenging math activities for him	Soledad	Bring in Spanish reading materials for her (in addition to her English ones)
Davis	Provide adult support in play/investigation to prevent frustration	Taisha	Help with numeral recognition and understanding of correlation to quantities
Elijah	Bring in 2nd and 3rd grade reading materials for him		
Hayley	Pair her with Elijah for higher-level reading		
Jessica	Work with her on sight word recognition		
Michael	Follow up on his interests in science—can he design experiments?		
Paulo	Encourage him to branch out in play and work partners		

Completed form for kindergarten class

Planning with the Child's ZPD in Mind

Suzanne: "Sometimes scaffolding steps give children the confidence to go forward on their own."

In the previous chapter I discussed the term *zone of proximal development* (ZPD)—what a child can do with support from an adult or another child (Vygotsky 1978). I talked about the importance of a teacher identifying each child's ZPD so she can provide scaffolding to the child when he tries something that is difficult or challenging. Planning with a child's ZPD in mind is another way of making individual modifications.

Certain materials may be too challenging for the child. Noticing that a child is frustrated with fifteen-piece puzzles, a teacher may get out puzzles with eight to ten pieces. Or materials may not be challenging enough. Seeing that a child is bored with simple alphabet matching games, a teacher may encourage a child to match cards with classmates' names instead. The idea is to pay close attention to the child's level of developmental accomplishments and make adjustments in the curriculum not only to match that level but also to challenge the child to move ahead in skills, knowledge, and concepts. Then, the teacher is standing by ready to provide scaffolding and support.

Challenge is indeed a part of best practices. But the trick is to identify the amount of challenge that is just right for each child so that she continues to try the new skill or understand the new concept. If the challenge is too hard, the child may give up, feel overwhelmed, get frustrated, or withdraw. If the challenge is too easy, the child may become uninterested, become bored, misbehave, or give up and withdraw. A child who counts to twenty can be challenged to count higher. A child who can almost tie her shoe successfully can be challenged to master the last few steps in the process. A child who is making shapes that look like letters at the writing center can be challenged to make those shapes more accurately. A child who always plays alone can be challenged to play with a small group of children. Individual challenges are also included in the modifications portion of the framework. When individualizing the curriculum, a teacher is making certain that a "one size fits all" approach is not used.

This is where the assessment process joins the planning and reflection process. Determining a child's ZPD is really an assessment task. As you observe the child at work and play, you notice which challenges are just right for him and where he needs your support. In chapter 8 we will consider assessment practices in more depth.

> **Sue:** "I like to record 'the spark' that came first—a child's frustration with something, or question about, or delight in—that validates the importance of pursuing a topic, skill, or material."

> **Brenda:** "Kindergarten teachers often plan for ability groups, and because of this, individualization is sometimes not adequately addressed. I used to have the teachers bring one or two pieces of children's work to meetings to discuss where the child is in relation to the learning goals and to brainstorm ways to individualize and provide scaffolding for that child."

How Often Do You Plan for Each Child?

The frequency of writing a plan for each child in the classroom will vary from teacher to teacher. Be careful that your individual modifications are not limited only to the children who are more behaviorally challenging. Individual adjustments also include offering challenges to children who are extremely successful in certain skills or activities so they can go further with those skills or explore other possibilities using favorite materials.

You may want to set up a time period (the first half of the year or the first two months) during which you attempt to rotate through every name on your class list in your "Modifications for Individual Children" box. Each week, you can write about four or five children. Some of us need this kind of task orientation to make sure no child is missed. Or you may just keep a checklist of the children's names handy and, during the reflection process, check off each time you noted a specific step to relationship building or individual adjustment for each child. Over time, you will see patterns develop and become more aware of the children who are receiving more attention and the children who are being overlooked. Then, you can plan accordingly, focusing on other children in future weeks.

As you get to know the children, you will come up with many different adjustments for each one. This is really at the core of developmentally appropriate curriculum. When teachers take planned steps to build relationships with children and their families, they use the knowledge gained about the children to individualize the curriculum. Each child feels safe and trusts the adults around them. With that sense of safety firmly in place, the children can take advantage of the classroom environment with all of its inviting possibilities. They will explore those possibilities and take risks, knowing that their teachers are watching carefully and making adjustments to help them be successful.

Again, keep in mind that if you are required to publicly post your weekly plans, you will not post the last page of the framework or the Individual Adjustments form that includes personalized information about the children. Individualizing is an important part of your everyday planning and implementation of curriculum but is not appropriate to share with anyone except you and your teaching team and each child's parents or family members as you confer with them privately.

Planning Ongoing Projects Based on Children's Interests

Another way to individualize curriculum is to plan activities that focus on interests the children have demonstrated. In the field of early childhood education, many curricular approaches suggest specific ways to go about planning with children's interests in mind. These approaches include the Project Approach, emergent curriculum, and the Reggio Emilia approach. Sensitive and responsive teachers have always recognized the interests of the children in their classroom and incorporated activities spontaneously or in a carefully planned manner.

Every day, children express their interests—sometimes in a very blunt fashion. In my own kindergarten classroom, I would sit down with the children to read a big book at large-group time. I remember one hot May day, I wore open-toed sandals. We did some settling-in chants and fingerplays to get ready to listen. Then I showed the cover of the book, discussed the author's name, and asked what the children predicted the book might be about. All of a sudden, Jessica called out, "Mrs. Gronlund, you have big toes!"

What happened to my story time? I could have said, "Jessica, be quiet. Let's not talk about that now. We're going to read this story." However, I would have received little cooperation from the five- and six-year-olds in the room. Instead, they all had gathered around to check out my toes! I decided to go with the flow. I closed the book and suggested that we look at everyone's toes. We ended up with a series of foot activities that day—measuring foot and toe size, sorting and classifying types of shoes, and painting with our feet. Every activity tied to feet still met developmental goals of the program, so the fact that the focus changed from my original plans did not affect the quality of the curriculum for that day. Only the subject changed—in a spontaneous response to an expressed interest on the part of Jessica and all of the children.

Carefully planning a series of activities and investigations based on the children's interests is another way to organize curriculum. Sometimes, a situation presents itself, and the whole group becomes interested. In chapter 2, I gave the example of a bird building a nest right outside Mrs. Chang's classroom. The teachers and the children were fascinated by the materials the bird was using and the progress she was making. To build on this fascination, the teachers planned a series of activities based on birds and nest building. Binoculars were provided to watch the bird more closely. Writing and drawing about observations were encouraged. Books about birds were added to the class library. Tapes of birdcalls were put in the listening center. Materials to build nests were placed in the sensory table. In this case, the teachers were able to plan around a spontaneous event.

Other times a child or two may show a particular interest. Many young children (especially boys) are fascinated by dinosaurs and train engines. They become very knowledgeable about these topics and almost seem to obsess about them. It may be possible for a teacher to take advantage of this intense interest and approach many areas of the curriculum through that child's interest. The dinosaur expert may be willing to write dinosaur names more than alphabet letters, his own name, or other words. The train engine aficionado may be engaged in math activities by counting the number of train cars, measuring the length of the train track, and

Mary B.: "I follow what emerges out of the children after I've set out some provocations (such as books in the block area or a construction alphabet). We took a walk and took photos of structures that matched what we had built."

Mary B.: "You tease out the children's interests. You and the child are both motivated. You can connect on some level."

identifying shapes on the locomotive. This is another way to individualize and meet the needs of each child.

Using the Frameworks

At the top of the first page of the preschool framework is a line for recording ongoing projects. If a teacher knows he will be responding to an interest of the children, then he writes that topic there. More than likely it will be one that many children showed an interest in and therefore warrants attention in several of the play areas and planned activities. There is a line for recording thematic topics on pages 1 and 3 of the kindergarten framework pages. A teacher could easily coordinate her plans for a Readers and Writers Workshop or Investigation Time around a central theme. Often an ongoing project or theme will emerge through reflection about the previous week. Here are Mrs. Chang's comments about the previous weeks when the interest in birds arose.

REFLECTIONS: What worked? What didn't? What did you learn about individual children and group interests?

Name recognition is improving.

Cooking activity took too long—too much adult involvement rather than kids.

Some throwing of sand at sand table again—supervise more closely?

Good response to movement activities by most children—except Josie. Should we let her watch until she's ready?

Great interest in bird building a nest outside of the classroom. Jennifer and Harland checked on it every day. Should we add bird activities for next week?

Mrs. Chang's reflections

Teachers will write specific activities in the other portions of the framework, as we saw in Mrs. Chang's plans in chapter 2. You may remember that not all areas of the classroom have to be coordinated with a project. It only makes sense to change areas that easily relate to the topic at hand. The classroom environment will offer plenty for the children to do in nonrelated learning areas.

Reflection will continue as the plan is implemented. Then, future planning will determine whether the project should be continued or whether it's time to move on to something else. Here are Mrs. Chang's reflection comments after the first week of the bird project. On the next page you will find her follow-up plan for the play areas, group times, and routines for the next week. You will see that she and her teammates added more bird activities in response to the children's continued interest.

> **REFLECTIONS: What worked? What didn't? What did you learn about individual children and group interests?**
>
> The children were constant in their viewing of the nest-building process.
>
> Binoculars and birdcall tapes were hits! Some beautiful feather collages were created.
>
> Our nest materials did not hold together very well, and children lost interest.
>
> Jennifer is our bird expert—very knowledgeable—from a bird-watching family. Shall we invite them in to teach us more?
>
> Some children still painted and built as usual. Sam, Nathan, Angie, Jessica were not as interested in birds.

Mrs. Chang's reflections after the first week of bird activities

Preschool Weekly Planning and Reflection Framework

Program/School: Learning Time Preschool   Date: 10/3/11   Teacher(s): Mrs. Chang and Mrs. Allen

Ongoing Project (optional): Birds and nests (week 2)

	Learning goal(s)	Additional materials or focus	Vocabulary words
BLOCKS	understanding community (build roads and buildings)	traffic signs and maps, cars and trucks	neighborhoods, roads, highways, bridges, stop signs
DRAMATIC PLAY	learning to play and get along with other children		
SENSORY TABLE	measurement	pour and measure bird seed	more, less
ART	hand-eye coordination	make toilet-paper-tube binoculars	binoculars, focus, lenses
MANIPULATIVES	spatial relationships	complete puzzles with varying numbers of pieces	
CLASS LIBRARY	vocabulary development	study books and magazines about birds	migration
WRITING CENTER	writing	make bird books with scissors; provide cards with names of birds	cardinal, sparrow, robin, pheasant, duck, swan
OTHER CENTER	listening	listen to bird-call tapes	songbirds

Mrs. Chang's reflections and plans for week two of bird activities

Preschool Weekly Planning and Reflection Framework

DATE: 10/3/11		MONDAY	TUESDAY	WEDNESDAY	THURSDAY	FRIDAY
Large group	Learning goal	balance, coordination, and reading comprehension	phonological awareness	listening and vocabulary development	balance, coordination	speaking and writing skills
	Activity and teacher strategy	Act out "Sammy" Daily routines Read *Brown Bear, Brown Bear*	"Did You Ever See a Lassie" Daily routines Identify rhymes in *Brown Bear* as you retell with flannel board	Daily routines Special visitor: Jennifer's dad tells us about bird-watching	"Did You Ever See a Lassie" Daily routines Act out "Sammy" using different children's names (use name cards)	Favorite songs Daily routines Write a group story about our bird walk and graph birds seen
Small group	Learning goal	fine-motor skills	→			
	Activity and teacher strategy	Throughout the week, Sylvia will invite children to cut out pictures in magazines, pick up buttons and toothpicks with tweezers, and use hole punchers.	→			

Plans for Building Community and Relationships	Plans for Outdoor Explorations	Plans for Meals and Transitions
Have children share their favorite birds throughout the week and graph.	Look for birds every day. Thursday: go for a bird walk with our "binoculars."	Daily, assign a child as "nest watcher" and have him or her check the nest at every transition and report back.

Mrs. Chang's reflections for week two of bird activities

Teachers sometimes plan a project or topic of study based on their past experiences and knowledge of young children's interests. For example, young children are often interested in transportation. Yet, in planning for investigation of transportation, teachers find that they still have to be responsive to the specific direction the children take. In his kindergarten classroom, Mark organized materials around different kinds of transportation and provided a variety of activities for the children to engage in. As the class discussed different ways to get places—cars, trucks, trains, and airplanes—Jack announced proudly that his father was an airline pilot. Mark noticed that for several days, Jack and his friends organized chairs and "flew airplanes." As he reflected on the week, he noted the children's interest in these activities. He decided to support and add to this interest and wrote plans for the next week for both a Readers and Writers Workshop and Investigation Time. Mark offered materials in the writing area so that the children could make tickets and also guided them in involving other children to be the passengers, ticket agents, and luggage handlers. He also invited Jack's dad to tell the class more about his job. When he arrived in full pilot uniform, the children beamed. Jack smiled most of all. The interest in airplanes, pilots, and airports lasted for a long time in this classroom. On the next page are two pages of Mark's plans for Readers and Writers Workshops and Investigation Time incorporating the interest in airplanes.

Notice that not every activity is about airplanes. It's not necessary to stretch every activity to fit a topic: only plan for those that make sense and are easily accommodated.

In her preschool program, Susie tried to interest her children in the topic of transportation. They half-heartedly built roads for toy cars and trucks and counted wheels on construction vehicles. She noted their unenthusiastic responses on her general reflection form. But the children's eyes lit up and they became actively engaged when a flock of geese settled on the pond outside their classroom windows. This, too, was noted in Susie's reflections and included in her plans for the next week. You will see Susie's reflection comments, and the first two pages of her plan with the activities on the following pages.

Kindergarten Weekly Planning and Reflection Framework
READERS AND WRITERS WORKSHOP

Program/School: meadowbrook Elementary   Date: march 12, 2012   Teacher(s): mr. m. and mrs. T.

Ongoing Project (optional): airplanes

	Learning goal(s)	Additional materials or focus	Vocabulary words
LISTENING CENTER	vocabulary development	listen to *Lisa's Airplane Trip* on tape while looking at book	flight attendant, airport, seatbelt
DRAMATIC PLAY	self-regulation and writing	help children act out airport ticket counter, going on an airplane, making tickets, etc.	tickets, seats, safety
JOURNALING CENTER	writing	open writing	
ALPHABET CENTER	letter recognition	alphabet games and puzzles	
FLANNEL BOARD/ POCKET CHARTS	reading comprehension	choose favorite story or poem to retell	
CLASS LIBRARY	vocabulary development	read books about airplanes	airplanes, wings, pilots, flight attendants, passengers, trips, itinerary, destination
TEACHER-LED LITERACY ACTIVITY	help with dramatic play		
WRITING CENTER	writing	provide cards with airplane-related words	see library, dramatic play, and listening center lists
OTHER CENTER		focus on airplanes	

Mark's plan for the week of airplane activities

Kindergarten Weekly Planning and Reflection Framework
INVESTIGATION TIME

Program/School: meadowbrook Elementary   Date: march 12, 2012   Teacher(s): mr. m. and mrs. T.

Ongoing Project (optional): airplanes

	Learning goal(s)	Additional materials or focus	Vocabulary words
BLOCKS	mathematical problem solving	build an airport with runways and terminal	runways, terminal, gates, ramps, luggage carts
MATH ACTIVITY	geometry and spatial relationships	make patterns and geometrical designs with pattern blocks	
SENSORY TABLE	experiment	experiment with texture of wet and dry sand; write name and letters in wet sand	
ART	writing	take photos of dramatic play with airplanes and make a book about it (children dictate and write what they can)	
MANIPULATIVES	observation and analysis	manipulate and solve problems with marble run and gears	machines, inclines, gears
SCIENCE EXPLORATION	making scientific predictions	make paper airplanes	wingspan, flight, propulsion
INFORMATIONAL READING	demonstrating curiosity and interest in new things	read storybooks from afternoon story time	
MATH AND SCIENCE JOURNALING	representing mathematical information	take survey of children who have ridden on an airplane—make transportation graph	
OTHER CENTER			

Mark's plan for the week of airplane activities

> ### REFLECTIONS: What worked? What didn't? What did you learn about individual children and group interests?
>
> Children loved dancing with scarves and playing balloon catch. They were NOT interested in cars and trucks activities—much wandering.
>
> There was MUCH, MUCH interest in the flock of geese outside. Cailyn and Zach were the first to notice them—they got lots of other children interested as well. Do a geese project?
>
> Kelly's mom had her baby!
>
> Talk with speech therapist about articulation needs of several children.

Susie's reflections about interest in geese

Preschool Weekly Planning and Reflection Framework

Program/School: Child Development Lab School   Date: November 7, 2011   Teacher(s): Susie

Ongoing Project (optional): Geese

	Learning goal(s)	Additional materials or focus	Vocabulary words
BLOCKS	expressing emotions appropriately	help children express feelings as they resolve conflicts in block building	
DRAMATIC PLAY	speaking	act out grocery store and shopping	cashier, cash register, deli, meats, produce, dairy
SENSORY TABLE	understanding family	wash baby dolls and manipulative toys	chores, responsibilities
ART	hand-eye coordination and using tools	make eyedropper paintings and paper-strip collages	
MANIPULATIVES	measurement, fine-motor skills	playdough, rollers, etc.; compare and contrast sizes of creations	
CLASS LIBRARY	demonstrate curiosity and interest in new things	read and listen to books about geese and ducks (among other favorites)	
WRITING CENTER	writing, concepts of print	help children write names with name cards	
OTHER CENTER	counting and quantity, representing math information	have children count the geese at the pond each day and keep a record	

Susie's plan for the week of geese activities

Preschool Weekly Planning and Reflection Framework

DATE: November 7, 2011		MONDAY	TUESDAY	WEDNESDAY	THURSDAY	FRIDAY
Large group	Learning goal	gross-motor skills, self-regulation, listening, reading comprehension				
	Activity and teacher strategy	Gathering and settling in songs and fingerplays Daily routines Read *The Ugly Duckling*	Read *The Ugly Duckling*	Read *Make Way for Ducklings*	Read *Make Way for Ducklings*	Discuss and record: what have we learned about geese?
Small group	Learning goal	writing, using tools, counting, vocabulary development				
	Activity and teacher strategy	Throughout the week, help children at the writing center, counting geese and recording				bake banana bread

Plans for Building Community and Relationships	Plans for Outdoor Explorations	Plans for Meals and Transitions
Have questions of the day for children to answer at arrival: "How do geese stay warm? What do they eat? Where will they go for the winter?" Then, share answers at gathering time.	Visit the pond each day to observe the geese (but stay far enough away not to annoy or bother them). Play "Duck, Duck, Goose"!	Discuss favorite fruits and vegetables at snacktime. Introduce "Hicklety, Picklety Bumblebee" for transitions.

Susie's plan for the week of geese activities

Susie wisely changed her focus from transportation to geese and helped the children figure out ways to count and record the number of geese each day. She provided books on geese in the class library and took the children outdoors to observe the geese at the pond more closely. Notice that she did not attempt to change everything in the classroom to be associated with geese. The "show" was right outside the classroom windows on the pond!

These examples demonstrate truly emergent curriculum—teachers responded to children's interests and were willing to adapt activities accordingly. By combining planning and reflection in one framework, they now have a record of what occurred for others to witness.

Some early childhood educators think that curriculum is the list of topics or projects teachers do across the year. The fallacy here is that the various topics for projects or studies are the source of curriculum. However, the theme or topic is not at the heart of the planning/observation/individualization curriculum process. Learning goals are.

The theme or topic is a way to engage the children—to capture their interest and develop their attention, to make learning fun and enjoyable so that the all-important developmental goals are continually being worked on. Preschool and kindergarten curriculum is focused on children's development: the strategies they are using to learn more about their world and the skills they are developing to observe, talk about, and represent what they are learning with a variety of materials. And they are asked to do this in a classroom that has other children with whom they have to get along. No matter what the theme or topic, these same goals (and more, including fine- and gross-motor skills, early math and reading, and so on) are the focus.

How often do you plan for a project? There is no need to plan for a topic of study each week. As I pointed out in chapter 2, if you have set up the classroom environment to be rich and inviting with a variety of materials in each learning area, exploring the classroom can be the focus for long periods of time and can be returned to as the focus throughout the year.

You can bring in a new project or change one when the children are no longer fully engaged or interested in what is available. You can use the criteria for changing the setup of the classroom or the materials that are present to decide when to change a project as well. Criteria might include the following:

- The children are not choosing to work on the project or to play in areas of the classroom devoted to the project.
- The children are bored with the topic (they may say they are bored, they may appear bored in activities relating to the project, or they may change the related activities themselves).
- The children's behavior is not productive or positive when they are working on the project.
- Another topic of interest has emerged in the classroom and is engaging the attention of some or all of the children.

Children may show an emerging interest by using materials in new ways. They may organize all of the food in the dramatic play area into a store and pretend to buy from and sell to one another. Changing to activities that relate to a grocery store, planning a field trip to a grocery store, and adding materials, stories, and songs related to this important family experience would be warranted.

Sometimes, the determining factor for a project or study is a field trip or a special site visit. This may not arise specifically from the children's interests. Rather, it is planned by the teacher (often well in advance in order to arrange transportation and parent helpers) because she knows the focus of the visit will be of interest to the children and may very well lead to ongoing investigations and project work.

The preschool program where Sharon taught was located on a high school campus. So, Sharon went and talked with the auto shop teacher, asking if he thought a visit to his shop would be appropriate for her young children. He was willing to take the safety precautions necessary and was enthusiastic about sharing his students' work with Sharon's. The visit was a roaring success, and children's involvement in a variety of activities related to repairing cars went on for a long period in Sharon's classroom.

How long does one keep planning with a topic in mind? Again, a teacher has to carefully observe the children and assess their ongoing interest and engagement in the topic. Barbara noticed that her children were using the stuffed animals and stethoscopes to play veterinarian's office in the dramatic play area. She decided to respond by providing materials and activities to follow up on that interest. The children acted out caring for the animals for three to four weeks. They read books about veterinarians, visited a veterinarian's office, practiced giving the animals shots, and bandaged their legs. One day, Barbara noticed that the children had packed up all of the veterinarian's equipment and turned the dramatic play area back into a house and kitchen. She knew then that her project was over. She changed the focus of her planning back to exploring the classroom environment and watched to see what new topics might emerge as the children used the learning areas to their fullest.

Being flexible, like all of these teachers, helps the topics or projects truly follow children's interests. Teachers know that the best projects are those that can be directly experienced by the children and relate to their lives. They report that the following projects or topics of study often are successful with preschool and kindergarten children:

- anything to do with the child and his or her everyday life, such as my body, my family, what I like to eat, my mom's and dad's jobs, my feelings
- anything in nature that can be experienced firsthand, such as weather and seasonal traits of your area

- classroom and/or household pets
- animals, insects, and plants that can be directly experienced and observed outdoors (preferably right on your playground and school grounds)
- local natural attractions (If you live near water, study it. Caves? Visit them and learn more about them.)
- your community (urban? tall buildings and subways; rural? farms and cider mills)
- neighborhood services (grocery store, restaurant, post office, fire station, etc.)
- machines and mechanical objects that interest the children
- special celebrations and events in your area (the rodeo, the pow-wow, the lilac festival, etc.)
- cultural events and experiences that relate to the children

Again, remember, it is not necessary to coordinate every activity in the classroom with a topic! Don't rack your brain trying to come up with materials in every area that relate. Instead, plan for activities that are meaningful and make sense. The rest of the classroom environment will stand as the rich and inviting place that it is.

Thoughts about Children with Behavioral Challenges

When individualizing curriculum, teachers often find that some children demand more of their attention than others because they have behavioral challenges. While this book is not an in-depth guide to managing children's behavior, it does include many aspects of curriculum that can prevent poor behavior. The elements of curriculum that I have identified are meant to help children feel safe, develop trust, and take risks in the classroom. When all of these elements are implemented, children realize that the adults are there to provide them with guidance, structure, and support. The goals set for them and the way the classroom is run are all based on knowledge of three- through six-year-old children. Over time children learn that their teachers are watching and making changes when they are not successful. They are not setting children up to fail but rather are providing challenges that are just right for their capabilities, learning styles, and personalities. This helps preschool and kindergarten children behave better. In chapter 9 we will look at ways to determine what elements of the curriculum process might be missing or need more attention. For now, let's continue to consider children with challenging behaviors.

When young children act up, teachers may have to intervene to protect them, to protect others, and to help them learn to control their own behavior. Perhaps they don't know how to express their feelings appropriately, and when frustrated, angry, or upset, they strike out or use hurtful words. Perhaps they don't have a sense of what is a safe risk to take and what is not. Perhaps their egocentricity is dominating their decision making so that they grab materials or boss around other children (who are unwilling participants). In these situations, teachers have to respond. But rather than merely react, teachers of young children should reflect and analyze the situation so that their intervention will be most helpful for the child. Intentional and caring teachers are reflective more than they are reactive.

In the second edition of *Reflecting Children's Lives: A Handbook for Planning Your Child-Centered Curriculum*, Deb Curtis and Margie Carter (2011) suggest that teachers consider their own perceptions of children when challenging behaviors occur:

> If you consider children to be competent and believe that their behavior has an important purpose that should be respected, you will respond with patience and coaching. If you see children as naughty or lacking control, then you will likely take less time to support children in solving problems for themselves. You can practice transforming your view of children . . . when these moments arise. (84–85)

They go on to share a helpful comparison of contrasting views of the same behavior in children:

Negative View	Competent View
The child has no idea of what is safe.	The child is an energetic explorer, a tireless experimenter, or a dedicated scientist.
The child lacks patience.	The child is eager to learn from every experience and interaction he has.
The child cannot keep his hands off of things.	The child is figuring out how to control his behavior and look after himself, others, and the world around him.
The child has temper tantrums.	The child is moving from dependence to independence. (85)

By being reflective practitioners, teachers gain better understanding of the underlying causes of a child's poor behavior. Yes, in the moment you must step in and prevent injury or offer guidance. However, taking the time to consider the child's perspective and analyze the situation from different angles is critical to learning how to prevent outbursts in the future and help the child most effectively in the long term.

In chapter 2 I talked about looking at the environment on a regular basis. When a child misbehaves, one question to ask is, Where in the classroom did this occur? Then, look at that area closely. Is there a limited amount of space for the number of children who want to play there? Are there enough materials for everyone to do what they want to do? Perhaps the resolution will involve increasing the size of the area, adding more materials, or limiting the number of children. The problem may not have been an out-of-control child; rather, the problem could have been a play area that needs a teacher's attention.

Another question to consider when a child acts up is, At what time of the day or in what part of our daily schedule did this occur? Play and investigation times can be difficult for those children who have a hard time getting started and settling in. Transitions can be very difficult for some children. Finishing up an activity in which they are deeply engaged can be hard for them. Times that involve waiting for one's turn or working in a small group can be a source of trouble for some children. It's important to look at when behavior problems occur and consider what you and your colleagues might do differently at that time of day for that child.

Many behavior problems arise at group times. Young children do not sit still well for long periods of time. They are not always good listeners or passive receivers of information. In chapter 6 we will analyze ways to plan for large and small groups that help children transition from more active to less active participation. Being thoughtful in planning effective large- and small-group times will help prevent many challenging behaviors during these times.

Another way to be reflective about challenging behaviors is to consider how many times you say "no" to children, or how many requirements you have in the daily schedule that forbid them from pursuing something that interests them. Katharine Kersey and Marie Masterson (2011) suggest that teachers embrace "the power of yes":

> If the goal is to create cooperation and reduce resistance, it helps to replace *no* with strategies that redirect behavior successfully. Effective strategies can turn resistance into cooperation even for children with whom the teacher typically struggles. Saying yes often empowers success and weakens the setup for resistance. Situations that make us want to say no can become opportunities to say yes. (41)

They suggest four strategies I've adapted below for embracing the "power of yes":

1. *The make-a-big-deal strategy,* where teachers give attention, thanks, specific praise, recognition, and encouragement.
2. *The incompatible alternative strategy,* where a teacher gives the "child something appropriate to do that ends the inappropriate behavior" (e.g., if she is running around the room, she is asked to help pass out books) or a teacher tells a child *what* to do rather than what *not* to do.
3. *The choice strategy,* where a teacher states a desired goal and gives the child two positive and acceptable choices for accomplishing it.
4. *The when/then strategy* to invite cooperation (e.g., a teacher says "When you clean up, then you may play with the sand."). (41–43)

Being reflective rather than reactive and thinking in terms of "yes" rather than "no" are conscious decisions on the part of each individual teacher. These decisions will impact children's behavior and have long-reaching, potentially positive results.

Self-Regulation

A primary task of the preschool and kindergarten years is children's development of self-regulation of their thinking, emotions, and behavior. Self-regulation is not the same as self-control. Self-regulation involves all aspects of development, including emotional and cognitive development, because a child has to think about the situation and then act in a way that inhibits his impulses.

> Thinking affects emotions, and emotions affect cognitive development (Blair & Diamond 2008). Children who cannot effectively regulate anxiety or discouragement tend to move away from, rather than engage in, challenging learning activities. Conversely, when children regulate uncomfortable emotions, they can relax and focus on learning cognitive skills. Similarly, children experience better emotional regulation when they replace thoughts like "I'm not good at this" with thoughts like "This is difficult, but I can do it if I keep trying." Regulating anxiety and thinking helps children persist in challenging activities, which increases their opportunities to practice the skills required for an activity. (Florez 2011, 47)

Teachers have an important role in helping children in this task. They provide scaffolding, or "co-regulation," helping the child move toward internalized, independent self-regulation. "Thus, to develop self-regulation skills, children need many opportunities to experience and practice with adults and capable peers" (Florez 2011, 48). Teachers can model ways to self-regulate by talking through their own inhibition process: "I'm going to stop talking now because it's your turn to talk." They can give children strategies for controlling their impulses: "When you feel angry at your friend, you can tell him with your words, you can walk away, or you can come and get one of the teachers to help you." Providing a safe place where children can remove themselves from the group when they feel overwhelmed or out of control is a way of working toward internalized self-regulation. You can also provide a Peace Table, where children have been taught a conflict resolution process where each party presents his problem. They listen to each other and attempt to come to an agreeable solution. This process may need adult assistance for quite awhile but can be successful as children see the model in action and learn to use the process for themselves.

Finally, a rich and wonderful way to see self-regulation in action is in pretend play. As children play at a role, they have to regulate their impulses. When playing "cats and dogs," a child who announces "I'm a dog" and then proceeds to meow will be greeted with strong reaction from the other children. He isn't playing cats and dogs according to the rules: cats meow and dogs bark. There are always inherent rules in children's pretend play. And children can rise to the occasion and follow those rules more often in pretend play than in real life. Have you ever noticed that when a child pretends to be the teacher reading a book to a group of students, the students listen better to her than they may to you as you read? That's because they are pretending to be students. They are playing by the "rules of student."

> Because the children want to engage in this play, they must regulate their behavior to play the roles correctly, as agreed upon by the group. . . . Children are encouraging each other to play in the right way, the way that fits their conceptions about the roles they are acting out. Vygotskians say that by the end of kindergarten, truly self-regulated children can think first and act later. They can restrain their own impulses. . . . The development of self-regulation is so important to later academic success—indeed to success in life itself—that teachers have an obligation to help children reach this high level of play. (Gronlund 2010, 17–18)

For those children in your class who exhibit challenging behaviors, you may find that if you ask them to pretend, they may be able to inhibit their impulses better. Depending on what your goal is, you choose a role that will help the child successfully meet that goal. Here are some examples:

- It's time to clean up, and this child is often reluctant to participate. You can suggest that he pretend to be a grown-up who is having company for dinner. He has to get the house all cleaned up before they arrive.

- Another child needs help, and this child is not showing empathy or caring. You can suggest that she is the big sister who has to show her little sister how to do things at snacktime or independent reading time.
- A child is being loud and disruptive as you are transitioning down the halls. You can suggest that he needs to be as quiet as a leopard stalking its prey. You help him get where he's going (outdoors, the gym) and then participate in the pretend. "Oh, you got me, Mr. Leopard! You were so quiet you sneaked up on me."

Conclusion

In addition to prevention, the reflection process of implementing curriculum is essential when considering children with behavioral challenges. Talking with colleagues, daily if necessary and certainly weekly, when considering plans for the next week will help teachers consider what they can do with their environment, daily schedule, group times, and playtimes to help each child be successful.

In the next chapter we will look at small- and large-group times and consider ways to plan for them most effectively for all children.

Mary B.: "What a teacher notices is a spark, a motivation, a focus that drives the child to experiment and want to know more. The child communicates this often using nonverbal cues. This is what the teacher notices. It is exciting when this is what drives the planning cycle."

CHAPTER 6

Planning for More Child-Initiated Than Adult-Led Activities

. . . .

Early childhood educators continually decide in which instances they will follow the child's lead and when to take a more directive role themselves. This is one of the many ongoing accommodations and adjustments teachers make and is an important element of the planning/observation/individualization cycle in the curriculum process. The balance between child-initiated and teacher-led activities is important. For young children, this balance should lean more heavily toward child direction.

In high-quality preschool and kindergarten classrooms, teachers recognize that offering choices to the children brings about more participation and deeper engagement in activities. Young children do not respond well to constantly being told what to do. As Erik Erikson (1950) identified, they are in the stage of initiative—trying things out for themselves. Their developing independence and movement toward greater competence propel them to reject constant direction from the adults in their lives. Yet, it is not complete freedom from adult guidance that they seek. Children trust adults to provide reasonable choices within the safety of adult guidance.

Teachers carefully plan the possibilities from which children can choose and the ways they will facilitate children's interactions with materials and other children. Never is any part of the day unplanned. However, within this planning, teachers offer more opportunities for child-initiated activities than adult-led ones. For a good part of the day teachers enable the children to make choices about which activities they will do and when, different ways in which they will use the materials, and with whom they will interact while they do so. A teacher also provides some activities where she is the leader and initiator, not the child. The heavier emphasis on child-initiated activities does not mean that chaos reigns in the classroom or that learning is no longer the focus.

As teachers look at the balance between child-initiated and adult-led activities, they take into consideration both the ages and developmental levels of the children. The balance will be different with young three-year-olds than it will be with kindergartners. Teachers also consider the children's personalities, dispositions to learning, past experiences, and cultural backgrounds. The tricky part is to find just the right balance between child-initiated and teacher-led activities for each group of children.

Offering Balanced Opportunities

The first step in determining this balance is to look at the whole schedule for the day. The focus of the activities throughout the day (or half day, as the case may be) will vary between the teacher as the initiator and the children as the initiators. In teacher-led activities, the children tend to play a more passive role. They are the receivers of information, ideas, or suggestions. In child-initiated activities, the children make decisions and take actions.

In her book *Teacher*, Sylvia Ashton-Warner (1963) talks about the need for children to have opportunities to "breathe out" and "breathe in," or to experience activities for output or intake. She defines *breathing out* as expressing oneself. Such expression can take place in the form of talking, singing, dancing, moving, writing, drawing, creating, or building. Ashton-Warner even includes crying, quarreling, daydreaming, and loving as output, or breathing out, activities. She defines *breathing in*, on the other hand, as taking in new information: listening, learning a new concept, watching a demonstration, pondering, or thinking. This can be tied directly to providing choices for children. When the children are the initiators, they are breathing out. When the teachers are the initiators, the children are breathing in. The critical point Ashton-Warner makes is this: children must first be given opportunities to breathe out before they are ready to breathe in.

Ashton-Warner sees the daily schedule in a classroom as a "daily rhythm" that flows from breathing-out activities to breathing-in activities. She says that flowing with this daily rhythm, "the teacher is at last with the stream and not against it: the stream of children's inexorable creativeness" (93). If breathing out precedes breathing in, children have had an opportunity to expend both physical and creative energy before they are asked to sit and be quiet. They have also had time to express and process any urgent feelings or experiences that they brought into the classroom that day. They are more ready to take in information from others, listen to a story, or follow directions.

Take a look at the following daily schedule for a preschool half-day program, and think about its daily rhythm. Notice where you see opportunities for the children to breathe out versus breathe in. Does breathing out usually precede breathing in? The classroom routines of cleanup, getting ready for snack, or going home probably are neither output nor intake activities—they just are things that have to be done, aren't they?

Sample Daily Schedule for a Preschool Half-Day

8:00–8:25 a.m. Arrival Time
Children put away their backpacks and coats and go to tables where hands-on materials are available (greetings and conversation; writing and drawing; small manipulatives for constructing, such as Lego building blocks; and playdough). *Breathing out.*

8:25–8:45 a.m. Large-Group Time
Children join in movement games, songs, and fingerplays (*breathing out*), then listen to discussions and stories before planning for the day (*breathing in*).

8:45–10:00 a.m. Work or Activity Time
The children choose among a variety of learning areas and may be invited to join in a small-group activity led by a teacher for approximately ten to fifteen minutes of this time. *More breathing out than anything; small group may be either breathing out or in.*

10:00–10:15 a.m. Cleanup Time
The children help clean up the entire classroom.

10:15–10:30 a.m. Snacktime
The children converse and eat snack. *Breathing out.*

10:30–11:00 a.m. Outdoors
The children engage in a variety of large-muscle activities, outdoors if weather permits. *Breathing out.*

11:00–11:15 a.m. Prepare to Go Home
Get materials, backpacks, coats, and so forth. Review the day's activities and make plans for tomorrow.

11:15 a.m. Dismissal

In my own preschool classroom, I had to try different schedules before I figured out how best to balance the activities so that they flowed from self-expression to taking in new information. The children in my class arrived at various times across a fifteen-minute period. Initially, I thought that we should begin the day with a large group or circle time. I reasoned that such a group experience would help everyone settle down and feel like part of the group right off. My plan was for the children to sit quietly while attendance was taken, a story was read, and plans were made for the day. All of these activities, according to Ashton-Warner, were breathing-in activities. I tried this for a few weeks, asking the children who arrived first to sit and wait until their classmates arrived. The waiting was excruciating for those children! Even for those who arrived later, the large-group time was not successful. They all had stories about the previous evening to tell to me and their friends. Several of them had brought things to show to the class and wanted to do so immediately. Wiggles and giggles and a general need for movement and conversation were evident as I continually attempted to "shush" the children.

Looking at this situation from Ashton-Warner's perspective, I had not given the children an opportunity to breathe out as they began their school day. I changed the schedule so that arrival time was a prolonged period. As children arrived, they put away their knapsacks and coats and chose among a variety of table activities (writing, manipulatives, drawing, and books). Conversation among the children was encouraged. My teaching assistant and I circulated among the children, greeting them, hearing their stories from home, admiring the objects they had brought to school, and encouraging their self-expression through the activities at hand. As new children arrived, they easily joined in at the tables. We allowed all the children an opportunity to converse, write, or draw for at least ten minutes. Then, we held large-group time. By this time, the children were ready to breathe in. The group-time transition went more smoothly than it had previously. The children sat and listened with more ease.

Children in kindergarten programs often attend for a full day. Analyzing breathing-out and breathing-in opportunities can be done in the same way for the schedule of a full-day kindergarten.

Sample Daily Schedule for a Full-Day Kindergarten

8:00–8:25 a.m. Arrival Time
Children put away their backpacks and coats and go to tables where hands-on materials are available (greetings and conversation; writing and drawing; small manipulatives for constructing, such as Lego building blocks; and playdough). *Breathing out.*

8:25–8:50 a.m. Large-Group Time
Children join in movement games, songs, and fingerplays (*breathing out*), then listen to discussions and stories before planning for the day (*breathing in*).

8:50–10:15 a.m. Readers and Writers Workshop
The children choose among a variety of literacy activities (listening to books on tape, writing and drawing in their journals, playing roles in dramatic play, using flannel boards and pocket charts to tell stories, writing letters to classmates and family members) and may be invited to join in a small-group activity led by a teacher for approximately ten to fifteen minutes of this time. *More breathing out than anything; small group may be either breathing out or in.*

10:15–10:30 a.m. Cleanup Time
The children help clean up the entire classroom.

10:30–10:45 a.m. Snacktime
The children converse and eat snack. *Breathing out.*

10:45–11:30 a.m. Special Activities
Children engage in gym, music, library, or other special activities. *Breathing out and in.*

11:30 a.m. Lunch
The children converse and eat. *Breathing out.*

12:00 p.m. Recess. *Breathing out.*

12:30 p.m. Large- or Small-Group Story Reading and Quiet Time
The children listen to teachers read stories in large or small groups. *Breathing in.*

1:00 p.m. Investigation Time
The children choose among a variety of math, science, and play activities (sorting, classifying and counting manipulatives, creating shapes with small and large blocks, measuring items in the room, engaging in an ongoing science experiment, caring for pets, writing in math and/or science journals, reading nonfiction books about nature and other topics, playing at the sensory table, making creations in the art area) and may be invited to join in a small-group activity led by a teacher for approximately ten

to fifteen minutes of this time. *More breathing out than anything; small group may be either breathing out or in.*

2:00 p.m. Cleanup Time

The children help clean up the entire classroom.

2:15 p.m. Prepare to Go Home

Get materials, backpacks, coats, and so forth. Review the day's activities and make plans for tomorrow.

2:30 p.m. Dismissal

....

Take the time to consider your own daily schedule from this perspective. When are you offering opportunities for children to breathe out and breathe in? Do you plan for active, expressive times before you ask children to be more passive and listen and take in information? If you are seeing problems at different times of the day, you may find that the children need more opportunities to breathe out, to actively express themselves through drawing, writing, building, dancing, singing, creating, and talking before being asked to sit quietly, listen, and watch.

Planning for Active Experiences

In chapter 2, I discussed the many possibilities for children to try in a well-organized, rich classroom environment. The question to consider now is, How much of children's explorations should be based on their choices, and how much should be based on teacher suggestions or directions? Again, the younger the child, the more the balance should be in favor of children's choices (within teacher-planned sets of choices).

Remember that within a carefully planned classroom environment, a structure for the possible choices is provided. The classroom setup helps children know where materials are and how they can be used. In addition, teachers make clear to the children the rules and procedures of the classroom. Having provided this environment, teachers do not need to add structure to playtimes by telling children what they should do or where they should play. Offering them choices, letting them make decisions for themselves, and then guiding them as they engage in their chosen activities will work better with young children. Their motivation and willingness to get deeply engaged will be greater.

Many teachers introduce their playtime of the day (sometimes called Investigation Time, Activity Time, Focused Choice Time, or Exploration Time) and allow children to choose the play areas at which they want to play. They describe the materials available, make suggestions about things children could do in each area, and ask each child where he would like to play first. Children can verbally identify a plan for their play or write or draw a play plan that shows their choices. Teachers recognize that children often choose areas for good reasons:

- The area may represent a strength or interest for that child.
- It may have opportunities to practice skills the child is trying to master.
- It may be a playmate's favorite.
- It may have something the child has not tried before.

There are ways to structure the choice-making process for children that may help them be even more successful in getting started and sustaining their involvement in play. Teachers recognize the goal is for children to make good choices, choices that allow them to be independent and responsible at the same time. Children may need a little help in that process.

Some teachers determine how many children can work in a specific play area at a time. Many teachers report that limiting the number of children leads to fewer behavior problems and more positive engagement with the activities. When considering the perfect number of children in an area, teachers pay attention to the following:

- the amount of square footage in the area (young children often need a circle of personal space that is approximately the size of a hula hoop within which to function)
- the number of materials available so that children can participate fully in the activity (for example, if a game has four game cards, it's appropriate for only four children; if there are two easels, only two children can paint)
- the number of chairs that will fit comfortably at a table (six chairs at the art table means only six children in the art learning area)

The procedure for making choices in these classrooms includes considering how many children are already present in an area and referring to some recognized sign that reminds everyone how many children can work in that area at any one time. Some teachers use choosing boards where children place their name card or photograph on hooks or in pockets that signify an area in the classroom. Some teachers use sign-in sheets posted around the classroom. In this way, children practice their writing skills while also learning to take turns and wait for an opening in a favorite area.

Photo 6.1

Photo 6.2

Photo 6.3

Letting the children figure out how long they want to stay with specific activities is another way of providing choice. Timing the children and making them rotate to different learning areas does not allow them the opportunity to make a plan and stick with it through completion. Adult agendas of "fifteen minutes at a center" limit children's engagement from an outside source. Many preschoolers are perfectly capable of staying with one activity for much longer than fifteen minutes, provided it is a self-chosen activity that really interests the child. And kindergartners can devote even longer attention to activities that they choose and find challenging. When teachers remember that such engagement is an important learning goal for this age group, they can relax and not worry about the children not getting to every play area each day. Instead, they can wonder at the intensity of a serious block builder who works cooperatively with friends over long periods of time and creates interesting structures that include symmetry and gravity-defying balance. Or they can marvel at the engagement of a socializer who spends many hours cooking and developing family scenarios in the dramatic play center.

Managing an active classroom full of children choosing activities sometimes involves limiting their choices. Children who throw sand at the sand table are not following the procedures for that learning area. A teacher can then step in, remind the child of the dangers of throwing sand, and watch for careful use of the materials. If the child continues to throw sand, the teacher may limit the child's choices by saying something such as:

> "I already discussed with you how we use the sand safely. I can see that you're having trouble doing that. You are showing me that you can no longer work at the sand table. Tomorrow, you can show me how you remember to use the sand safely. Now, you may choose to put together some puzzles or listen to a story on the headphones. Which would you like to do?"

In this case, the teacher took away the choice of using the sand and offered two other options from which the child could choose. This is one way of structuring children's choices.

Teachers are continually attempting to find just the right balance between child-initiated and teacher-led activities. No matter what the age of the class, it may be wise to offer fewer choices some days than others. For example, the day after a major celebration, such as Halloween, is often

Suzanne: "Last year we added 'Plans for the Day' where children used a chart to select three activities they planned to do throughout the morning. This helped those who had trouble deciding what to do as well as helped all of them focus on their day. It helped to empower the children to make good and meaningful choices. It was also very useful as a reflection tool."

chaotic for young children. A day of more restricted choices with quieter activities may yield better behavioral results than a day of many loud, active choices. The opposite will be true on other days. If a teacher sees that children are wandering and not engaging in activities she has planned or not paying attention to teacher-led discussions or stories, she may want to ask the children, "What would you like to do next?" She can give some possibilities for special choices that are not frequently available, such as Twister or dancing to music with scarves. Or she can listen carefully to the suggestions of the children and follow one or more of those. The balancing act is a daily event that must be paid careful consideration in the classroom.

Planning for Adult-Led Large- and Small-Group Activities

The younger the children, the less time in a day should be spent in teacher-led, breathing-in activities. Three-year-olds need more breathing-out time than five-year-olds. And thinking of strategies that help children settle in before they are asked to be quiet listeners will help large- and small-group times go much more smoothly.

At large-group time, teachers are usually the focus. Children are expected to sit in a group and receive information about the day, listen to a story, and take turns participating by raising hands or waiting to make comments or ask questions. Teachers often find that large-group time helps in the following ways:

- builds community among the children
- helps them get to know one another better
- gives children experience in listening and following directions
- develops reading comprehension skills
- gives children an opportunity to experiment with turn taking

How long should large-group time last? There is no magic number for three- to five-year-olds. However, there is a very clear point at which large-group time should end: when the children no longer show interest!

That means large-group time may vary in length from day to day. At the beginning of the year, it may be a much shorter experience than at the end of the year. On a day when the children are particularly calm and

Sarah: "As we move away from instructing children and instead move toward working with them in a child-centered approach where there is a balance between adult- and child-led activities, I have found that it is often helpful for teachers to document the open-ended questions that they plan to use with the children as they play and explore. I have had some teachers do this directly on the lesson plan so that they are reminded of these questions as they write them, as they practice them, and as they reflect on how things have gone throughout the week. This has also proven to be useful in working with colleagues, family volunteers, and visitors to the classroom."

the story is a class favorite, large-group time may last longer than usual. As group time progresses, teachers must be alert to the body language of the children. Are they sitting quietly with little movement, or are there lots of wiggles? Are the children keeping their hands to themselves, or are many of them fiddling with their neighbors in some way? Are the children actively engaged in the activity or conversation, or are they looking around the room, asking when circle time will be done, or staring with little light in their eyes as if they've given up until this "ordeal" is over? Teachers need to read these signals to determine when to end a group activity, even stopping a story midstream if necessary.

Some teachers choose not to do large-group times at all. They feel that the goals of building community, developing listening and comprehension, turn taking, and so on can be met in many other ways throughout the classroom day. Annalynn, Stephanie, and Christina had eighteen three- to five-year-olds in their classroom. They felt that large-group time was not productive with that many children involved and instead planned for small-group activities at different times throughout the day to involve children in music and movement activities, daily routines, and story reading.

An effective group time is one that meets the needs of the children. Depending on the children and the program, a short group time, a long group time, or even no group time at all can be successful. A teacher who understands this and plans group times that work for the children in her class is showing her sensitivity; she knows how best to plan for preschoolers and kindergartners.

On the frameworks, there is a section titled "Large group." This area is where teachers can write learning goals and activities planned for group time. (Two models are provided in appendix A or at www.redleafpress.org, one for daily planning and one for weekly.) Discussion topics, demonstrations, or stories can be written here along with teaching strategies for addressing the identified goals. In some classrooms, teachers have routine tasks that they do each day at large-group time. These might include taking attendance, identifying classroom helpers, looking at a calendar, and making plans for the day. There is not enough room for all of these routines to be written on the planning form. It may be best for a teacher to write a more generic term, "Daily routines." On the next page are examples of Valerie's plans for large groups. Notice how each day Valerie begins her large group with an active song and some kind of movement, which pulls the group together.

DATE: *12/12/11*			MONDAY	TUESDAY	WEDNESDAY	THURSDAY	FRIDAY
Large group	Learning goal		*listening, speaking, gross-motor skills, and reading*	→			
	Activity and teacher strategy		*Daily routines* *"Knee to Knee Game," "Wiggles," "My Thumbs Go Up"* *Read It Looked Like Spilled Milk*	→	*Play "Simon Says," "Where Is Thumbkin?"* *Read Jump, Frog, Jump*	*Children choose a favorite story*	*"Give Yourself a Hug," "Who Stole the Cookie?"* *Reread Spilled Milk; children predict and read along*

Valerie's plans for large groups

She then progresses to calmer activities and fingerplays. Daily routines are followed by either a large-group learning activity or a story. The children know exactly what to expect each day because her routine remains the same.

Valerie is demonstrating a way to develop longer engagement in circle-time activities: she is applying the concepts of breathing out and breathing in. Beginning large-group time with songs and movement games that give the children the opportunity to express themselves physically helps them breathe out. Moving toward less and less physical activity helps the children get ready to breathe in and listen more attentively to discussions and stories.

Beginning large-group time by calling the children together with movement songs, such as "The More We Get Together," grabs the children's attention, brings them into the circle, and lets them expend energy by moving their bodies:

> Oh, the more we get together, together, together,
> The more we get together, the happier we'll be.
> Move this way and that way and this way and that way.
> Oh, the more we get together, the happier we'll be.

Additional verses can be added using the children's names and allowing each of them to decide on a movement the class can replicate. These movements are all done standing up. The children might suggest raising their arms, swinging their legs, jumping up and down, or touching their toes:

> Andrea moves this way, and Joseph moves that way,
> Yolanda moves this way, and Ari moves that way.

Following such vigorous activity with a less vigorous movement song or game will lead the children to sit down quietly. For example, the following fingerplay begins with the children standing up and ends with them sitting down:

> I wiggle my fingers, I wiggle my toes,
> I wiggle my elbows, I wiggle my nose,
> I get all of my wiggles out of me.
> And, then, I sit quiet, as quiet can be.

Now, the children may be more ready to participate in a discussion that requires listening and taking turns responding, or to listen to a story. If there are still some wiggles, add a sitting-down song or fingerplay with minimal movement (such as "Open, Shut Them" or "Eeensy, Weensy Spider"). These activities have progressed from breathing out (active, self-expression) to breathing in (quietly taking in new information). Many teachers report that this progression lengthens the attentiveness of children and increases the effectiveness of their large-group times. Then, having a ritual or routine for dismissing children from the large-group gathering to the next activity (snack, play centers, outdoors, or whatever) will help children handle that transition more smoothly. In chapter 3 we included some songs and chants that use children's names. These can be used to end group time and send one to three children off at a time to wash hands, choose a play area, or get ready to go outdoors.

An effective group time agenda that moves from breathing-out to breathing-in activities would proceed as follows:

- call children together through ritual and routine
- move from more active to more passive activities
- keep the group time going as long as most of the children are interested and engaged, and end when many are no longer interested
- have a routine for dismissing to the next activity

At the end of this chapter, I have included the words to several songs and fingerplays. Some work best to call the children to group time or to dismiss them to the next activity. Others start with the children standing end with them sitting. And still others are meant to continue the quieting-down process after the children are seated in the large group. Thanks to all of the teachers who have shared these songs, chants, and fingerplays with me over the years.

Teacher-Led Small-Group Time

Teachers often find they can devote more attention to individual children and get a better sense of what they can do by leading them in small-group activities. Teachers may plan to address specific skills at this time or give children opportunities to practice something they are learning to do. Teachers may plan to implement small groups during play (for preschoolers) and during a Readers and Writers Workshop and Investigation Time as well for kindergartners. In this case, it's important not to interrupt children engaged in productive activities to bring them to a small-group activity. Instead, inviting children to choose when they come to the small group supports what they were doing and validates its importance. Many teachers plan for a fifteen- to twenty-minute part of the daily schedule during which small groups occur. Then, the child's participation is not a choice. The class is divided into two or three groups, each led by a teacher or educational assistant (and perhaps a third engaged in independent work). Kindergarten teachers may find that planning for small-group work both in the morning and the afternoon (in addition to the small-group choices during more active times) will help them address their goals more in depth and gain assessment information about how each child is learning and progressing.

On the framework, there is a box to write plans for teacher-led small groups. (As for large-group gathering, two models are provided, one for daily and one for weekly plans.) Keeping the purpose of small group clear and establishing time limits will ensure that the children gain from the experience rather than just pass time. If a specific project, such as an experiment or cooking, is involved, the small-group time can last until the project is completed.

If the activity involves working with specific skills, the teacher can be sensitive to how long the children stay interested and actively engaged. It is not necessary to plan a different small-group activity for each day of the week. In fact, most teachers find that if their planned activity is rich enough in opportunities, children will be interested in participating in it

Robin: "We do three, rotating small groups in the morning and three in the afternoon. Sometimes we split the children up by ability levels for reading and math groups."

Rosemary: "We have the same three small groups all week, and the students rotate through them. We usually include a dialogic reading experience, a math or science activity, or game with a parent volunteer and a literacy skills group. We have three-, four- and five-year-olds in our class, so there can be big differences in our goals for the small-group experiences."

multiple times. And you may find it easier to fit in working with all of the children in a small-group activity if you only work with a few each day.

Laurel realized that sometimes she identified a goal that was too specific or provided materials that were too limited. She and her colleagues found that it helped to plan small-group activities that had many possibilities for engaging the children's interest. For example, when she set the goal for children to use scissors to cut on a line, she found that many children could do so very quickly and were ready to move to another activity, while others did not have the control to do more than make random snips on the paper and felt frustrated. As she reflected with her colleagues, Laurel decided that cutting on a line was too specific a goal. She knew that cutting skills are part of hand-eye coordination and that there are many ways for children to demonstrate that goal. Here is an example of Laurel's plan for a week of small-group activities focusing on hand-eye coordination.

Small group	Learning goal	hand-eye coordination, and using tools
	Activity and teacher strategy	Give children choices of lacing beads, lacing cards, cutting and paper, small pegboards and small connecting blocks.

Laurel's plan for small-group activity

In chapter 3, I shared some ideas for effective small-group activities. Here are a few more, with possible learning goals identified as well. All of the ideas I am sharing can be used multiple times with children. They could go on for one week or for more than a week. And you can cycle back and revisit them again in later months as well.

Name Study

This activity requires some preparation on your part but is one you can do with the children many times. Make a name card for each student by printing each one's name on a sentence strip. Try to make sure that the letters are the same size, and cut the strip off right after the last letter of the name (see the photo on the following page). Then, the name cards can be easily lined up and compared to each other. You may want to laminate them so they can be used again and again. Invite the children to do a "name study" with the challenge, "How many ways can you organize these cards to compare them?" You can guide children to organize them in a number of ways:

- by comparing the number of letters in each name (short to long)
- by those that begin or end with the same letters
- by those with the same number of syllables
- by those that have letters that hang down beneath the line
- by those that have more than one of the same letter
- by choosing one letter and finding all of the names that have that letter in them
- any other ways you and the children can think of!

Learning goals could include letter identification, name recognition, awareness of letter sounds, understanding concepts of print, counting, and understanding quantity and measurement.

Photo 6.4

Label the Room

This activity also requires sentence strips (a material I think no teacher should be without!) but is done in collaboration with the children in your small group. Invite each child to choose an object or area in your classroom to label. You write the word on the sentence strip (so that it's readable and the print is consistent). As you do so, talk with the children about the letters you are writing, sounding each one out, discussing how it looks on the page, and so on. Then, a child helps you affix the label (with clear contact paper or packing tape) to the object (shelf, tub, chair, table, etc.). Once each child has labeled one object, go back and look at the labels again, naming them, comparing them, discussing them so they will be remembered for the following small-group activity, Reading the Room. Learning goals could include letter identification, awareness of letter sounds, understanding concepts of print, vocabulary development, and memory.

Reading the Room

Once each child in the classroom has had an opportunity to choose an object to be labeled, change the small-group activity to reading those labels. Many teachers add a prop to make this a fun activity. Children use the prop to look at and point to a label and then read the word out loud. Some props teachers use are

- a pointer
- a magic wand
- big glasses or sunglasses
- a plastic finger (from a costume for a witch, perhaps)
- a pointer with a latex glove filled with flour tied to the end
- a special hat

Learning goals could include the same ones identified for the previous activity.

Measuring the Room

Measure each child's length with a piece of string and cut it to match their height. Then, have them find things in the room that are just as long as their piece of string. They record what they find that matches through drawing, and count how many items they found that match their height. The same can be done by cutting string to the same length as their feet, as their arms, or as the circumference of their heads. Learning goals could include listening, speaking, awareness of counting and quantity, measurement, mathematical problem solving, representing mathematical information, using body coordination, and grasp and control of a writing tool.

Nature Walk and Graph

Take children on a walk outdoors, giving each child a bag in which she can collect sticks, leaves, small stones, feathers, and other items. Then, return to the small-group area and sort and categorize what was found. Count how many of each item was collected. Represent the findings on a graph, and read through the graph with the children. You can complicate the activity by writing a group story that includes sentences telling what each child found: "Marissa found 2 feathers, 1 stick, and 5 leaves." "Jorge found 6 big sticks." Then, the children can practice reading the story. Learning goals could include listening, speaking, vocabulary development, awareness of counting and quantity, sorting and categorizing, representing mathematical information, developing observation and analysis skills, and using body coordination.

Exploring Tastes, Smells, and Textures

Young children love to explore the world with their senses. Setting up a tasting or smelling activity or comparing interesting textures can make for a great small-group activity. Encouraging the children to talk, draw, and write about the experience will add more depth and involvement. And graphing favorite and least favorite tastes, smells, or textures will involve comparison and mathematical thinking as well. Learning goals could include sensory exploration, vocabulary development, counting, and understanding of quantity.

Project Work

Another possibility to consider when planning for small-group activities is the project work you may be doing related to an interest of the children or an upcoming field trip. When you focus your curriculum to study a topic with the children, you will find small groups helpful. You can engage children in discussions about what they know about the topic before you begin the project, writing down their comments and saving them on a chart to refer to later. Then, you can plan activities that ask them to make predictions, conduct experiments, and record the results. At the end of the study, you can revisit the chart from the beginning of the project and discuss what they have learned through their explorations. This is a wonderful way to use small-group work to its fullest potential.

Using the Reflection Framework

The reflection framework or general reflection form can provide a means to analyze the success of your teacher-led large- and small-group times. Here you can note how long the children stayed engaged in the activity. Writing down which particular children had trouble sitting through a story or waiting their turn to stir the cookie batter can guide you to a better plan, both for the group as a whole and for that individual child. You may find that large-group times are more successful when the group is divided into two smaller groups (one led by the head teacher, the other by the assistant). "Divide and conquer" can be a smart strategy for some groups of children. Or you may find that large-group gathering times are very difficult for a child, especially one who is particularly sensitive to having his personal space invaded. The following story comes from my experience with a three-year-old boy:

> Aiden did not like other children sitting too close to him. Our large-group area was not very spacious and required children to sit next to one another to see the pictures in a storybook or observe what the teacher was demonstrating. Aiden often struck out at other children who touched him or brushed against his legs. We offered that he sit on our laps, but that also was not comfortable for him. We tried putting a chair at the back of the group on which he could sit, but he did not like that option either. Finally, we decided that Aiden could do something quietly at a table during large-group time. We gave him the choice of working with puzzles and manipulatives or drawing. This strategy seemed to work for a while as long as we provided a little supervision as group time went on. One day, however, after Aiden got settled at his table, my assistant and I got involved with the rest of the children in the large group and forgot to supervise Aiden. When we paid attention to what he was doing, we found that he had gone to the block area (which was located behind the large-group area) and built a wall of blocks around himself. He sat inside the wall and sang every song that the large group of children sang. He also listened to the story and called out relevant answers to our questions about it. He found a way

to participate in large-group time that gave him the personal space that he needed. From then on, we encouraged him to get his block wall ready before large-group time. Other children seemed to understand his needs and never asked to do the same. Aiden had come up with a viable solution on his own!

As you reflect about your small-group activities, you may realize they are not keeping the children's interest. Or the children may tell you they want to return to the activity from the week before (such as the name study or measuring the room). You may want to mix up the grouping of children in small groups so that they have opportunities to work with and learn from differing sets of their peers.

Here are some examples of ways that preschool teachers Juan and Shawna and kindergarten teachers Lucinda and Carey reflected about their teacher-led activities and changed their approaches either for the whole group or for individual children.

REFLECTIONS: What worked? What didn't? What did you learn about individual children and group interests?

Good cooperative play in many areas this week.

Measurement activities went well—start introducing counting number of nonstandard measurement units (like blocks, etc.).

Large group: Hokey Pokey was hard because so few children know right from left. Need more settling time to calm down before story reading. More dancing? Fingerplays? Quiet games?

Still missing observations on Laila, Michael, Zoe, and Robert.

Juan's reflection comments

As a result, Juan planned different movement activities that did not require knowledge of left and right, including dancing and freeze songs, dancing with scarves, and singing and acting out "Under the Spreading Chestnut Tree." He also introduced the chant "One, Two, What Do We Do?" to help the children transition from standing to sitting.

> REFLECTIONS: What worked? What didn't? What did
> you learn about individual children and group interests?
>
> Journaling is going so much better—children have their favorite word
> collections and are using them as well as sharing them with each other.
>
> We might have to look at more skill-oriented small groups geared to
> some of our math skills. Several of the children are not getting those.
>
> Investigations in science were very popular with the earthworms this week.
>
> Large group needs some revving up—too much time on calendar and not
> enough on community building and stories.
>
> Melissa, Andrew, Sara, and Cole are ready for higher-level readers.

Shawna's reflection comments

Shawna decided to introduce her children to two community-building songs, "The More We Are Together" and "Friends, 1, 2, 3." She lessened the amount of time she spent on the calendar and, instead, added more active math games that required children to create a standing equation of the number of children present and absent. She included several story-reading activities that were active as well, such as Eric Carle's *I Can Do That*.

> REFLECTIONS: What worked? What didn't? What did
> you learn about individual children and group interests?
>
> Children are really exploring ways to measure water at the
> sensory table and using the water wheel too. Blocks could use
> a little change—maybe add cars and trucks?
>
> The marble run was very popular in the manipulatives area—
> maybe do a sign-up list for next week so everyone can get a
> chance.
>
> The leaf sorting in small group did not capture the children's
> interest—they are so interested in animals. These children
> sorted and classified 3 types of leaves: Erik, Yesenia, Diana,
> William, Alex, Juan, Vanessa, and Miriam.

Lucinda's reflection comments

Lucinda followed up on the children's interest in animals by providing animal classification cards and playing Animal Bingo, Go Fish, and Memory games with the children at small-group time.

REFLECTIONS: What worked? What didn't? What did you learn about individual children and group interests?

Readers and Writers Workshop is really flowing smoothly—children are independent and get engaged in activities quickly. Should we add a post office for writing letters to each other at the Writing Center?

Need more books in the class library that children can actually "read"—get out emergent readers and level-one readers.

Small-group math activity needs more focus—seems to turn into play with manipulatives that's more about construction than math.

Suzanna, Harley, Mahela, and Carlos are ready for more challenges in writing—do some small group work with them?

Carey's reflection comments

Carey changed the goal of her small-group activity to patterning for three of the days of the week. She provided the children with lacing beads and pattern blocks. She also gave them colored paper shapes to create patterns in collages. On the other two days, she changed the activity completely to a writing experience that targeted the work for specific children (and included others who wished to participate!).

Conclusion

Planning for child-initiated and adult-led activities in preschool and kindergarten classrooms involves knowing the traits of young children and working with those traits. It also involves knowing your own group of children well. Again, the balance is more heavily weighted on child-initiated activities. But that does not mean that learning is neglected. Rather, it means that teachers intentionally figure out ways to provide inherent structure, weave in learning goals as children make choices, and plan for group activities that are engaging and interesting to the children.

In the next chapter, we will explore ways to build caring, respectful relationships with families.

Transition Songs, Chants, and Fingerplays

Quieting Children Down

One, Two
One, two, what do we do?
Three, four, sit on the floor.
Five, six, our legs are fixed.
Seven, eight, our backs are straight.
Nine, ten, now let's begin!

Wiggles
I wiggle my fingers. I wiggle my toes.
I wiggle my elbows. I wiggle my nose.
I get all my wiggles out of me.
And then I sit quiet as quiet can be.

My Thumbs Go Up
Sing this with words the first time, hum it the second time,
and the third time do hand motions only.
My thumbs go up, up, up.
My thumbs go down, down, down.
My thumbs go out, out, out.
My thumbs go in, in, in.
My thumbs go round and round.

Hello Neighbor
Hello neighbor, what do you say?
It's going to be a happy day.
Greet your neighbor *(shake hands)* and boogie on down.
Give a little bump and turn around.
Hello neighbor, what do you say?
It's going to be a happy day.
Greet your neighbor *(shake hands)* and boogie on down.
Give a little bump and sit on the ground.

Clap, Clap, Clap
Clap, clap, clap your hands.
Stomp, stomp, stomp your feet.
Give yourself a great big hug because you are so neat.
Clap, clap, clap your hands.
Stomp, stomp, stomp your feet.
Give yourself a great big hug and then please have a seat.

Under the Spreading Chestnut Tree
With each verse, eliminate a word and do the action until
you are only doing actions.
Under the spreading chestnut tree,
Under the spreading chestnut tree,
With my doggie on my knee, oh how happy we will be
Under the spreading chestnut tree.

Circle Time (to the tune of "Jingle Bells")
Repeat, whispering the last line.
Tap your toes. Shake your head. Turn yourself around.
We're ready now for circle time so quietly sit down.

Friends
Repeat in American Sign Language.
Friends, friends, 1, 2, 3. All my friends are here with me.
You're my friend. You're my friend. You're my friend. You're my friend.
Friends, friends, 1, 2, 3. All my friends are here with me.

CHAPTER 7

Building Relationships
and Communicating with Families

. . . .

Preschool and kindergarten children do not arrive at the classroom door in
isolation. They come surrounded by the love and concern of their families.
Even families with multiple problems love their children. And like their
children, parents and other family members need to learn to trust their
children's teachers and the program. They want to know that the teachers have their child's best interests at heart. They want to understand that
their child is learning. They want to know she is being accepted for her
uniqueness and supported to develop to her full potential; they want to
feel respected and informed. They look for ways they can contribute to
their child's educational experience and communicate regularly with her
teachers.

Building trust with families, then, is another part of relationship building with children. The frameworks do not include a special box addressing
this family connection. That does not, however, negate or ignore its importance. Most preschool teachers share the first two pages of the framework
with families, and kindergarten teachers share the first three pages. They
post them on a parent bulletin board that is visible as parents drop off and
pick up their children each day. They also post them online or in weekly
newsletters so that family members know what is going on at school.

You can develop other program policies to focus on the families of the
children in your care. Hopefully, many of them are already routine parts
of your program. They contribute to a quality experience for both children
and parents. They include

- getting to know children and their families
- having an open-door policy
- providing regular written communication

- creating opportunities for regular verbal communication
- providing many opportunities for family participation
- scheduling official family-teacher conferences
- creating and communicating clear policies about solving problems

Let's consider each of these family-friendly policies in more depth.

Get to Know Children and Their Families

Many teachers find that they can get to know children and their families better by scheduling home visits and/or introductory classroom visits as the child enters the program. For many preschool children, and for some kindergarten children, leaving home to go to a place with strange adults and children is a daunting experience. Fear of the unknown and worries about separation from loved ones can affect a child's behavior and adjustment to school. When a teacher visits with the child and his family at their home, she can learn more about them, assure them, and begin the process of building a caring and respectful relationship with them. She can use the Individual Child Information Record (see chapter 5) as the focus of the conversation and get acquainted with who lives in the home and what kinds of experiences the child has had. She can invite the child to show her some of his favorite toys or things to do. She can reassure the parents of her kind intentions and her goals for their child. And she can invite them to express their concerns and ask questions about her program.

When doing home visits, many teachers go in pairs to provide support and safety to each other. This is a wise policy. One does not want to feel uncomfortable or unsafe. Making clear the time frame for the visit is important. Communicating with families ahead of time about the time and date of the visit and assuring them that they need not entertain the teacher with food or plan anything special are also important.

In addition, many teachers invite children and their parents to visit the classroom before they begin attending. Most do so in individual appointments so that the child is not overwhelmed by other children. If that's not possible, scheduling small groups of visitors is better than having the whole class visit at once. The visit is brief—perhaps fifteen to twenty minutes—and includes a tour of the classroom, a chance perhaps to place a name card on their cubby, have a photograph taken for the attendance board, meet the class pet, and play a little with a couple of materials set out on tables. These visits can do wonders to ease children's and parents' fears about starting a new program.

Have an Open-Door Policy

Another important policy for preschool and kindergarten teachers is to keep an open door. Let family members know they can drop in any time to see what's going on in the classroom. Welcome siblings and extended family. Even though having younger children in the room may be a hassle, the benefits to establishing a warm relationship with the family should outweigh the potential problems. You can make clear to the adults that if they bring a toddler, they are responsible for his supervision. You can provide some safe materials for that child and have a special place where she can play. For the adults, you may want to provide some comfortable, adult-size chairs to sit on near that area so they can observe what their older child is doing as well as keep an eye on the younger one.

Introduce all visitors to the whole class. Make sure you ask them in what way they would like to be addressed. And celebrate with the child whose family is visiting. Recognize his excitement and joy. Allow him to hug his parents, give them a tour of the classroom, or show them something he is working on. Then, make clear how you are going to continue with your day. Invite the parents to sit and watch quietly or join in a particular activity, providing some spontaneous volunteer help. If the visit becomes too disruptive, let them know in a kind and respectful manner. Ask if they might like to come back another time to assist with a special activity or help with supervision on a field trip or an outdoor experience. Work out something in a positive manner as best you can.

Suzanne: "In my community it can be easier for me to get to know families than for others. I live around the corner from our preschool. So, I see families at the beach, the grocery store, and the post office. Those unexpected outside moments can be helpful as we see each other in our 'real lives.' Beyond that, the ability to acknowledge and make allowances for special circumstances in families goes a long way. Frequent, brief, substantive communication is key."

Provide Regular Written Communication

Newsletters, bulletin boards, displays of the children's work, and documentation boards tell the parents about all of the goings-on at school. Teachers with technological skills are now posting blogs with photos of the children in action. Classroom websites provide a gathering place for information. And e-mail messages can go back and forth between teachers and families.

Photo 7.1

Mary B.: "One way to be reflective about children's interests is through documentation. Documentation shows families what teachers value."

Whatever the style of your written communication, include information about the learning goals you are working on with the children. Post examples of work that they have done, and make the connection to the learning goal. Many parents do not understand that play experiences can involve learning. You can help by showing them a photo of a dramatic play scenario and describing the ways that you see the children learning in that

The image includes handwritten child's text reading "ALICIA", "ORANGE", "APPLE", "EGGS", "RICE M", "COOKIES" and a callout box stating:

Your child is working on

- knowledge of books and print
- writing skills

Photo 7.2

activity. You can do the same with a child's drawing or scribbling sample. You are making the connection for them and helping them understand your curricular approach better.

Some teachers post photos and work samples on bulletin boards in the classroom (as well as online) and always include the learning goals being addressed. To make this an easy task, they create a document with all of their learning goals printed on labels. On the Redleaf website, you can download a template ready for you to print on address labels (Avery 8160 mailing labels or their equivalent). This document includes labels with the learning goals we have been using in this book (see chapter 3). You can also make your own labels using the goals from your state standards or curricular objectives. You can easily affix the labels to the children's work samples or the photos of children in action. To post online, take photos of these displays or download photos to your class blog or website. Be sure to always post examples of children's work that includes a connection to an early learning standard or a curricular goal. In this way you are making learning evident to others who may not see it so clearly and easily as early educators do.

Create Opportunities for Regular Verbal Communication

Regular verbal communication is an essential part of building caring relationships with family members. Teachers are available to greet them at arrival and wish them well at departure. During those exchanges, they may give brief information about how the child is doing. But they arrange for more lengthy conversations by telephone or in person when needed.

Most teachers have found that it is not wise to engage in conversations that evaluate the child's behavior at the end of the day. "Oh, she had a good/bad day, today." Such a broad statement is not really informative and can be misinterpreted by the family. If it was a "bad day," the child may be punished at home in some way. If it was a "good day," neither parent nor child knows what parts of the day went better than others. It's better to give a generally positive report about something specific that happened. Here are some examples:

> *"Joshua worked so hard at cleanup time today. You were my special helper, weren't you, Josh?"*
> *"Sabrina, would you like to show your Mom where we hung your painting on the wall?"*
> *"Thomas really used his words today when he was angry with a friend."*

Notice that for both Joshua and Thomas, encouragement to continue to be a cleanup helper or to use words when angry is being expressed. And for Sabrina, by having her show her mother the painting (and perhaps a couple of labels with learning goals affixed to it), the teacher is connecting creative expression and learning for the parent.

When lengthy conversations are needed because of particular concerns or issues, teachers schedule phone appointments or after-school face-to-face meetings. Often the issue is one that should not be discussed in front of the child. It's important to recognize when there is a need for such conversations and to keep in mind three purposes for the conversation:

1. To build partnership with the family member
2. To work together toward a solution
3. To keep in touch as progress is made or not

Establish a time frame for the discussion. By setting a time limit ("Shall we set up a ten-minute phone call for this evening?" or "Can you stay after for fifteen minutes today?"), you are communicating that the discussion will be focused, to the point, and respectful not only of the parent's busy schedule but also your own. Then, as the conversation progresses, keep track of the time and give the parent fair warning as the end time is approaching. Make clear how you will continue to communicate with each other about this issue. Perhaps e-mail or written notes will be the best follow-up methods.

Provide Many Opportunities for Family Participation

Many family members may be interested in volunteering in the classroom or for special events but are unsure how to make arrangements for that or what their responsibilities are once they arrive. It's important to clearly describe volunteer opportunities in the classroom and those for special family events, such as field trips, dinners, open houses, and so forth. Some moms and dads are naturals with children and will have no problem coming into your classroom and being helpful and engaging with the children. Others will need more guidance. They may need to be assigned to an activity that does not involve working directly with the children, such as preparing materials, organizing a cupboard, or supervising at snacktime. The goal is to provide diverse ways to be involved, so families with many different skills and kinds of availability all have a way to participate.

I began my preschool teaching career as the only professional working in a cooperative nursery school. In this setting, parents enjoyed a lower tuition because they were expected to be my teaching colleagues on a regularly scheduled basis. This was truly a family approach that had many benefits for the children. I learned so much from this experience and will always be grateful to the family members with whom I worked so closely.

We did notice one interesting trend: whenever a parent came to work in the preschool room for the day, their child acted differently. This was true almost all of the time. Some children acted out, demanding more of my attention and doing things they did not do when their mother or father was not present. Other children became more clingy and demanding of their parent, even though they were very comfortable and independent on other days. And some children showed off for the family member, not acting inappropriately but seeking their approval throughout the day. In our debriefing meetings, I always reassured my family assistants that this was a trend we were seeing with all of the children and that they need not be concerned. The child may be feeling excited and nervous about his mom being in the classroom, or he may be feeling like she is invading his territory. Informing parents of the possibility for different behavior on the part of their children before they join in volunteer opportunities will help them feel more comfortable and relaxed as they help with all of the children.

Schedule Official Family-Teacher Conferences

At least twice a year, a formal family-teacher conference should be scheduled to review the child's progress and development in the classroom, share a portfolio or work collection, and identify goals for the child's continued success. This is an important time for both parties to focus their communication about the child. For a true back-and-forth conversation to occur and for samples of the child's growth to be studied and discussed, a conference should be scheduled for at least thirty minutes. Arranging adult-sized chairs and a table and providing refreshments (lemonade and cookies or something simple) can soften the experience.

The discussion begins with inviting parents to share their hopes and dreams for their child as well as any concerns or questions they have. The child's successes and accomplishments then are the major focus of the teacher's discussion. When problems are addressed or concerns raised by the teacher, she does so in a considerate way, offering strategies that she and her colleagues will be implementing to help the child continue to grow and learn. She invites parent input and asks about ways they handle things at home. They make plans together for continued support for the child and for future communication.

Again, a clear time frame is important for conferences. If a half hour is the planned time frame, the teacher respects that commitment and keeps track, letting the parents know when ten minutes are left. In this way, she gives them the opportunity to get any pressing concerns or questions addressed and can conclude the conference in a timely manner. She also protects her time and is ready to go on to the next family meeting or teaching task.

It's important to remember that a conference with a teacher can be a frightening experience for some parents. They may not have fond memories of school or experienced much success in their own educational endeavors. They may have worries they are afraid to raise with a professional educator. They may be defensive or feel they are being judged on their parenting skills. Preschool and kindergarten teachers must work hard to communicate in an open, welcoming style and to recognize the emotional atmosphere that a family-teacher conferences can bring about.

In the community of Greenwich, Connecticut, all of the preschool programs have developed a preschool profile that is shared with family members and then submitted to kindergarten teachers in early May. Here is the story of the implementation of this communication among families and preschool and kindergarten teachers from Kathy Stewart, director at St. Saviour's Church Nursery School:

> One practical success on a district-wide level is the use of the Connecticut Preschool Assessment Framework as the basis of our three- and four-year-old conference form (used in the fall and spring months) and a preschool profile that is submitted to kindergarten teachers in early May. Families are being educated about appropriate learning goals for their children and the sequence of development in each learning goal. And the preschool profile provides kindergarten teachers with valuable information that will assist them in providing ready classrooms for their incoming students. Parents from multiple programs have reported that the format provides them with greater clarity about their children's expected and actual learning, and strategies that are proposed for their progress. This year over four hundred preschool profiles were received in the elementary schools, and feedback about their value is being gathered from the kindergarten teachers currently.

In the next chapter, I will share a report format that can be the basis for formal family-teacher conferences. I will discuss in more detail the integration of curriculum and assessment and ways to organize portfolio documentation that demonstrates what children can do and are learning to do.

Create and Communicate Clear Policies about Solving Problems

Teachers and administrative staff must work closely with family members regarding issues of concern about their child. Parents should be clearly informed about how to raise issues of concern. When they do so, the teachers and administrative staff are ready to listen respectfully to problems brought to them by the parents and to work toward a mutually satisfying solution. At all times, the teachers and administrative staff show respect, cultural sensitivity, and a "win-win" attitude when working toward a solution with families.

As I said earlier, family members may often feel unsure of themselves when raising issues with early educators. They may worry that their parenting style or skills are being evaluated along with their child. And it's important that early educators do not become defensive when approached by families with concerns. Emotions from both sides may run high in such discussions. Being professional and ethical requires a cool head and thoughtful discussion. If at any time this is not possible, the conversation should be ended and resumed at a later time. Bringing in a third party, such as an administrator or another teacher, can sometimes mediate the situation. Agreeing to gather more information and observe the child more closely can sometimes help. Looking at the relationship as an equal one—all adults who care about the child—will help keep the playing field even. Here's an example of a difficult conversation between parents and professionals.

Miguel's mother arranged for a meeting with his preschool teacher, Teresa. "His father and I have something important to talk with you about," she told Teresa on the telephone. The meeting was set for the next afternoon. Teresa talked with her colleague, Sergio, and asked him if he had any idea what the parents might be concerned about. Sergio (the primary Spanish-speaking teacher in the class) told Teresa that he had noticed more harsh words among the Spanish-speaking boys as they built with Legos and blocks lately. He had intervened more than once as Miguel and other boys engaged in tug of wars with the same toys.

Teresa felt nervous as the time of the meeting approached. When Miguel's parents arrived, she welcomed them, encouraged them to sit in the adult-sized chairs she had arranged at a table, and asked them to tell her more about their concerns. Miguel's mother looked down at the hands in her lap. Miguel's father explained that their son was being hit, punched, and kicked on the playground by the other boys. His voice was strong, his fists clenched as he spoke. His English was not perfect, but his message was clear. "This is not acceptable. You must stop this." Teresa said, "I am so sorry. I am not aware of this and promise you that my colleague, Sergio, and I will pay more attention to Miguel when we are outdoors. You are right, this is unacceptable. We do not want any of our children to feel unsafe or be hurt in any way at our preschool." Teresa assured the family that she and her colleague would supervise Miguel's interactions with others more closely both indoors and out. She promised to contact them by phone and send notes home regularly to let them know how things were going. She did so and was able to report that there were far less problems and that she and Sergio were there to intervene when any arose.

Teachers do not have more power than parents, and parents do not have more power than teachers. They work together in a united front for the best for the child. Sometimes taking a stance of explaining rather than defending is helpful. When parents question the amount of play in a classroom or the lack of paper-and-pencil tasks, teachers can explain the value of play and make the connection to learning. If all of the above policies for communication with families have been implemented, such discussions may not arise. You will have set the stage for understanding your curricular approaches and for working as teammates with families.

Conclusion

Building a strong relationship with families strengthens the program itself. Families can be the biggest allies and best advertisers. They can also contribute to the success of the child. If a family is nervous about leaving the child in the classroom, often the child will be nervous as well. If a family is having difficulty communicating with their child's teacher, often the child senses this and may act out in her relationship with the teacher. Making sure that clear communication is ongoing, with a truly welcoming and respectful attitude, will pay off in the long run for the children and the early education program. Teachers and family members are on the same team: they are both on the child's team.

In the next chapter we will explore the integration of curriculum and authentic, observational assessment practices.

CHAPTER 8

Integrating Authentic Assessment and Curriculum

. . . .

The integration of curriculum planning with assessment of children's learning is the key to good teaching. Teachers observe how children respond to and participate in the activities they plan. They note where children show strengths and interests and in what activities they struggle or which ones they avoid. Assessment is ongoing. It is not limited to occasional assessment tasks or one-on-one assessment sessions. Therefore, implementing assessment processes that will help with the planning process is essential.

In the field of early education, *authentic* assessment processes are recommended, ones that are based in the everyday interactions between children and teachers:

> The methods of assessment are appropriate to the developmental status and experiences of young children, and they recognize individual variation in learners and allow children to demonstrate their competence in different ways. Methods appropriate to the classroom assessment of young children, therefore, include results of teachers' observations of children, clinical interviews, collections of children's work samples, and their performance on authentic activities. (NAEYC 2009, 22)

Young children do not test well. On-demand assessments such as tests have variable results and therefore do not provide reliable information. The most reliable data can be collected through teacher observation of children every day in a variety of situations. In this way, teachers can see trends in children's performance and can rule out times when a child was not feeling well or did not give their full attention to a task.

Sarah: "The cycle does not end when the planning is complete but continues as it is implemented (through observations, interactions, and scaffolding), assessed, and incorporated into future plans. It can be very rewarding as the progress and learning of the children becomes evident."

Because observation is ongoing, teachers need to document what they see and hear. They do not write down everything—if they did, they would have time for nothing else. (Later in this chapter I will give some tips on documenting observations in a time-efficient manner.) They do focus on documenting particular observations at times when the task can be accomplished. And focusing observations is part of the process of authentically assessing each child's progress and development. Observations can be focused in several ways:

- by developmental domains and learning goals
- by individual children or groups of children
- by play area or activity

The framework includes a box to identify the focus for observations. If your focus will be on specific children for each staff member each day, that is where that list can be written. If your focus will be on specific classroom areas or activities for each teaching colleague, you will note that in the box. And if your focus will be on a specific developmental learning goal, you will note that in this portion of the framework. Let's look at the observational process with each of the above bullet points in mind.

Focusing Observations on Developmental Domains and Learning Goals

To complete an assessment of a child's progress, teachers need to focus their observations so that they gain information about the *whole* child. Therefore, they pay attention to the developmental domains, including language arts, math, social studies and science, social/emotional development, approaches to learning, and physical development. The framework helps with this process. Because learning goals are identified for child-initiated play activities as well as for adult-led group times, teachers can ensure they address each of the domains. Then, as they facilitate children's play and group participation, they have a focus for their observations and documentation. The connection is made between assessment and curriculum in the planning process.

In Pam's inclusive preschool classroom, she and her assistants often identify a developmental domain on which they will focus for a week or two. Their observations will be exclusively about that area. For example,

Laura: "I have seen teachers successfully use more authentic one-on-one observations of children in their natural play settings and realize that through these observations they gain more information about what children know and the concepts they are learning by interacting with peers, with hands-on materials in centers, and in small and large groups."

one week they may concentrate on the children's growing language skills. Another week, they may focus on fine-motor development. In this way, their assessment of each child's growth and learning is well rounded rather than skewed to only behavior or only motor or cognitive skills. They write this focus on the third page of the framework in the box labeled "Focused Observations."

FOCUSED OBSERVATIONS:

Pay attention to all of the children's use of language as they speak—write down some of their quotes as you converse with them in play or at snacktime.

Pam's observations

FOCUSED OBSERVATIONS:

Pay attention to children's fine-motor skills and make notes about how they

show hand-eye coordination

use tools to cut and write

use self-help skills such as buttoning and zipping

Pam's observations

Of course, if they see something else significant, they jot a note down as well. But they try to keep focused on the identified domain or learning goals. Then, they change them every week or two to make sure they address all of them.

When teachers do not have an identified focus for observations by specific learning goals or domains, they may very well miss some of them. They may find holes in their documentation for each child. They will not find it as easy to keep up with the assessment process and end up with a complete, well-rounded picture of what each child can do.

One way to avoid this problem is to consider what your favorite things to do with the children are. Every teacher has favorite areas or activities. Some of us are more artistic. Some of us are mathematical. Some of us really like to help children develop self-control. If we focus only on the areas that appeal to us, we will lose that picture of the whole child. Instead, we have to force ourselves to think about all areas of development and learning.

Here are two ways to analyze what you tend to focus on when watching children. If you have observations already written down, read through them. As you do so, ask yourself honestly: "What is the primary focus of this observation? Is it behavior and social/emotional development? Is it math or science? Is it language? Is it reading and writing? Is it fine- or gross-motor skills?" With each observation, make a tally mark next to each of these developmental categories. Did you tend to have more observations in one category than in the others?

Here's another way to evaluate yourself. Look over the following list of developmental learning areas. Then, rank order this list placing a number 1 by the area you really think you pay the most attention to (or like the best in your teaching practice), a number 2 by your second choice, and so on. Look over your ranking. More likely than not, you focus your observations much more on your first, second, and third choices and much less on your less favorite ones.

Developmental Learning Areas

___ social/emotional development

___ language development

___ reading and writing development

___ math

___ science

___ social studies

___ approaches to learning

___ fine-motor development

___ gross-motor development

In my conversations with teachers, many will admit that they tend to observe with greater intensity in the social/emotional area. Language is another area teachers of young children tend to focus on. Reading and writing has become a dominant domain in kindergarten classrooms. And all are important for good reason! Young children are learning how to function with groups of other children and adults and often are away from their homes for the first time. Their language development is exploding in ways that are astonishing and exciting to witness. And their understanding of letters, sounds, and the written word is paramount to them learning to read. If we only focus, however, on social/emotional and language arts development, we miss so much else about a child's accomplishments, strengths, and weaknesses. Focusing our observations to make sure we are paying attention to all areas will give us a far more detailed, accurate, and complete picture of each child's unique capabilities.

Identifying Children to Observe

By identifying specific children to observe, teachers ensure that no child is missed. Many teaching teams split up the class list into several small groups for observation purposes. Then each teacher or teaching assistant focuses their eyes and ears more closely on four to five children a day. The workload of observing all the children is shared. Different adults often see different things in the children's behavior and performance.

Some preschool programs assign primary caregivers to children so that one teacher really gets to know each child fully and can be the main contact with the family. If that's the case, the primary caregiver should be the one to observe his or her assigned children. Teaching colleagues who see the child in action, then, report to the child's primary caregiver so that information is shared and observations are noted.

Focusing observations on specific children each day helps teachers get a well-rounded picture of what that child can do and what that child may struggle with. Without focus, the children who have more problems with other children often take center stage. They need adult intervention, which they receive in order to protect other children and help them learn self-control. However, if teachers only focus on those children, so many others will be missed. The picture that will arise about these more needy children will be lopsided toward their negative behavior.

Some children ask for lots of attention—not for negative behavior but for positive interaction with the teacher they know and love. Again, it's easy to focus on these children because they ask for it. The ones who are often missed are the children who don't ask for negative or positive attention. They can easily become invisible unless some intentional action is taken to make sure they are being observed as well.

Sometimes teachers divide up the children in the classroom, and each observes the same group of children over time, perhaps with attention to a specific learning goal each week. You and your colleagues will need to communicate clearly about this aspect of your teaching. Recording it on the framework will give it importance—almost as if you have been given an assignment. The assignments can be given in reflection meetings as you discuss what you saw the children doing and who needs to be observed next.

Here are some examples of how teachers divided the workload for observation and documentation about specific children.

FOCUSED OBSERVATIONS:

Lori: monday—Joseph, Alyssa, mariella, Hayden
Tuesday—Jamie, Lisa, michelle, Bernardo
Wednesday—Alan, Derek, Sean, Chloe
Thursday—Jessie, Alana, Benjamin, Katie

Susan: monday—Jessie, Alana, Benjamin, Katie
Tuesday—Alan, Derek, Sean, Chloe
Wednesday—Jamie, Lisa, michelle, Bernardo
Thursday—Joseph, Alyssa, mariella, Hayden

Lori's and Susan's plan to divide their observations

FOCUSED OBSERVATIONS:

Yesenia—focusing and paying attention

Erik—cutting and counting

Vanessa—writing and drawing

Derek—recognizing names, shapes, and colors

Observation plans focused on particular children

FOCUSED OBSERVATIONS:

Need anecdotes (at small-group time?) about writing and recognition of numerals for

  Mariah, Anthony, Scott, Sharonne, Keith, and Anna

Need anecdotes (large-group time? Readers/Writers Workshop?) about reading comprehension for

  Peter, Celina, Keyonna, Layla, and Max

Observation plans focused on activities and children

Observing the Play Areas of the Classroom

As a teaching team, you and your colleagues may decide to focus on a specific play area of the classroom for the purpose of gaining information about the children in a variety of activities. Again, since learning goals are identified on the plan, the observations documented in the areas will probably relate to those goals. You are actually accomplishing two tasks with these kinds of assignments: documenting observations *and* providing adult supervision during the playtime. Here is a story of how two teachers focused their observations during children's play.

In Glenna's classroom, Glenna and her assistant, Debbie, would discuss how they would facilitate children's play. Some weeks, both of them would "float," as they called it. This meant that they were not assigned to any specific area; rather, they moved around the classroom and helped the children as needed. Were new materials necessary to keep a group interested in the manipulatives area? Did the children in blocks need help making more space between their ever-expanding construction and the block shelves? Did a child need a lap to sit on and read a book in the library? Had the paint spilled at the easel?

In the weeks when Glenna and Debbie both "floated," they were each available to solve various problems, provide support to the children, and, most important, observe the children in action in a variety of activities. They each carried a clipboard with a class list on it, a sticky note pad, and a pen or pencil. That way, they could quickly note what they saw the children do and make a check mark next to the child's name as they documented their observation. The class list helped them remember to observe all the children, even those not asking for direct attention.

One thing they always kept in mind, however, was that they should try to avoid ending up in the same corner of the room. They attempted to distance themselves in such a way that one or the other could see all parts of the classroom. This provided safety and communicated to the children that the adults were ready to help them when problems arose.

Some weeks, only one of them served as "the floater." For example, if they planned an art activity that needed close monitoring or a cooking activity that required attention, one of them was assigned to that, and the other was the floater. This again helped focus observations. If Glenna was leading a small group on shape and color recognition, she could easily note each child's knowledge on a clipboard with a list of the children's names on it. If Debbie was cooking with the children, she could focus her observations on their abilities to follow directions or their fine-motor skills when handling small measuring spoons and eggbeaters.

Another benefit to focusing observations on play areas is learning which areas are favorite ones for individual children. In the second edition of our book *Focused Observations: How to Observe Children for Assessment and Curriculum Planning* (2013), Marlyn James and I include a Preschool Choice Record that provides a format for recording information about the play areas in the classroom. You will find a photocopy-ready form in appendix C and at www.redleafpress.org, as well as a format for use in a kindergarten classroom to include the areas for a Readers and Writers Workshop.

Teachers can use this record to note the areas where a child tends to spend more time and develop more engagement. Recording the initials of a child's name when he chooses that area and stays there for fifteen to twenty minutes or longer will show the trends in his choices. Why is this informative or important? There are three possible reasons:

1. Children often choose to do things at which they are competent, that is, demonstrating a strength in their development.
2. Children sometimes choose to do something that they are just learning to do and want to practice.
3. Children avoid areas or activities in which they are not competent, that is, demonstrating a weakness in their development.

This record could also include a note about times that you provided scaffolding or assistance to a child as he tried to do something in a play area. In this way, you will be observing and recording the things that a child can do with your assistance.

Writing Down Your Observations

Teachers are constantly observing the children in their classrooms. However, they don't always write down or document what they observe, which must become a habit in order to overcome that little problem most of us have—poor memory!

When I am in a classroom, I feel like my brain is a video camera in constant action. Even though I'm not writing down everything I see, I am taking it in mentally. And it often comes back to visit me later in the day, that night, or even in my dreams. Sometimes, my video-camera brain takes in so much information that I feel overwhelmed. Many teachers talk about observing their children but not being sure exactly what they should be

Preschool Choice Record

(may be used to tally one child's choices or a group of children's choices)

Child(ren): _____ Date: _____

Art	Blocks	Dramatic Play
Manipulatives	Science/Math	Music/Movement
Library	Sensory Table	Writing Center

Preschool Choice Record form

Kindergarten Choice Record

(may be used to tally one child's choices or a group of children's choices)

Child(ren): _____ Date: _____

Listening Center	Dramatic Play	Journaling Center	Alphabet Center	Flannel Board or Pocket Charts
Class Library	Writing Center	Blocks	Math Activity	Sensory Table
Art	Manipulatives	Science Exploration	Informational Reading	Math and Science Journaling

Kindergarten Choice Record form

looking for. They see so much that they must filter through their recollections to figure out what was important and plan responses and interventions with particular children.

I do not recommend that you write observations on the frameworks. There isn't room, especially when including quotes from the child and other details. The space there is provided to focus your observations, not to document them. Many teachers prefer to have clipboards placed around the classroom with notepaper or sticky pads and pens. As they interact with children at play, they can easily access the clipboard and write a brief note about what the children are doing or saying. They may only write a couple of words, such as "Jeremy, block area." This will serve as a memory jogger when they review their notes at the end of the day. Then they can fill out the documentation with more details about Jeremy's symmetrical construction and identification of shapes as he built.

Jeremy—Block Area 11/14

Today, Jeremy spent more than twenty minutes in the block area working with Jose and Theodore. Together, they built a structure with matching symmetrical towers. Jeremy carefully placed blocks so that they did not fall. He noted when something did not match—"Hey, we need another round one up here," pointing to a cylinder. "And another triangle there."

Details added to a memory jogger

Photographs can become memory joggers as well. Having a digital camera handy is helpful for documenting what the children are doing. Then at the end of the day (or week) you can download the photos, review them, and write a more detailed description of what the children were doing.

Photo 8.1

Julianna 1/17/12

Today, Julianna chose to work with the magnetic letters. She spent a long time at a table by herself, arranging them from left to right. When she finished, she called me over and said, "Look, miss Brooke. I put all the colors together." I asked her if she could tell me the names of the colors, and she said, "Green, yellow, pink, red, blue. And these letters are falling down." (We had just read the book *Chicka Chicka Boom Boom.*)

Details added to a photograph

A child's work samples can also serve as memory joggers. Preschool and kindergarten children produce drawings, writing samples, and art creations, such as paintings or collages. You may plan for a math activity that involves the children recording what they have done with manipulatives as they count and work with quantities. In the kindergarten example in the photo on the following page from a small-group experience, the children were asked to build with small colored blocks. The teacher photographed their constructions. Then, they talked with her and described the positions of the blocks. And finally, they were asked to draw their block construc-

Photo 8.2. Details added to a work sample

tion. All of this was saved as documentation that could then be accompanied by an anecdotal or observational note describing what each child did and said.

You may find there are some days when the playtime in your classroom is going so smoothly and children are so deeply involved in productive play that you do not need to be as facilitative as usual. That's a wonderful signal that you should be writing down what you are observing the children doing and saying. You will always be ready to step back into the action with the children if needed, but you are taking advantage of a momentary lull and making good use of your time. Here's an example of an observation that a teacher was able to document as the children played.

> Lucia, Marco, and Robert play "camping." 4/05
>
> Lucia, Marco, and Robert were playing in the kitchen. Lucia said, "Hey, let's go camping!" The boys agreed and got busy packing up some dishes in a bag. Robert said, "We have to make a campfire." Lucia said, "And a tent." I offered them a blanket to put over the table and suggested they get long blocks for their "fire." "What are you cooking on the fire?" I asked. Marco said, "Marshmallows." Robert said, "Yeah, with chocolate. And graham crackers." Lucia poured "hot chocolate" into cups, and the three sat around the campfire, then climbed into the tent and went to sleep. Their play went on for thirty-five minutes.

Observation note about children at play

Notice that she did interact with the children as she observed, and included that information in her documentation. There is nothing wrong with talking with children, asking them questions, and including that as you write for assessment purposes. You can also document the ways you provide scaffolding and assistance to children, as in the following anecdotal record.

> Suzannah   2/24/12
>
> Suzannah chose to work on a floor puzzle with forty-five pieces. She dumped the pieces out of the box and spread them on the floor. I saw her pick up various pieces and look at them, then put them back down. She did not find any that fit together. I suggested that she look at the picture on the box and notice what goes on the bottom of the puzzle. Together, we found some pieces that had the blue of the water and the flat bottom. Suzannah found several that fit together and finished the bottom. Then, I showed her how to find the corner pieces. Together, we placed those and looked for side and top pieces with a flat side. Between us, and with some help from two other friends, we completed the puzzle in about twenty minutes. All of us cheered!

Observation note that includes teacher scaffolding and assistance

Other Times of the Day to Focus Observations

Circle time, snacktime, and outdoor play are also ripe with opportunities for teaching colleagues to focus their observations on different aspects of the activity involved. At circle time, if one colleague is reading a story, the other can note which children are following along with the print, which are comprehending the story and making predictions, and which don't seem to have a clue. At snacktime, sitting at different tables allows each teacher to interact with different children. Vocabulary can easily be noted as friendly conversation occurs among the children and adults. Outdoors, one team member can be posted near the highest climbing structure to provide safety. The other can float around to other areas of the playground and keep an eye on safety concerns elsewhere. The two teachers' observations will be different in focus then. The one by the climber will probably see more evidence of risk taking (or lack of risk taking) and problem solving as the children wait in line to climb the slide. The floater may see more gross-motor skills, such as running and jumping, and learn more about the children's interests in nature and weather. (Again, don't forget to take that clipboard, sticky note pad, and pen outdoors with you!)

Antonio 5/3/12

Today, outdoors, Antonio came up with a great idea for taking turns on the merry-go-round. "I know," he told the five children who were trying to fit into the four spots. "I'll be the counter—and I'll count to ten—and when I say 'Blast off,' someone has to get off, and it's my turn to get on." The other children agreed and took turns this way for quite awhile.

Observation note from outdoors

Are you noticing that the observation notes above are factual descriptions of what the child did and/or what the child said? They are not evaluative or judgmental. Instead, the teacher continually edits herself as she writes, making sure that the words only describe the child's actions or quote the child's utterances. There is no place for opinion or interpretation in this part of the assessment process. This is the collection of evidence or documentation that will be used later to make judgments and evaluations in summarizing reports and family-teacher conferences.

Using a method that works for you is most important in getting observations written down. Time is always a factor for teachers of preschool and kindergarten children. There are many demands for a teacher's attention and help. Finding time-efficient ways to gather complete documentation to assess each child's progress can be challenging. Again, in *Focused Observations* (Gronlund and James 2013) you will find many strategies for documenting observations for assessment purposes.

Lauren: "The 'Take Five' concept is an idea that helps teachers find time to write on the reflection page throughout the week."

One time to consider for documentation is at the end of the day, in reflection after the children have left. I call it "Take Five" time: take five minutes to sit with your teaching team and discuss the day. What did you see the children do or hear them say? Have a class list handy so that you are thinking of all the children (but not necessarily writing about all of them—you have only five minutes!). You are trying not to focus only on the most demanding child or the one who had the hardest day. Instead, you're trying to pay attention to even the most quiet, reserved ones. As a team you can decide which member will record each observation you have discussed. Perhaps in five minutes, you will have discussed three observations or revisited three memory joggers (brief notes, photos, or work samples) that need more details.

Here's an example of such a discussion in action and the resulting documentation.

Amber, Tasha, and Perry gathered at the end of their day with their twenty-five kindergartners. Amber said, "Let's not clean the room quite yet. Let's do our 'Take Five.' Tasha, the assistant teacher, and Perry, the student teacher, joined her at a table. Amber asked, "What happened today that we don't want to forget? That we need to document? Here's the class list. Let's think back." Perry spoke up. "You know, today as you read the story, Amber, Helen was shouting out predictions that were right on. She was really comprehending what was going on." "Good, Perry, would you please write that down?" Tasha said, "Amber, didn't you tell me that Ryan made something about math with you today?" "Oh, yes, that was great. He told me he wants to get better at math and wrote out all of these equations. I saved the paper somewhere. Here it is. I'll write that observation down," Amber said. "How about something about the making of the zoo in the block area? Wasn't there someone over there that we haven't been getting much documentation on?" "Yes, you're right," Tasha replied. "It's Theodore. I'll write how he made a giraffe cage. I took a photo of it. He worked for a long time on that and worked cooperatively with Clayton, too. I can probably write one up for Clayton as well." The three teachers wrote their documentation, filed it, and went on to do their daily cleanup of the room. As a result of their daily Take Five sessions, they had some sort of documentation written about each child by the end of the week (in addition to documentation they had written during the day).

Helen   1/25/12

In large group, we read the book *Mrs. Wishy Washy*. Helen listened and responded to questions as I asked, "What do you think will happen next?" Helen said, "She's going to have to give them all a bath. They are so dirty!" When we got to the part where this happened, Helen called out, "See, I told you. Now they'll be all clean, and then I bet they'll want to jump in the mud again!"

Observation note resulting from a Take 5 discussion

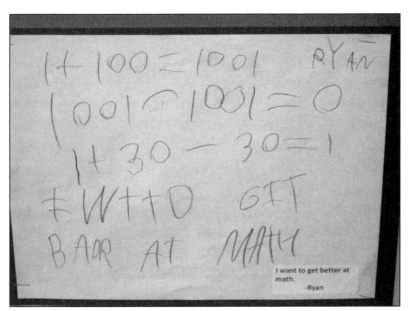

Photo 8.3

Ryan   1/25/12

We had asked the children to think about things they want to get better at. Ryan went to the writing table and worked for over twenty minutes writing equations with numbers and wrote the sentence, "I want to get better at math." See photo above.

Another observation note resulting from a Take 5 discussion

Theodore   1/25/12

In response to our provocation to build a zoo in the block area, Theodore and Clayton worked together to build a "giraffe cage." They talked through what they would need. Theodore said, "We gotta build some trees 'cause giraffes eat leaves." He found some long blocks and stacked them with support. "What can be the leaves?" he asked out loud. He found two paper plates and placed them at the top. Together, the boys found blocks to enclose the area. They worked for approximately twenty minutes.

One of two observation notes resulting from a Take 5 discussion

Photo 8.4

Clayton   1/25/12

In response to our provocation to build a zoo in the block area, Theodore and Clayton worked together to build a "giraffe cage." They talked through what they would need. Theodore built the trees so the giraffes could eat the leaves. Clayton noticed that the giraffe figure couldn't reach high enough. "Here, we gotta put the giraffe on some blocks so he can reach the top of the tree. The little giraffe can reach his—but not the big one." He built a stack of blocks and placed the giraffe on top. Together, the boys found blocks to enclose the area. They worked for approximately twenty minutes.

One of two observation notes resulting from a Take 5 discussion

What Do You Do with Your Documentation?

Documenting observations gives teachers evidence to support assessment conclusions and helps them remember what they are seeing children do. Teachers can refer back to their documentation to answer questions such as:

- How is this child showing what he can do? What is he accomplishing?
- Where have we seen particular progress?
- What are some of the areas or skills that he is working on and need further support?

It is helpful to organize the documentation for each child first. You can do this as you collect it for each child to ensure you are capturing evidence that demonstrates the child's competence in all domains. One way to do this is to adopt a portfolio collection process that includes written observations, work samples, and photographs.

In our book *Focused Portfolios: A Complete Assessment for the Young Child* (2001), Bev Engel and I show how to organize focused observations of children's growth and tie those observations to developmental milestones. Since its introduction, the format for these portfolios has been adopted and adapted by many different early childhood programs. On the next page, you see the latest adaptation, loosely built on the one now used by programs in New Mexico. I invite you to try out this portfolio collection form and to make adaptations of your own so that the process works for you. (You will find this photocopy-ready form in appendix C and online at www.redleafpress.org.)

You can see that this portfolio collection form has been designed to connect a teacher's observations with learning goals, standards, or milestones. The assumption is that a teacher records anecdotes of children in action, accompanied by photos and/or work samples when appropriate. She writes those notes on sticky notes, index cards, or mailing labels and then affixes them right to the portfolio collection form, or she writes on the portfolio collection form itself. (Some teachers rewrite the notes on the forms or type them there. This requires extra time and effort and is not recommended. Instead, try to write neatly the first time to avoid that extra task!)

Portfolio Collection Form

Child's Name: _____ Date: _____ Observer: _____

Domains(s): _____

Learning goal(s) demonstrated in this documentation: _____

_____

_____

Check off whatever applies to the context of this observation:

☐ child-initiated activity   ☐ done independently   ☐ time spent (1 to 5 minutes)

☐ teacher-initiated activity   ☐ done with adult guidance   ☐ time spent (5 to 15 minutes)

☐ new task for this child   ☐ done with peer(s)   ☐ time spent (more than 15 minutes)

☐ familiar task for this child

Anecdotal note: Describe what you saw the child do and/or heard the child say (attach a photo or work sample if appropriate).

The portfolio collection form includes the child's and observer's names and the date of the observation. A photograph of the child in action, or a work sample that the child produced, can accompany the anecdote. Or the anecdote can stand alone as the documentation of the child's performance. Additional information is then included on the portfolio collection form— information that identifies exactly what developmental or learning information the teacher sees as significant in this observation. For example, an anecdote that includes direct quotes from the child may serve as evidence of the child's growing language abilities. The teacher then notes right on the portfolio collection form what specific language skills the child has that this observation demonstrates. She also notes what additional learning goals, standards, or milestones are embedded in the observation. Children rarely demonstrate only one skill or goal at a time. Instead, they integrate and apply what they know and can do to the situation at hand. It's much more useful to gather documentation that is rich in information about the child rather than limited to only one goal or milestone. On the next page, you can see that Akila demonstrated many learning goals as she worked with playdough.

A program can use any kind of observational assessment tool and still document observations on this portfolio collection form. The learning goals or standards that the teacher refers to both in her plans and on her portfolio collection forms do not come out of thin air. Instead, she refers to her state's early learning or kindergarten standards (or the national Common Core Standards for Kindergarten). A source such as this for goal-setting and assessment purposes can easily be integrated into the planning and reflection frameworks and used on the portfolio collection form as well. Or a teacher may turn to familiar developmental checklists, such as the Early Learning Scale, the Creative Curriculum Developmental Continuum, the High/Scope Child Observation Record, or the Work Sampling System. These are well recognized and reflect the best thinking about child development from the early childhood education field.

Whether or not you use the portfolio collection form in this book, you will want to organize the documentation of observations you have completed for each child and move into the reflection and evaluation process to assess how each child is growing and learning. This is the collection of evidence you will use to make judgments and evaluations in summarizing reports. And this evidence will be shown to family members at the family-teacher conference. In fact, families often want to keep a child's portfolio,

Portfolio Collection Form

Child's Name: __Akila__   Date: __10/14/11__ Observer: __Margaret__

Domains(s): __fine-motor development, language, literacy, social/emotional__

Learning goal(s) demonstrated in this documentation: __hand-eye coordination, using tools, speaking, letter__

__identification, playing cooperatively with other children__

Check off whatever applies to the context of this observation:

☒ child-initiated activity ☒ done independently ☐ time spent (1 to 5 minutes)

☐ teacher-initiated activity ☐ done with adult guidance ☒ time spent (5 to 15 minutes)

☐ new task for this child ☒ done with peer(s)

☒ familiar task for this child ☐ time spent (more than 15 minutes)

Anecdotal note: Describe what you saw the child do and/or heard the child say (attach a photo or work sample if appropriate).

Akila chose to work at the playdough table today. She started rolling the playdough with the roller, cutting and snipping at it with scissors, and pressing it with her hands. Tamara joined her, and the two talked together as they rolled and cut. Akila asked, "Where are the alphabet cookie cutters?" I helped her get them down from the shelf, and she said, "Here, Tamara. You find your letters and I'll find mine." Together, the two girls found several of the letters of their names and pressed them into the dough to make the letter shapes.

Akila's portfolio collection form

as it gives them such rich, informative documentation of what their child is doing at school. Teachers give them to parents at the end of the child's year in the program and report that it is a highly valued gift.

I recommend that you build a collection of evidence for each child that includes a minimum of the following:

- You may want to have one portfolio collection form with a primary observation related to each of the domains. If you use the list I have been using in this book, that would be eight forms (language arts, math, science, social studies, social/emotional, approaches to learning, fine- and gross-motor development).
- Or you may want to choose several observations (say a minimum of four or five) that document multiple domains and learning goals so that all domains are addressed.
- It's not necessary to have a photograph or work sample with every portfolio collection form, but it is necessary to have a factual description of what the child did and or said. Parents do love photos, so including some enhances the portfolio. And children do produce interesting and informative work samples. So think about where you might include those as well.

Using Your Documentation for Reflection and Reporting to Families

You will refer to your observational notes and portfolio collection forms as you engage in the reflection process. When reflection is included with the framework, teachers are able to review observations and coordinate their planning, continually reevaluating how their curricular activities are contributing to each child's growth and development. All of this information is important to the assessment process. Teachers will see the connections between their room arrangement and activity planning and the progress the children make. The portfolios will be the evidence of that progress.

Below are two teachers' reflections from a week that include ones about individual children. On the following pages you will find the two portfolio pieces they wrote that documented those reflections and observations.

> REFLECTIONS: What worked? What didn't? What did
> you learn about individual children and group interests?
>
> Children rearranged dramatic play to no longer be a hospital—
> they boxed up the medical equipment themselves and went back to
> playing house and family!
>
> Children are still very interested in insects and spiders. Rubber
> worms and potting soil were a hit! Our insect collection is growing,
> but we need more magnifying glasses for outdoor bug hunts. At
> group time, children ask to read *Hungry Caterpillar* and *Grouchy
> Ladybug* over and over again—and they can sit through two
> readings of each.
>
> Rose Marie sitting with Jesse at the Writing Center helped.
> Other children praised Jesse and wrote him letters on stationery.
>
> Johanna counted to 100 on the 100's chart.

Ann's and Rose Marie's reflections and plans

In chapter 5, I introduced you to the Individual Child Information Record as a way of recording information about each child and updating that information as you get to know her better. Along with the portfolio documentation, the Individual Child Information Record can guide the writing of a summary report about the child's progress and the next steps planned to stimulate and enhance this child's development. It can then be included in the conference presentation to the family. Revisiting the Individual Child Information Record before each family-teacher conference allows the teacher to review the family's comments at the beginning of the year and compare what she has learned about the child over several months in the classroom. She can corroborate what the parents told her and add information.

Then, as she prepares to conference with families, she uses the portfolio items and the information record to write a report that summarizes the child's capabilities, strengths, and weaknesses or challenges. The teacher doesn't emphasize the negative when reporting to parents. Instead, she will find it far more effective to emphasize the positive and set goals with parents for helping the child overcome challenges and make progress in areas that are more difficult for him. Most parents come to family-teacher conferences with one major question: "How is my child doing?" They often add "in relation to the other kids." As teachers, we know that comparing children to one another is not always helpful. However, because we

Portfolio Collection Form

Child's Name: _Jesse_   Date: _4/30/11_   Observer: _Ann and Rose Marie_

Domains(s): _fine-motor development and literacy_

Learning goal(s) demonstrated in this documentation: _using tools to write, understanding conventions of print, letter identification_

_____

Check off whatever applies to the context of this observation:

☐ child-initiated activity   ☐ done independently   ☐ time spent (1 to 5 minutes)

☒ teacher-initiated activity   ☒ done with adult guidance   ☒ time spent (5 to 15 minutes)

☒ new task for this child   ☐ done with peer(s)

☐ familiar task for this child   ☐ time spent (more than 15 minutes)

Anecdotal note: Describe what you saw the child do and/or heard the child say (attach a photo or work sample if appropriate).

Rose Marie invited Jesse to come to the Writing Center with her on two separate days this week. He easily found his name card. Rose Marie helped him trace the letters on his card both with his finger and with a fat pencil. Initially he held the pencil in a fist grasp. Rose Marie corrected his grasp, and his writing became much more readable. He smiled broadly and showed everyone in the room how he had written his name!

Portfolio documentation about Jesse

Portfolio Collection Form

Child's Name: _Johanna_   Date: _4/30/11_ Observer: _Rose Marie_

Domains(s): _math_

Learning goal(s) demonstrated in this documentation: _understanding counting and quantity_

_____

_____

Check off whatever applies to the context of this observation:

☐ child-initiated activity   ☒ done independently   ☐ time spent (1 to 5 minutes)

☒ teacher-initiated activity   ☐ done with adult guidance   ☐ time spent (5 to 15 minutes)

☒ new task for this child   ☐ done with peer(s)   ☒ time spent (more than 15 minutes)

☐ familiar task for this child

Anecdotal note: Describe what you saw the child do and/or heard the child say (attach a photo or work sample if appropriate).

A challenge was offered to the children this week: "How many bugs (rubber) can you count?" Johanna got out the 100's poster board chart and carefully placed one bug on each number, counting aloud until she had reached 100. Her naming of the numbers was correct. We have never heard her count this high before.

Portfolio documentation about Johanna

are using well-established learning goals or standards as the basis for our curriculum and assessment process, we can say, "Let me tell you how he is doing related to those reasonable expectations. I have documentation for you that shows what he's good at, and what we're working on further with him." Then, you can invite parents to review the portfolio pieces you have collected, read through the Individual Child Information Record, and contribute their ideas for setting goals and helping their child progress further.

Most parents want a written report of some sort to take home. They need something to refer to and revisit so they can remember the teacher's key points and understand what their child is accomplishing. Rather than give report cards with grades, plusses or minuses, or checklists of some sort, effective early educators have learned that a family-teacher summary report is more helpful. A narrative description by domain helps parents move away from comparing their child to others and toward seeing their child's accomplishments more clearly and celebrating them. On the following pages is a model you could use with whatever learning goals, standards, or milestones that you are using in your program. Feel free to adapt this to your needs so that you can communicate effectively with the families in your program.

What does a teacher write on this report? She writes a brief description, referring specifically to the learning goals or standards she has documented in her observations. She basically categorizes those goals into the ones the child has clearly accomplished, the ones he has shown progress in, and the ones the teachers are still working on with him. The latter category is where some weaknesses or challenges might show up. But notice how positively these are communicated to families in this format. The emphasis is not on the child's need to work on these goals—it is on the teachers' plans to support him in his accomplishment of them. And here is a wonderful opportunity to invite parent's ideas about how they can work with him at home as well. Now, the true partnership between teachers and family members shines. An example of a completed Family-Teacher Summary Report for Alberto is included for your review on the following pages.

When programs combine the report with a portfolio collection, they keep copies of the report in their files and send the original report and the portfolio home with the family. In this way, communication about the child's progress is shared in a meaningful way with parents.

Laura: "The family summary report form has been a great success. Teachers have reported that families love the form. It shows the children's strengths and has a positive tone for what the child is doing right."

Family-Teacher Summary Report

Child's Name: _____ Date: _____

Teacher: _____ Program: _____

DOMAIN: _____

Growth and accomplishments	
We will continue to work on	

DOMAIN: _____

Growth and accomplishments	
We will continue to work on	

DOMAIN: _____

Growth and accomplishments	
We will continue to work on	

DOMAIN:

Growth and accomplishments	
We will continue to work on	

DOMAIN:

Growth and accomplishments	
We will continue to work on	

DOMAIN:

Growth and accomplishments	
We will continue to work on	

DOMAIN:

Growth and accomplishments	
We will continue to work on	

Family-Teacher Summary Report

Child's Name: _Alberto_   Date: _November 15, 2011_

Teacher: _Miss Hernandez and Mrs. Blythe_   Program: _Children's Garden Pre-K_

DOMAIN: _language and literacy_

Growth and accomplishments	Alberto talks with us and the other children in both English and Spanish. He expresses his needs, listens to others, and follows two-step directions. He's beginning to recognize his name and shows interest in books. See his writing sample in his portfolio.
We will continue to work on	helping Alberto become more interested in writing and figuring out sounds of letters and rhyming words.

DOMAIN: _math_

Growth and accomplishments	Alberto counts up to five objects at a time, pointing to each one. He builds with blocks and identifies shapes as he does so. See his math portfolio sample.
We will continue to work on	counting to ten, working with measurement, and solving mathematical problems.

DOMAIN: _science_

Growth and accomplishments	Alberto is very interested in magnifying glasses and balance scales. He often chooses to play at the sensory table—especially when we have water with tubes and water wheels. He makes some observations as we talk with him as he plays. See his science portfolio sample.
We will continue to work on	describing and predicting as he works with different materials and uses scientific tools.

Family-Teacher Summary Report for Alberto

DOMAIN: *social studies*

Growth and accomplishments	Alberto has become a helpful member of our class community. He often volunteers for chores or to help others at cleanup time. He acts out roles in dramatic play, often being a police officer or firefighter.
We will continue to work on	supporting Alberto's caring for others and our class community.

DOMAIN: *social/emotional*

Growth and accomplishments	Alberto is learning to express his feelings in words, to get along with other children in play, and to wait his turn as we go through our daily routines.
We will continue to work on	helping Alberto to resolve conflicts with other children and to express his feelings appropriately.

DOMAIN: *approaches to learning*

Growth and accomplishments	Alberto can really focus his attention when he's interested in something. He'll stay at the sensory table or block area the whole playtime, productively engaged. He shows much curiosity and interest in new things.
We will continue to work on	finding more things that interest Alberto and helping him develop self-regulation as he works and plays.

DOMAIN: *gross- and fine-motor development*

Growth and accomplishments	Alberto runs and jumps and climbs outdoors with ease, balance, and coordination. He is working on a correct pencil grasp and learning to cut with scissors.
We will continue to work on	pencil grasp and use of scissors.

Second page, Family-Teacher Summary Report for Alberto

Conclusion

Making observation and documentation a regular part of every classroom day and identifying who on the teaching team will focus their observations on which children are essential steps to making observational assessments work well. Focusing observations, writing factual and descriptive anecdotes, and using some reference to developmental standards will fit beautifully with the planning and reflection process for a truly individualized curriculum.

In the next and final chapter, I will revisit the planning/observation/individualization cycle and look at the results when any of the essential elements are missing.

CHAPTER 9

Revisiting the Planning/Observation/ Individualization Cycle

Throughout this book we have considered an all-inclusive, holistic view of curriculum for preschool and kindergarten children. Steps have been presented in a curricular process that revolves around age-appropriate learning goals and that includes six elements for effective implementation. Here's the graphic showing all of the aspects we have been discussing in depth in the previous chapters.

Elements of the Curriculum Process

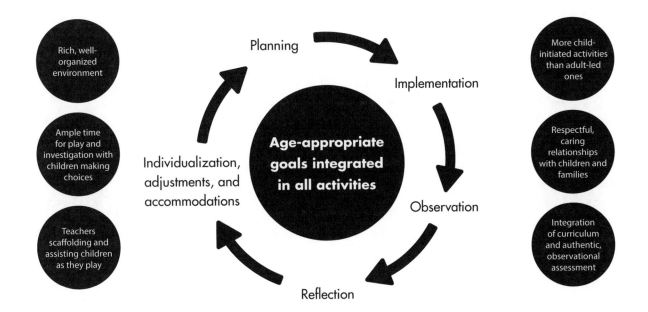

Suzanne: "No one piece of the process can be successful on its own. They all rely on each other. Without careful observation and reflection on what we've seen, we'd be unable to plan effectively. Without assessing within the cycle, we would be unable to move forward with clear and logical direction."

Lauren: "When looking at the six elements of curriculum, I found that each of these needs to be present in order to have a successful preschool or kindergarten program. I also found that if one of these elements is not present, it will be very difficult to sustain the other five. For example, if you do not give children ample time for play, you will be very limited in how you can scaffold and assist them. Also, if your day is made up of mostly adult-led activities, you will have a more difficult time building caring relationships with the children. All of these elements are connected to one another. Therefore, a teacher must consider one just as important as the next."

As I have stated, all of the steps and elements in the process work together to create effective practices for teaching three- to six-year-olds. How does a teacher know when she is successfully implementing this curriculum process? When an element is missing, what will she see? In this chapter we will look at the signs of successful implementation as well as the signs that an element might be missing or need more attention.

Successful Implementation

First, let's consider what successful implementation looks like. Preschool and kindergarten classrooms should be happy places. Children want to be there. They look forward to going to school and are excited to see what their teachers have planned for them. After a short time, they feel comfortable separating from their family members and transitioning to the classroom. They know the routines and trust the consistency of the daily schedule. They also trust their teachers to provide an atmosphere of safety and support. They relish learning because so many opportunities are given to them to figure things out for themselves, learn in playful ways, and be challenged at the level that is just right for each of them.

Successful implementation means an active, busy classroom—and yes, a noisy one. Administrators and parents should notice a hum of activity with lots of conversation among children and between children and their teachers. But once that hum becomes a roar, the teacher steps in with a reminder to the children (perhaps involving a song or a special clapping game) to quiet their voices down again. And in a successful classroom, the children easily do so.

Successful implementation also focuses on long-term learning. The preschool and kindergarten years are times for children to learn foundational skills that will serve them throughout the rest of their lives. So, teachers do focus on some specific skills, such as alphabet recognition and counting, but they also spend much time working with children on learning to be learners. They help them develop focus and attention, work cooperatively with others, express themselves, and try new activities. They help them learn what being a citizen in a democracy involves—contributing to the classroom by being responsible and considerate of others. The following quote reminds us of the importance of nourishing a love of learning in children. It addresses primary-grade students but also can be applied to preschool and kindergarten children:

> One of the most important goals for this age group is developing an enthusiasm for learning. During the primary grades, it is essential for children to learn to read, but it is equally important for them to develop the *desire* to read. Similarly, it is as important for children to be *motivated* to solve mathematics problems as it is for them to learn how to add and subtract or measure with a ruler. Teachers build children's motivation when they show they care about each child's needs and interests, demonstrate genuine enthusiasm for the subject at hand, and capitalize on teachable moments within the planned curriculum. (Copple and Bredekamp 2009, 257–58)

As time goes on, a teacher will know that her curriculum is working if she sees the following:

- Children are resolving disagreements and conflicts easily with agreement from all parties involved. Sometimes they need adult help and may ask for it (a sign of maturity on their part). Then, they accept the adult guidance and move on to continue their involvement with each other.
- Children are making positive choices about what to do with their time at play areas, in more open-ended activities like at a Readers and Writers Workshop, and outdoors.
- Children are engaging in activities for increasing periods of time.
- Children are applying their growing skills in different activities. For example, in a small-group activity, a teacher may have worked on adding quantities together with objects. She then sees children playing at adding quantities together as they work with manipulatives or act out grocery shopping.
- Children are settling into adult-led activities because they have had plenty of opportunities to engage in breathing-out activities. The balance of child-initiated and adult-led ones is more heavily in favor of the former.
- Children are saying, "I love school!"

When Elements Are Missing

Teachers will notice that children's behavior is different when the elements previously identified are missing or need more attention. They will find themselves pulled in different directions, having to intervene more frequently and using their time with the children differently. Let's look at what can result when each of the six elements are not given their due.

Rich, Well-Organized Environment

When the classroom environment is not well organized and rich with possibilities, teachers may see the following:

- Children are running because there are large, open areas rather than well-defined ones with shelves and tables breaking up the running paths.
- Children are wandering because they are not sure of the purposes for areas or there are not enough interesting things for them to do.
- Children are taking poor care of materials and not putting them away neatly because there is no clear organization that includes labeling of shelves and tubs.
- Children are arguing over toys, games, and materials because there are not enough for several children to play with or explore.
- Children are saying, "I'm bored," or asking the teacher, "What can I do now?"
- Children are doing the same things again and again, engaging in simple, repetitive actions because no new materials or ideas have been provided.

Ample Time for Play and Investigation with Children Making Choices

When there is not an ample amount of time for play and investigation, teachers may see the following:

- Children are wandering because they are still figuring out where to play or are worried that they will be interrupted shortly and do not think it is worth their time to get deeply involved.

Rich, well-organized environment

Ample time for play and investigation with children making choices

- Children are competing to play at their favorite area because they know their time is limited—thus not all children get to play at all areas throughout the week.
- Children are not engaging deeply in their play, so it remains shallow and unfulfilling with little learning involved.
- Children are not cooperating with cleanup time or transitioning to other activities because they want to stay at the play experience longer.

Teachers Scaffolding and Assisting Children as They Play

Teachers scaffolding and assisting children as they play

When scaffolding and assistance are not provided to the children as they play, teachers may see the following:

- Children are engaging in less productive play (chaotic or more simple, repetitive engagement).
- More conflicts are arising among children.
- Less learning, problem solving, and vocabulary development are occurring.
- Children are avoiding some activities and staying at others for shorter periods of time.

More Child-Initiated Activities Than Adult-Led Ones

More child-initiated activities than adult-led ones

When the balance of child-initiated and adult-led activities is more heavily in the adult category, teachers may see the following:

- Children are acting up during adult-led activities that require long periods of sitting rather than active engagement (or a combination of breathing out and breathing in).
- Children are refusing to participate in some activities or participating in a half-hearted way.
- Children are saying, "I'm bored," or "When can I . . . ?"
- Children are being silly to the point of hilarity.

Respectful, Caring Relationships with Children and Families

When attention is not paid to building respectful, caring relationships with children and families, teachers may see the following:

- Children do not want to come to school because either they or their family members have not established a trusting relationship with the teachers.
- Children are more needy, asking for a teacher's attention through whining, clinging, or inappropriate behavior.
- Children are tense, afraid to take risks, or try new activities.
- Family members are raising concerns about the program or their child in ways that are negative or critical, rather than working in partnership with the teachers.

Respectful, caring relationships with children and families

Integration of Curriculum and Authentic, Observational Assessment

When curriculum and authentic, observational assessment are not integrated, teachers will notice the following:

- They will not learn as much about each individual child's personality traits and developmental capabilities.
- On-demand assessments will lead to less reliable information about each child than ones embedded in everyday activities.
- Assessment will feel like an additional task rather than one that is occurring as teachers interact with children all day, every day.

Integration of curriculum and authentic, observational assessment

Conclusion

Effective curriculum integrates assessment as well as all of the steps and elements previously identified. When it all comes together, children's needs are met more fully. They experience more success and are willing to try new things that may be challenging. Teachers find their jobs more rewarding because children are happier and more engaged. Parents and family members are able to see their child's delight in the preschool or kindergarten program. And through the authentic assessment process, teachers show families evidence of the learning that is occurring as children play, explore, study, and experience in ways that are just right for young children. As I quoted earlier:

> Excellent teachers know . . . it's *both* joy *and* learning. . . . They go hand in hand. . . . Teachers are always more effective when they tap into this natural love of learning rather than dividing work and enjoyment. As some early childhood educators like to put it, children love nothing better than "hard fun." (Copple and Bredekamp 2009, 50)

The planning/observation/individualization approach to curriculum helps teachers provide "hard fun" and joyous learning experiences. Young children deserve nothing less.

Appendix A
Planning and Reflection Frameworks

. . . .

- Preschool Weekly Planning and Reflection Framework
- Kindergarten Weekly Planning and Reflection Framework
- Weekly Planning and Reflection Framework
- Infant/Toddler Weekly Planning and Reflection Framework

Preschool Weekly Planning and Reflection Framework

Program/School: _____

Date: _____   Teacher(s): _____

Ongoing Project (optional): _____

	Learning goal(s)	Additional materials or focus	Vocabulary words
BLOCKS			
DRAMATIC PLAY			
SENSORY TABLE			
ART			
MANIPULATIVES			
CLASS LIBRARY			
WRITING CENTER			
OTHER CENTER			

Preschool Weekly Planning and Reflection Framework

DATE:

		MONDAY	TUESDAY	WEDNESDAY	THURSDAY	FRIDAY
Large group	Learning goal					
	Activity and teacher strategy					
Small group	Learning goal					
	Activity and teacher strategy					

Plans for Building Community and Relationships	Plans for Outdoor Explorations	Plans for Meals and Transitions	

Preschool Weekly Planning and Reflection Framework

OBSERVATIONS, MODIFICATIONS, AND REFLECTIONS

FOCUSED OBSERVATIONS:

MODIFICATIONS FOR INDIVIDUAL CHILDREN:

REFLECTIONS: What worked? What didn't? What did you learn about individual children and group interests?

PLANS: Based on your reflections, what will you change for next week?

Kindergarten Weekly Planning and Reflection Framework

READERS AND WRITERS WORKSHOP

Program/School: _____   Date: _____   Teacher(s): _____

Ongoing Project (optional): _____

	Learning goal(s)	Additional materials or focus	Vocabulary words
LISTENING CENTER			
DRAMATIC PLAY			
JOURNALING CENTER			
ALPHABET CENTER			
FLANNEL BOARD/ POCKET CHARTS			
CLASS LIBRARY			
TEACHER-LED LITERACY ACTIVITY			
WRITING CENTER			
OTHER CENTER			

Kindergarten Weekly Planning and Reflection Framework

DATE:		MONDAY	TUESDAY	WEDNESDAY	THURSDAY	FRIDAY
Large group	Learning goal					
	Activity and teacher strategy					
Small group	Learning goal					
	Activity and teacher strategy					
Afternoon Story Time	Learning goal					
	Activity and teacher strategy					

Plans for Building Community and Relationships	Plans for Outdoor Explorations	Plans for Meals and Transitions

Kindergarten Weekly Planning and Reflection Framework
INVESTIGATION TIME

Program/School: _____ Date: _____ Teacher(s): _____

Ongoing Project (optional): _____

	Learning goal(s)	Additional materials or focus	Vocabulary words
BLOCKS			
MATH ACTIVITY			
SENSORY TABLE			
ART			
MANIPULATIVES			
SCIENCE EXPLORATION			
INFORMATIONAL READING			
MATH AND SCIENCE JOURNALING			
OTHER CENTER			

Kindergarten Weekly Planning and Reflection Framework

OBSERVATIONS, MODIFICATIONS, AND REFLECTIONS

MODIFICATIONS FOR INDIVIDUAL CHILDREN:

PLANS: Based on your reflections, what will you change for next week?

FOCUSED OBSERVATIONS:

REFLECTIONS: What worked? What didn't? What did you learn about individual children and group interests?

Weekly Planning and Reflection Framework

Program/School: _____   Date: _____ _____   Teacher(s): _____

Ongoing Project (optional): _____

	Learning goal(s)	Additional materials or focus	Vocabulary words

Weekly Planning and Reflection Framework

DATE:		MONDAY	TUESDAY	WEDNESDAY	THURSDAY	FRIDAY
Large group	Learning goal					
	Activity and teacher strategy					
Small group	Learning goal					
	Activity and teacher strategy					

Plans for Building Community and Relationships	Plans for Outdoor Explorations	Plans for Meals and Transitions

Weekly Planning and Reflection Framework
OBSERVATIONS, MODIFICATIONS, AND REFLECTIONS

FOCUSED OBSERVATIONS:	MODIFICATIONS FOR INDIVIDUAL CHILDREN:
REFLECTIONS: What worked? What didn't? What did you learn about individual children and group interests?	PLANS: Based on your reflections, what will you change for next week?
REFLECTIONS: What worked? What didn't? What did you learn about individual children and group interests?	PLANS: Based on your reflections, what will you change for next week?

Infant/Toddler Weekly Planning and Reflection Framework

Program/School: _____   Date: _____   Teacher(s): _____

Learning objectives (overall goals in each content area): _____

LEARNING THROUGH DAILY ROUTINES

Diapering/Toileting	Arrival/Departure	Meals
Hand Washing	Self-Help	Naptime

LEARNING THROUGH EXPERIENCES

Sensory	Movement (indoor/outdoor)	Fine-Motor Skills (math, writing)
Creative Play	Scientific Exploration	Literacy (songs, stories, fingerplays)

Infant/Toddler Weekly Planning and Reflection Framework

OBSERVATIONS, MODIFICATIONS, AND REFLECTIONS

RELATIONSHIP BUILDING AND FAMILY INVOLVEMENT:

FOCUSED OBSERVATIONS:

MODIFICATIONS FOR INDIVIDUAL CHILDREN:

REFLECTIONS: What worked? What didn't? What did you learn about individual children and group interests?

PLANS: Based on your reflections, what will you change for next week?

Appendix B
Learning Goals for Play Areas

. . . .

The following learning goals can be addressed (and therefore written on the framework) in each of the play areas of a preschool or kindergarten classroom.

Blocks

- language arts: listening, speaking, vocabulary development, and writing (as in making signs)
- math: sorting and categorizing (ordering and patterning), counting and quantity, geometry and spatial relationships, mathematical problem solving, and measurement
- social studies: getting along with others and understanding community (as in building neighborhoods)
- science: developing observation and analysis skills, making scientific predictions, and experimenting
- social/emotional: learning to play and get along with other children and expressing emotions appropriately
- approaches to learning: demonstrating curiosity and interest in new things, showing initiative, and focusing attention and persisting in tasks
- gross-motor development: showing balance and control
- fine-motor development: demonstrating hand-eye coordination

Dramatic Play

- language arts: listening, speaking, vocabulary development, knowledge of books and print (as in reading to baby dolls or looking at grocery circulars), and writing (as in making grocery lists or writing letters)
- math: sorting and categorizing (as in putting the dishes away), counting and quantity, and measurement
- social studies: understanding families (as in imitating family roles), getting along with others, and understanding community (as in playing restaurant, grocery store, hospital, etc.)
- social/emotional: learning to play and get along with other children, expressing emotions appropriately, and developing self-regulation
- approaches to learning: demonstrating curiosity and interest in new things, showing initiative, and focusing attention and persisting in tasks
- gross-motor development: showing balance and control and exhibiting body coordination in walking, running, jumping, and climbing stairs
- fine-motor development: demonstrating hand-eye coordination, using tools to write and cut, and using self-help skills, such as buttoning and zipping

Sensory Table

- language arts: listening, speaking, and vocabulary development
- math: sorting and categorizing (ordering and patterning), counting and quantity, and measurement
- social studies: getting along with others
- science: developing observation and analysis skills, making scientific predictions, and experimenting
- social/emotional: learning to play and get along with other children and expressing emotions appropriately
- approaches to learning: demonstrating curiosity and interest in new things, showing initiative, and focusing attention and persisting in tasks
- fine-motor development: demonstrating hand-eye coordination and using tools

Art

- language arts: listening, speaking, vocabulary development, reading comprehension (as in drawing favorite parts of a story), and writing skills
- math: sorting and categorizing (ordering and patterning), counting and quantity, geometry and spatial relationships, and representing mathematical information
- social studies: understanding families (as in making things for family members)
- science: developing observation and analysis skills (as in marble painting), making scientific predictions, and experimenting (as in mixing colors of paint)
- social/emotional: learning to play and get along with other children and expressing emotions appropriately
- approaches to learning: demonstrating curiosity and interest in new things, showing initiative, and focusing attention and persisting in tasks
- fine-motor development: demonstrating hand-eye coordination and using tools to write and cut

Manipulatives

- language arts: listening, speaking, and vocabulary development
- math: sorting and categorizing (ordering and patterning), counting and quantity, geometry and spatial relationships, mathematical problem solving, measurement, and representing mathematical information
- science: developing observation and analysis skills, making scientific predictions, and experimenting
- social/emotional: listening to and following the guidance of teachers and expressing emotions appropriately
- approaches to learning: demonstrating curiosity and interest in new things, showing initiative, and focusing attention and persisting in tasks
- fine-motor development: demonstrating hand-eye coordination, using tools to write and cut, and using self-help skills, such as buttoning and zipping

Class Library

- language arts: listening, reading comprehension, phonological awareness of sounds and syllables, speaking, vocabulary development, knowledge of books and print
- math: sorting and categorizing (as in comparing books), counting and quantity (as in reading number books)
- social studies: understanding families and understanding community
- science: making scientific predictions (when reading scientific books)
- social/emotional: listening to and following the guidance of teachers, expressing emotions appropriately, and developing self-regulation
- approaches to learning: demonstrating curiosity and interest in new things, showing initiative, and focusing attention and persisting in tasks
- fine-motor development: demonstrating hand-eye coordination

Writing Center

- language arts: listening, reading comprehension, phonological awareness of sounds and syllables, speaking, vocabulary development, knowledge of books and print, and writing skills
- math: geometry and spatial relationships, measurement (as in comparing lengths of words, names, sizes of letters), and representing mathematical information
- social studies: understanding families (as in writing to family members and understanding community)
- social/emotional: expressing emotions appropriately (as in writing and drawing about them)
- approaches to learning: demonstrating curiosity and interest in new things, showing initiative, and focusing attention and persisting in tasks
- fine-motor development: demonstrating hand-eye coordination and using tools to write and cut

Appendix C
Assessment Forms

· ·

- Individual Child Information Record
- Individual Adjustments
- Preschool Choice Record
- Kindergarten Choice Record
- Portfolio Collection Form
- Family-Teacher Summary Report

Individual Child Information Record

Child: _____   Date: _____

Culture	Life Experiences	Family	Learning Style	Developmental Strengths
Interests	Emerging Developmental Areas	Approaches to Learning and Responses to Challenges	Emotional Makeup	Physical Needs and Health Issues

Individual Adjustments

For week of: _____   Teacher: _____

Child's Name	Planned Adjustment	Child's Name	Planned Adjustment

Preschool Choice Record

(may be used to tally one child's choices or a group of children's choices)

Child(ren): _____   Date: _____

Art	Blocks	Dramatic Play
Manipulatives	Science/Math	Music/Movement
Library	Sensory Table	Writing Center

Kindergarten Choice Record

(may be used to tally one child's choices or a group of children's choices)

Child(ren): _____ Date: _____

Listening Center	Dramatic Play	Journaling Center	Alphabet Center	Flannel Board or Pocket Charts
Class Library	Writing Center	Blocks	Math Activity	Sensory Table
Art	Manipulatives	Science Exploration	Informational Reading	Math and Science Journaling

Portfolio Collection Form

Child's Name: _____ Date: _____ Observer: _____

Domains(s): _____

Learning goal(s) demonstrated in this documentation: _____

_____

_____

Check off whatever applies to the context of this observation:

☐ child-initiated activity   ☐ done independently   ☐ time spent (1 to 5 minutes)

☐ teacher-initiated activity   ☐ done with adult guidance   ☐ time spent (5 to 15 minutes)

☐ new task for this child   ☐ done with peer(s)

☐ familiar task for this child   ☐ time spent (more than 15 minutes)

Anecdotal note: Describe what you saw the child do and/or heard the child say (attach a photo or work sample if appropriate).

Family-Teacher Summary Report

Child's Name: _____ Date: _____

Teacher: _____ Program: _____

DOMAIN:

Growth and accomplishments	
We will continue to work on	

DOMAIN:

Growth and accomplishments	
We will continue to work on	

DOMAIN:

Growth and accomplishments	
We will continue to work on	

(continued on next page)

(continued from previous page)

DOMAIN:

Growth and accomplishments	
We will continue to work on	

DOMAIN:

Growth and accomplishments	
We will continue to work on	

DOMAIN:

Growth and accomplishments	
We will continue to work on	

DOMAIN:

Growth and accomplishments	
We will continue to work on	

References

Ashton-Warner, Sylvia. 1963. *Teacher*. New York: Simon and Schuster.

Bergen, D., and D. Mauer. 2000. "Symbolic Play, Phonological Awareness, and Literacy Skills as Three Age Levels." In *Play and Literacy in Early Childhood: Research from Multiple Perspectives*, edited by K. A. Roskos and J. F. Christie, 45–62. Mahwah, NJ: Lawrence Erlbaum.

Berk, L. E. 2006b. "Make-Believe Play: Wellspring for Development of Self-Regulation." In *Play=Learning: How Play Motivates and Enhances Children's Cognitive and Social-Emotional Growth*, edited by D. Singer, K. Hirsh-Pasek, and R. Golinkoff. New York: Oxford University Press.

Blair, C., and A. Diamond. 2008. "Biological Processes in Prevention and Intervention: The Promotion of Self-Regulation as a Means of Preventing School Failure." *Development and Psychopathology*, no. 20: 899–911.

Bodrova, E., and D. J. Leong. 2003. "Chopsticks and Counting Chips: Do Play and Foundational Skills Need to Compete for the Teacher's Attention in an Early Childhood Classroom?" *Young Children* 58 (3): 10–17.

———. 2007. *Tools of the Mind: The Vygotskian Approach to Early Childhood Education*. 2nd ed. Upper Saddle River, NJ: Pearson/Merrill Prentice Hall.

Brown, Stuart. 2009. *Play: How It Shapes the Brain, Opens the Imagination, and Invigorates the Soul*. New York: Penguin.

Copple, Carol, and Sue Bredekamp, eds. 2009. *Developmentally Appropriate Practice in Early Childhood Programs Serving Children from Birth through Age 8*. 3rd ed. Washington, DC: National Association for the Education of Young Children.

Csikszentmihalyi, Mihaly. 1997. *Finding Flow: The Psychology of Engagement with Everyday Life*. New York: Basic Books.

Curtis, Deb, and Margie Carter. 2011. *Reflecting Children's Lives: A Handbook for Planning Your Child-Centered Curriculum*. 2nd ed. St. Paul, MN: Redleaf Press.

Elias, C., and L. E. Berk. 2002. "Self-Regulation in Young Children: Is There a Role for Sociodramatic Play?" *Early Childhood Research Quarterly* 17 (1): 216–38.

Erikson, Erik. 1950. *Childhood and Society.* New York: W. W. Norton.

Espinosa, L. 2002. "High Quality Preschool: Why We Need it and What it Looks Like." *NIEER Policy Briefs.* http://nieer.org/resources/policybriefs/1.pdf.

Florez, Ida Rose. 2011. "Developing Young Children's Self-Regulation through Everyday Experiences." *Young Children* 66 (4): 46–51.

Genishi, Celia, and Anne Haas Dyson. 2009. *Children, Language, and Literacy: Diverse Learners in Diverse Times.* New York: Teachers College Press.

Ginsburg, Kenneth R. 2007. "The Importance of Play in Promoting Healthy Child Development and Maintaining Strong Parent-Child Bonds." *Pediatrics* 119 (1): 182–91. doi:10.1542/peds.2006-2697.

Gronlund, Gaye. 2003. *Focused Early Learning: A Planning Framework for Teaching Young Children.* St. Paul, MN: Redleaf Press.

———. 2010. *Developmentally Appropriate Play: Guiding Young Children to a Higher Level.* St. Paul, MN: Redleaf Press.

Gronlund, Gaye, and Bev Engel. 2001. *Focused Portfolios: A Complete Assessment for the Young Child.* St. Paul: Redleaf Press.

Gronlund, Gaye, and Marlyn James. 2013. *Focused Observations: How to Observe Children for Assessment and Curriculum Planning.* 2nd ed. St. Paul, MN: Redleaf Press.

Hampson, Rick. 2010. "A 'Watershed' Case in School Bullying?" *USA Today*, April 5. www.usatoday.com/news/nation/2010-04-04-bullying_N.htm.

Isenberg, Joan Packer, and Nancy Quisenberry. 2002. "Play: Essential for All Children. A Position Paper of the Association for Childhood Education International." *Childhood Education* 79 (1): 33–39.

Kavanaugh, R. D., and S. Engel. 1998. "The Development of Pretense and Narrative in Early Childhood." In *Multiple Perspectives on Play in Early Childhood Education*, edited by O. N. Saracho and B. Spodek, 80–99. Albany, NY: State University of New York.

Kersey, Katharine C., and Marie L. Masterson. 2011. "Learn to Say Yes! When You Want to Say No! to Create Cooperation instead of Resistance: Positive Behavior Strategies in Teaching." *Young Children* 66 (4): 40–44.

Lindsey, E. W., and M. J. Colwell. 2003. "Preschoolers' Emotional Competence: Links to Pretend and Physical Play." *Child Study Journal*, no. 33: 39–52.

Miller, Edward, and Joan Almon. 2009. *Crisis in the Kindergarten: Why Children Need to Play in School*. College Park, MD: Alliance for Childhood.

Montie, J. E., Z. Xiang, and L. J. Schweinhart. 2006. "Preschool Experience in 10 Countries: Cognitive and Language Performance at Age 7." *Early Childhood Research Quarterly*, no. 21: 313–31.

NAEYC (National Association for the Education of Young Children). 2009. *Developmentally Appropriate Practice in Early Childhood Programs Serving Children from Birth through Age 8*. Position statement. www.naeyc.org/positionstatements/dap.

NAEYC and NAECS/SDE (National Association for the Education of Young Children and National Association of Early Childhood Specialists in State Departments of Education). 2003. *Early Childhood Curriculum, Assessment, and Program Evaluation: Building an Effective, Accountable System in Programs for Children Birth through Age 8*. Position statement. www.naeyc.org/positionstatements/cape.

Perry, Bruce D., Lea Hogan, and Sarah J. Marlin. 2000. "Curiosity, Pleasure, and Play: A Neurodevelopmental Perspective." *HAAEYC Advocate*. www.childtrauma.org/ctamaterials/curiosity.asp. (Web page discontinued.)

Roskos, Kathleen, and James Christie. 2004. "Examining the Play-Literacy Interface: A Critical Review and Future Directions." In *Children's Play: The Roots of Reading*, edited by Edward F. Zigler, Dorothy G. Singer, and Sandra J. Bishop-Josef, 95–123. Washington, DC: Zero to Three Press.

Ruff, H. A., and M. C. Capozzoli. 2003. "Development of Attention and Distractibility in the First 4 Years of Life." *Developmental Psychology*, no. 39: 877–90.

Vygotsky, Lev S. 1978. *Mind in Society: The Development of Higher Psychological Processes*. Edited by Michael Cole, et al. Cambridge, MA: Harvard University Press.

Wenner, Melinda. 2009. "The Serious Need for Play." *Scientific American Mind*, February/March.

Index